KIDS CAUGHT IN THE
PSYCHIATRIC MAELSTROM

KIDS CAUGHT IN THE
PSYCHIATRIC MAELSTROM

*How Pathological Labels and
"Therapeutic" Drugs Hurt
Children and Families*

Property of
Baker College
of Allen Park

Elizabeth E. Root

Foreword by Robert Whitaker

PRAEGER
An Imprint of ABC-CLIO, LLC

A B C  C L I O

Santa Barbara, California • Denver, Colorado • Oxford, England

Library of Congress Cataloging-in-Publication Data

Root, Elizabeth E.
    Kids caught in the psychiatric maelstrom : how pathological labels and
"therapeutic" drugs hurt children and families / Elizabeth E. Root ; foreword by
Robert Whitaker.
        p. cm.
    Includes bibliographical references and index.
    ISBN 978-0-313-38122-5 (hard copy : alk. paper) — ISBN 978-0-313-38123-2 (ebook)
1. Pediatric psychopharmacology. 2. Child psychiatry. 3. Medical
misconceptions. 4. Attention-deficit hyperactivity disorder. 5. Manic-depressive
illness in children. 6. Psychotropic drugs industry. I. Title.
    RJ504.7.R66   2009
    618.92'89—dc22   2009028032

13   12   11   10   09   1   2   3   4   5

This book is also available on the World Wide Web as an eBook.
Visit www.abc-clio.com for details.

ABC-CLIO, LLC
130 Cremona Drive, P.O. Box 1911
Santa Barbara, California 93116–1911

This book is printed on acid-free paper (∞)

Manufactured in the United States of America

All clients are composite characters drawn from clinical experience. Names and details have been
changed to protect confidentiality.

To all the children who passed through my door

******

In honor of Jim and Barbara who made so many things possible.
In loving memory of Linda Urban Sears

As a species, we have evolved culturally in large part because of our play-fulness, and all that it produces in the way of intelligence and creativity.

—James Garbarino
Raising Children in a Socially Toxic Environment

Contents

Foreword

In *Kids Caught in the Psychiatric Maelstrom*, Elizabeth Root asks two questions that we, as a society, desperately need to think about. There has been an astonishing rise in the number of children and teenagers diagnosed with mental illness and treated with psychiatric medications in the past 20 years, and here is what she wants to know:

"Are these children really mentally ill?"

"Is the care we provide really helpful?"

Those are two separate, yet related questions. The first raises the specter of a medical discipline that tells children they have broken brains when, in fact, there is no evidence that is so. The second raises the specter of drug treatments that simply don't work, even for those children who in fact may be depressed or extremely agitated and in need of help. Together, the two questions raise the specter of medical practices that are doing great and lasting harm to millions of children in our society.

Having raised the right questions, Elizabeth Root then answers them through a sober review of the research literature. She proceeds in a clear, logical manner. Is there evidence that children with ADHD or bipolar disorder have "abnormal" brains? Does psychiatry have a biological test for diagnosing a mental illness? As she explains, psychiatry lacks such objective diagnostic tests, and thus it becomes easy to understand that psychiatry today is diagnosing many children as mentally ill who are, in fact, perfectly normal. Next, she turns her attention to a review of what the drugs do, and whether the scientific literature shows that they provide a long-term benefit. One might assume there is plenty of evidence to show that the drugs help children get better, stay well, and prosper in their lives, as otherwise psychiatry would have to admit that it was flying blind, a process that usually results in tragedy. But, as she reveals, psychiatry lacks this evidence base. There is simply no scientific reason for the field to believe that prescribing psychiatric medications to millions of children and adolescents will improve their lives.

Once she has reviewed this scientific tale, Elizabeth Root describes what psychiatrists and the drug companies tell the public about psychotropic medications, and the financial forces that govern that storytelling. Here we begin to see the betrayal of the American public that is at the heart of this story of the medicated child. We see, time and again, that the story told to the American public by the pharmaceutical companies and by many leading psychiatrists is a dishonest one. Study results are twisted to make it appear that children have abnormal brains, or that psychiatric drugs are beneficial, when in fact the studies show no such thing. The medicating of children in America did not come about because of advances in diagnosing and treating mental illness, but rather because financial forces made it profitable to do so.

This book also will stir parents to think twice about allowing their children to be "screened" for mental illness. Elizabeth Root charts the development of TeenScreen and other initiatives of this sort, which at first glimpse seem to be progressive in nature. Who would object to a screening program that helps identify children who are suffering from an illness? We discover in this book, however, that the screening programs are better described as market-expansion efforts, with pharmaceutical companies and psychiatry collaborating in a search for new customers. The harm these screening programs can do is poignantly revealed here.

Finally, Elizabeth Root reviews a number of alternative non-drug programs that have proven to be helpful to children who are struggling with their emotions and their behavior. This important book will stir readers to think about how we as a society, if we so chose, could move away from a drug-based paradigm of care that is doing great harm, to a humanistic one with the potential to do much good.

Robert Whitaker
Author, *Mad in America*

Preface

"Capullio is out! Capullio is out!" my granddaughter Lilly cried in her loudest gravelly voice as she catapulted out the front door. Mindless of her diminutive four-year-old frame, no match for the giant chow that had escaped his yard next door, she was on her way to save the day.

May Lilly never lose the sense of power that sent her in hot pursuit of Capullio. Full of self-confidence, she saw herself as an important agent of her community. Such spirit is a sign of healthy development, and in Lilly's case I feel sure that it will continue. But for many children, strong spirit gets squelched somewhere along the hazardous road to maturity.

That road is indeed hazardous in this 21st century. Many professionals claim we have an epidemic of mental illness among youth and that it is showing up in younger and younger children. Across our nation millions of toddlers are acquiring pathological labels, mostly of the newly invented pediatric bipolar diagnosis and the attention deficit hyperactivity disorder commonly referred to as ADHD. But are these children really mentally ill? Is the care we provide really helpful?

These questions plagued me throughout my journey as a children's psychotherapist and led to some agonizing conclusions. But that journey illuminated some promising alternatives to the way mental health treatment is practiced today. I share both the good and the bad with readers. I speak to parents, caregivers, and all who have a stake in the health and welfare of children.

For many youngsters, childhood is not the carefree playful experience of my generation. Flying in the face of child development experts' recommendations, our system mandates youngsters to stop playing and start academic work prematurely. Children who persist in natural age-appropriate behaviors like wiggling, playing, or drawing spontaneously are chastised. Their parents are pressured to force conformity by acceding to pathological labeling and medicating with brain-altering drugs. This practice is gaining momentum, leading toward widespread child abuse via chemicals. Screening children for mental illness, a practice heavily influenced by the pharmaceutical industry, feeds the momentum. A plan to screen all public school children, set forth in the Bush administration's New Freedom Initiative, is accelerating the practice, and the Obama administration so far indicates support for mental screening. Ironically, screening children actually increases their risk for mental illness, even as it threatens the sanctity of the family unit.

The grim facts about mental health care inform parents and decision makers to recognize potentially harmful interventions. Facts help caregivers guide children safely through mental health treatment when assistance is desired. Good therapists can help without the use of drugs. A host of drug-free solutions for distress is illuminated in Chapter 7.

Noxious elements in American society, unhealthy food processing, and pollutants in our environment also threaten healthy child development. We face the urgent tasks of repairing a flawed mental health system, a toxic environment, and increased government intrusion into families. I hope this book will inspire the necessary grassroots activism to effect sorely needed change. Our progeny's welfare depends on our immediate response to the challenges posed in these pages.

Acknowledgments

I am indebted to friends and family, whose warm support buoyed me through the years of transforming my concerns to a purpose, to a manuscript, and finally to a book.

Three people encouraged me during the nascent period of manuscript writing. My friend and colleague, Jamee Sobko, has been an enthusiastic cheerleader from the start; she applauded my earliest literary attempts. My brother, Jim Eichstedt, read some of the first epistles, notated comments, and tracked my progress over the years with loving interest. My dear friend Linda Sears remained always a stalwart supporter and force behind my mission. We shared precious hours together in the closing years and months of her life. She was a great listener, and an energetic source of inspiration.

I am most grateful to my friends Hazel Brampton and Louise Richards, who believed in my ideals, scrupulously read my work, and cheered me on over the long haul. I thank my son, Bryan Root, whose frank criticism kept me on track from time to time, and for all the time he devoted to various helpful tasks. In the final days of manuscript preparation, friends Patti Burgevin and Louise Richards generously gave of their time to proofread lengthy chapters, for which I am most grateful. I thank my sister-in-law, Barbara Eichstedt, for graciously caring for my dogs when book-related work called me away.

I am honored that eminent medical journalist, Robert Whitaker, took time from his busy schedule to read my manuscript and write the foreword for me. I extend my deep gratitude to him. Peter Breggin has been an inspiration in fomenting mental health care reform and stopping the chemical abuse of children. He has warmly endorsed my literary efforts. Grace Jackson has been most kind and generous in reading and refining my interpretations of her fine medical research. I am profoundly indebted to them all.

With respect and fondness, I acknowledge my colleagues in the workplace for their comradeship and loyal devotion to the children and families we served together and for their continuing allegiance to their work.

Finally, I extend my gratitude to Debora Carvalko, my editor, for seeing promise in my manuscript, and to all her behind-the-scenes collaborators who approved it. I extend my heartfelt thanks to all the unseen toilers who guided me through my venture as a first-time author.

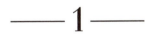

1

Toward a Greater Understanding: The Basics

Where are the Einsteins, Freuds, or Picassos today? There is a tragic possibility: they are being psychiatrically diagnosed and drugged. Any biography of Einstein, Freud, or Picasso will demonstrate enough childhood 'pathology' to warrant diagnosis and drugging with the inevitable suppression of his unique contribution to life.

—Peter R. Breggin & Ginger Ross Breggin

This chapter is a must-read in order to fully comprehend the thrust of this book. Informed consent and two divergent theories that drive choices of treatment are basic toward that understanding. Readers are also apprised of the risks associated with traditional mental health counseling, especially for children. Knowing the risks helps families avoid them.

WHAT IS INFORMED CONSENT?

High-spirited Alice Compton[1] has entered kindergarten with gusto. Her teacher, Ms. Smith, begins registering complaints to Mrs. Compton about Alice's rambunctiousness. One day she calls to suggest that Alice should be "tested" for attention deficit hyperactivity disorder (ADHD), because Alice cannot sit still and focus on her seatwork and she sometimes disrupts the rest of the class by speaking out of turn.[2] Ms. Smith says she cannot devote so much attention to Alice because she has 20 other kids to teach. She says that medication might help Alice to stay focused. Since Alice is Mrs. Compton's oldest child, she hasn't had previous experience with elementary school teachers. Alice's cooperative nursery school teacher said Alice, a spunky and enthusiastic youngster, was really ready for kindergarten. Alice's mother takes Ms. Smith's complaint to heart because Ms. Smith is the authority and Mrs. Compton certainly wants Alice to succeed at school. She and Alice are referred to the local mental health clinic and Alice is evaluated by a clinical social worker. Mrs. Compton asks about this medication the teacher mentioned and the evaluator tells her Alice has to meet with the clinic psychiatrist for that. An appointment is scheduled.

The two present to Dr. Hamilton, who explains that he needs a history, so they repeat the same procedure as with the social worker. It's a 45-minute session. Mrs. Compton tells Dr. Hamilton how Alice has always been strong willed, high spirited, and energetic. She admits that, yes, Alice can be a challenging child who doesn't easily take orders; she often argues and connives to get her way. Mrs. Compton tells him Ms. Smith suggested medication. Dr. Hamilton responds that Ritalin, a stimulant drug in various forms, is still the standard treatment for hyperactivity. He explains that it comes in both regular and long-acting concentrations. He suggests Concerta for the morning and Focalin, a shorter-acting form, for later in the day when the morning dose wears off. Mrs. Compton responds that she is uneasy about putting Alice on drugs. Dr. Hamilton reassures her that stimulant drugs have been used for decades and are approved for children. Mrs. Compton asks if there are side effects. The doctor replies that some children have diminished appetite and that sometimes they have trouble sleeping. But he states that he can prescribe another pill to help with sleep. Mrs. Compton still isn't sure. She tells Dr. Hamilton she needs to think about it and asks if he has any literature about ADHD and the medication. He readily hands her a booklet about the attention deficit hyperactivity disorders and standard treatment. He also refers her to the CHADD[3] Web site.

Mother and daughter return home, and Mrs. Compton reads the pamphlet and gleans information from the CHADD Web site. Both tell her that a stimulant drug sometimes combined with counseling is the treatment of choice. They state unequivocally that medication is the crucial element in treatment. They also claim ADHD is a biological or neurological disorder and that stimulant medication corrects a chemical imbalance or anomaly in the brain. It seems to make sense. If you were in Mrs. Compton's place, what would you do?

This scenario is played out every day in mental health clinics that serve children. As Alice's parent, would you believe you have all the information you need to consent to Dr. Hamilton's recommendation to medicate Alice? The average person puts trust in the doctor. That M.D. title after his name is revered, and the various framed diplomas on his office wall look impressive. Most likely some of your friends have told you their children are taking something for hyperactivity that is helping with schoolwork and behavior.

Actually, your consent to medicate Alice, if given based on the information provided by the two professionals at the clinic, is not an informed one. Mrs. Compton didn't think to ask about a medical "test" for ADHD. Had she, Dr. Hamilton would have had to tell her that his diagnosis is only based on his judgment of Alice's behavior in his office and the little information Mrs. Compton gave him. She didn't notice the tiny print on the back of the ADHD information booklet signifying it is published by one of the drug companies that makes stimulant medication. And the CHADD Web site didn't mention its close alliance with drug companies and the American Psychiatric Association. Dr. Hamilton didn't inform Mrs. Compton that the stimulant drugs are basically amphetamines, or synthetic versions thereof, and that their effect on the brain is virtually identical to that of cocaine. Every day doctors prescribe psychiatric medications without telling the parent the whole story. Often, they don't know the whole story because they are selective in their reading material and often base their recommendations on information (or misinformation) provided them by drug company salespeople who frequent their offices.

It is critically important for parents to be armed with the information they need to make informed choices in the treatment of their children for high energy or misbehavior. Filling the vacuum of non-information left by mental health professionals in most clinics is a tall order. Let's start with a discussion of two perspectives that divide clinicians (professionals who treat a medical or emotional condition) in their beliefs about the causes of emotional distress and how treatment should be done.

TWO TREATMENT MODELS

The Medical Model

The late George Albee, past president of the American Psychological Association and sage in the discipline of psychology, spoke at the 2004 Conference of the International Center for the Study of Psychiatry and Psychology. Throughout his long career, he advocated for a preventive approach to emotional distress to replace the medical model in its treatment. He pressed his conviction that psychologists made a tragic error when they borrowed the medical model from psychiatry at the dawn of their profession.[4] Clinical social workers, the largest component of psychotherapists in our country, followed suit along with most other mental health professionals. The medical model means a clinician (any professional who treats a medical or emotional condition) assigns a diagnosis to a patient and then prescribes a remedy. In mental health, the remedy usually includes a referral to a doctor for medication and some kind of talk therapy. This model is so ingrained that the reader may think, "Isn't that what the therapist is supposed to do?" In the case of a bona fide physical illness, yes. Physical illnesses usually have detectable symptoms, sometimes quantitative via testing. Not so with emotional distress; no tests exist to diagnose the so-called mental illnesses. Television commercials used to state unequivocally that mental illness such as depression was caused by a "chemical imbalance," and that medication advertised would correct the "imbalance." Someone must have informed the networks of the theoretical, not factual, basis for such a statement, for now the wording is subtly modified. The phrase "chemical imbalance" is usually omitted, and one commercial, for example, states that the product "can help" depression. (True enough, medication can help depression, but most of the time, as we shall see in chapter 4, the improvement is due to a placebo effect: the patient improves because she believes and expects the medication will help.) Mental health practitioners who apply the medical model presume that emotional distress is "mental illness," caused by a defect in brain chemistry, often with a genetic component. Neurobiological proponents naturally embrace the medical model of treatment. This is the standard of diagnosis and treatment in most public and nonprofit mental health clinics.

The Psychosocial Model

I and many other clinicians embrace the psychosocial perspective, a view that diverges from the neurobiological in many respects. We believe that emotional distress stems from adverse life events to which people vary in response. Some people are more resilient and experience a mild upset; others become so overwhelmed by catastrophic events that they become irrational and flee from reality temporarily as a defense mechanism. Decades of experimentation have produced no proof that emotional dysfunction is caused by faulty brain chemistry. Our opposition to the chemical imbalance theory is supported by this fact. Chapter 2 details some of the research that has failed thus far to identify the elusive biological marker for the common diagnosis of attention deficit hyperactivity disorder (ADHD).

In working with children, it is usually easy to identify the causes for temper tantrums, rages, or gross misbehavior. All the social, environmental, and familial influences that have impacted the child comprise the psychosocial history. When the primary caregivers disclose this history, the causes of misbehavior are usually obvious to the impartial professional, and sometimes to others close to the child. They are often not as obvious to parents, who are too close to and immersed in their child's life to be objective.

The psychosocially oriented therapist believes misbehaviors are normal child-like responses to extraordinary stress. Common stressors on children include divorce (especially when there is acrimony between parents), loss of significant friends or caregivers, multiple relocations, verbal or physical violence, and disability in a family member. The absence of such stressors can render even the professional at a loss to explain misbehavior. High energy, intensity, irritability, and temperament sometimes can be explained only by a child's innate personality, inherited character traits, or by some congenital anomaly. A specialist who can diagnose or rule out a medical condition should evaluate unusually troubling behavior that may contribute to the problem. If a cognitive impairment such as a learning disability or mental retardation is suspected, psychological testing may be part of the evaluation. Cognitive impairments can also be difficult to diagnose, but knowledge of disability enables caregivers and teachers to obtain appropriate accommodations and form realistic expectations.

Now we examine the risks to which children are exposed when brought to a typical mental health clinic where the medical model of treatment prevails.

THE RISKS OF TYPICAL MENTAL HEALTH CARE

The fortunate child comes to the clinic with a problem that is solved relatively easily, and the family gets back on track in a timely fashion. Too often, though, the child is mired in treatment and has a poor outcome due to being labeled, medicated long term, and possibly hospitalized repeatedly. The following are risks that can precipitate unfortunate outcomes.

Diagnosis and the DSM

Applying the medical model to the treatment of emotional distress starts the process. The first step in the traditional medical model is the diagnosis, which implies a medical condition. Therefore, most clinics employ a psychiatrist who is also a medical doctor. Once diagnosed, the child might be referred to the clinic psychiatrist any time in the course of treatment. The great majority of children who visit this doctor leave with a prescription for psychotropic medication.[5] Medication as a risk factor is discussed after further exploring the ramifications of diagnosis.

Panels of psychiatrists comprise a task force that decides about every 7 to 10 years what human behaviors or feelings should be classified as mental illnesses and includes them in the ever-enlarging *Diagnostic and Statistical Manual of Mental Disorders*[6] (DSM). The first DSM, published in 1952, listed 106 disorders. The second, in 1968, included 182. The third, in 1980, had 265. So it went until the fourth and latest edition, published in 1994, contained nearly 400 diagnoses. Still more are being considered for the DSM-V, due for publication in 2011 or 2012. On average, then, every 10 years sees an increase of 25 new disorders. Critics such as Herb Kutchens and Stuart A. Kirk (*Making Us Crazy*),[7] John Abramson (*Overdosed America*),[8] and Melody Petersen (*Our Daily Meds*)[9] reveal how the alliance of psychiatrists and pharmaceutical companies has compromised pure scientific research and invented "new" illnesses and "new" (but not improved) medicines, all for monetary gain. *USA Today*[10] reported in 2006 on a study that investigated psychiatrists who served on panels that developed the DSM-IV. The study looked at research funds, consultancies, patents, and other gifts or grants received by members of the 18 separate panels from 1989 to 2004. It found that among the 170 "medical experts" comprising the panels, 56 percent had financial ties with the pharmaceutical industry. Of those on panels overseeing disorders typically treated with prescription drugs, such as schizophrenia, 100 percent of members had financial connections with drug companies. The *USA Today* article revealed that in April 2006, the journal *PloS* (Public Library of Science) *Medicine* accused drug companies and psychiatrists of "disease-mongering" (inventing diseases such as "restless leg syndrome") and expanding definitions to take in more patients. On May 6, 2008, the *New York Times* reported on the psychiatrists now compiling the next edition of the DSM.[11] Citing the Web site for Integrity in Science, the *Times* reported that the American Psychiatric Association (APA) allows panel members to accept money from drug companies. The site highlighted the link between the 28-member task force overseeing the DSM-V and the drug industry, based on financial disclosures of the members posted on the APA Web site. The Integrity in Science group characterized the conflict of interest among members as ranging from "small to extensive." One member reportedly worked as a consultant over the past five years for 13 drug companies.

The *Eugene Weekly* featured "'Greening' of Mental Health?" on December 24, 2008.[12] David Oakes, executive director of MindFreedom International,[13] attempted to have dialogue with DSM V panel members about having input from mental health system consumers, who number in the millions. This effort to break the undemocratic domination of mental health care by the medical establishment was flatly disregarded. Oakes' response: "So these few hundred unelected mainly rich, mainly white males are cooking up behavioral guidelines for us all, with zero input from the public who is impacted by these rules." Oakes pointed out that Dr. Darrel A. Regier, a key figure in the new DSM, also heads the independent component of the APA that publishes the DSM and "tends to get millions of drug company dollars."

An ominous change occurred in the latest DSM edition, DSM IV. A category maintained for many previous years, Organic Mental Disorders, was eliminated. Dr. Shahul Ameen's e-book[14] explains how this happened. Until the DSM IV, a distinction was made between organic mental disorders clearly definable through medical tests and all the other "functional" or physiological mental disorders. Psychiatrists were of the opinion that the latter could not be detected by existing laboratory procedures. But Ameen explains, "During the past few decades, the advent of newer pharmacological treatments and advances in fields such as neuroimaging, genetics, and molecular biology have resulted in a growing recognition of brain pathology as the basis for mental disorders." Citing the introduction to the 2000 Text Revision of the DSM IV (DSM IV TR), Ameen reiterates the consensual opinion of the DSM authors that the term "mental disorder" is anachronistic, inasmuch as the authors now believe all abnormalities in the DSM are physical or biological in origin. They keep "mental disorder" only because they haven't yet come up with an appropriate substitute. Readers will discover in succeeding pages that their assumption of biological etiology was and remains premature. Those "advances in fields such as neuroimaging, genetics, and molecular biology" have yet to prove their rationale for "newer" pharmacological treatments. Ameen points out how this new perspective has diminished psychoanalytic and psychotherapeutic treatments and turned virtually all attention on biochemical treatments.

By whatever name they are called, diagnoses remain categories invented by doctors who have ties with pharmaceutical companies. A person who supposedly meets a number of criteria (symptoms) is placed in the corresponding category. But in real life, people don't fit neatly in boxes; their personality traits fall along a continuum that blends and changes over their life span. This is especially true for children, who change very quickly through their growing-up years. Moreover, they vary in their rates of task readiness, skill development, and in their learning styles. They also differ in their ability to bounce back from adversity. But in these times, it has become customary to assign diagnoses to children who do not conform to the "expected" trajectory or pattern of development. Sometimes the diagnosis is driven by the child's reaction to the medication prescribed for the condition. If it seems to not "work," the psychiatrist may decide the first diagnosis was wrong. Absurd as it sounds, doctors sometimes claim the medication revealed a more serious underlying condition. They then assign or add a more serious condition, in which case the prescribed drugs will get stronger and multiply. The child's risk of becoming truly mentally ill, and chronically so, has just risen significantly.

Medication

Medication, then, is the next risk factor following diagnosis. Years of observing children deteriorate following the introduction of chemicals into their brains via medication convinced me that doing so worsens the original problem. Many people do not realize that psychiatric drugs go right to the brain, a highly complicated, exquisite, little understood organ. Paul G. Allen, a philanthropist who provided seed money for the Paul G. Allen Brain Institute, was interviewed on NPR's *Morning Edition* in September 2003. He stated that neuroscientists know only about 5 percent of what there is to know about the human brain. Therefore, it would seem that psychotropic drugs, used liberally for decades, have a hit-or-miss affect as they infuse the brain.

The chemicals in psychotropic drugs perturb the brain's natural chemical makeup. Many experts are extremely concerned about plying the developing brains of children with drugs whose long-term effects are not known. Even though magazine and newspaper articles suggest we are using children as guinea pigs, the medical profession at large condones the practice. Psychology professor Daniel Burston[15] observes that the Food and Drug Administration, the mental health industry, and society at large seem to presume a new drug harmless unless proven otherwise. He explains that the Greek word *pharmakos* means "poison" as well as "medicine." This presumption of "harmless" is an especially gross injustice to children, who, unlike adults, never seek these treatments voluntarily. Burston concludes, "We are normalizing the use of powerful psychotropic agents in young children, whose brains are still fragile and unformed." He underscores the dangerous trend toward neurobiological etiology of emotional distress and especially its toxic impact on children.

My granddaughter Nicole teaches science at a residential treatment center for children. We have discussed my objection to the use of medication that is the norm at such places. When I ran into Nicole at the grocery store at the end of a workday, she related an incident that greatly disturbed her. In the middle of her classroom instruction, the nurse barged in unannounced, approached a boy, and demanded that he take his medication. The boy strongly objected, but the nurse pressured him "to make the right choice." Then Nicole told me that during training the new employees were told that the residents could not be forcibly medicated; they had the right to refuse medication. I responded, "Yeah, but are they told that? Are they given information to make an informed decision?"

Nicole's facial expression made my questions rhetorical. She went on to tell me about a girl whose hands are so shaky she can't perform some of the hands-on science activities. This girl told Nicole how she hates taking lithium.

Identification with the Diagnosis

Especially devastating is the final risk factor that logically follows a diagnosis and a chemical (drug) remedy. The child and his parents are led to believe that the problem lies within the child. Getting a diagnosis and taking medicine support this erroneous belief. An example will help explain this risk.

Twelve-year-old Mary returned with her mother to our clinic after a time away. This is how her mother introduced the problem: "Mary's acting up. Sometimes I don't know if it's her bipolar or her ADHD that is coming out. I don't think the medicine is working; it probably needs to be increased." I turned to Mary and asked how she felt things were going for her. Her response: "I got in trouble last week at school for fighting with a girl. And my grades went down this marking period." I asked if she could identify a reason for her difficulties, such as trouble with friends or a teacher she wasn't getting along with. She responded, "My friends don't understand about me being bipolar. The pills were helping me with my schoolwork before." Mary was revealing how she identified with a perceived disorder and felt that having something wrong with her negatively affected her friendships. Her diagnosis became a self-fulfilling prophecy—a phenomenon addressed in the chapter on the bipolar diagnosis. And she attributed her success or deterioration to her medicine rather than taking credit or responsibility for the ups and downs typical for her age. I had known Mary since she was nine and felt initially that she was a pretty typical youngster. She was vivacious and prone to outbursts that I deemed normal for the person she was. But her mother insisted on seeing the clinic psychiatrist because she said she herself was bipolar and on medication, as were others in the family, and she was sure Mary was just like her. Besides, Mary's older sister was taking Paxil for depression, and the mother was convinced that Mary needed medication too. The psychiatrist predictably agreed with the mother and started the drug regimen at that time. Mary had been on and off various pills ever since and discontinued counseling except when prompted by a concern between doctor's visits. Scheduling an extra visit with the psychiatrist mollified this concern. But I knew Mary's future was jeopardized by an illness unwittingly created through the collusion of her mother and the psychiatrist.

Sadly, this is a common scenario. Parents believe the problem resides in their child, and thus seem unwilling to look for other possible causes of unwanted behavior, such as negative family interactions or other factors. Many want the "quick fix" they have been led to believe lies in a pill. In Mary's case, her mother had believed for years that bipolar or some other disorder was inevitable because of family history—not necessarily a history of mental illness, but a history of dependence on medication to solve emotional distress. It is very hard to convince parents like Mary's to try a psychosocial approach that reaches to the source of the distress and ameliorates emotional pain that cycles through generations. I could not help children like Mary who are destined to believe they have a mental illness that requires a lifetime of powerful medication. We can hope for a favorable turn of events before their brains or their lives are irrevocably damaged. Otherwise, these children face poor prognoses.

SUMMARY

The model chosen, psychosocial or medical, influences the therapist's attitude toward her clients. Psychosocial-oriented therapists focus on the strengths of their child clients instead of on what is "wrong" with them. For example, super-abundant energy is an asset when rightly directed. Chapter 7 elucidates drug-free alternatives that can alleviate child distress and behavior management difficulties. It suggests approaches that transform children's high-energy troublesome behavior into constructive behavior that sprouts success. Psychosocial proponents believe our model enriches quality of life for children and their families, while chemical solutions more likely inhibit opportunities to work on positive behavior change on the part of all family members.

Even when organic illness is ruled out, the medical model devotee still sees the child as "ill." Being labeled and taking medication surely imply a sick child. Parents are led to believe the answer to the child's problem lies in a chemical solution that will "bring his brain back in balance," and their main responsibility is to administer medication. They may drop the child off at the clinic to see a therapist every other week, but with young children, little can be accomplished without the collaboration of caregivers. I was saddened every time I lost the opportunity to work with a family once the parents' wish for medicine was satisfied and I never saw the child again. I would check the chart to follow the course of treatment and usually observed the typical pattern: the first medication "didn't work" or "stopped working," so different, stronger ones were introduced.

As in the case of Mary, the medical model of treatment denies the child and family the opportunity to get to the source of emotional distress and make therapeutic changes. Even when caregivers do continue with psychotherapy, it can be a futile exercise because psychotropic medications mask symptoms and/or interfere with cognitive functioning. Parents often believe the problem is solved, when actually it is made worse. Typically, problems emerge on a continuous basis for years, and eventually it becomes impossible to know who the "chemically modified" child really is. I grieve for innocent children who have no say in the very serious decisions made on their behalf that will likely affect the rest of their lives. Evidence of treatment gone terribly wrong was to be found in client records at our clinic. I had only to view charts that were inches thick and sometimes divided into multiple volumes. These contained the stories of children made chronically ill by the treatment to which they were subjected.[16]

The belief system of the clinician drives the course of treatment. Those who hold with neurobiological theory apply the medical model. The medical model poses the risks identified above. Those who hold with psychosocial models avoid medication and work as collaborators with as many family members as they can muster. The child whose brain has not been chemically altered stands the best chance of a timely and complete recovery from the emotional distress that brought him into treatment.

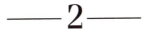

—— 2 ——

ADHD[1] and the Missing Holy Grail

Giving three-year-olds medications to help them be better nursery school students is a giant leap across an ethical threshold that will have profound consequences for our society. The responsibility, or . . . the irresponsibility, is enormous.

—Jonathan Leo

INTRODUCTION AND HISTORY

Super-energized, high-spirited, exuberant, spontaneous, active, intelligent, and impulsive are pro-child ways we might describe kids assigned the ADHD label. Pro-child advocates are terribly concerned about treatments that emerge from the dominant assumption of neurobiological origins of ADHD. Indeed, many believe ADHD is merely a condition of high energy that makes one need to be on the move. Children are particularly prone to restlessness, and up until the mid-20th century it was considered normal; many people still consider it normal.

Most professionals in pediatric mental health agree that ADHD has been grossly overdiagnosed, especially since 1991, when it was added to the group of disabilities that qualify children for special education services. School personnel could now refer difficult students to doctors for stimulant medication once they were labeled.

Children diagnosed by a medical doctor with ADHD also became eligible for Supplemental Security Income (SSI). Consequently, the 1990s saw an explosion of ADHD diagnoses among children. Pediatrician Lawrence Diller noted that the production of Ritalin, the most commonly prescribed drug for ADHD, increased by over 700 percent between 1990 and 1998.[2] This is amazing for a drug that has been available since 1955.

ADHD has long been a topic of interest among professionals. "An Overview of ADHD" by Larry J. Seidman, Ph.D. at Harvard University traces a history of ADHD.[3] About 100 years ago George Still described a condition known as "hyperactivity," or "hyperkinesis disorder of childhood," found mostly in boys. In the 1960s it briefly became known as "minimal brain dysfunction," referred to as "MBD." The consensus was that some kind of brain insult had occurred that could not be detected by any neurological exam. Now outmoded, it introduced the concept of hyperactivity as a brain disease. In the 1970s, deficits in attention became the central defining feature.

Attention deficit disorder first appeared in *Diagnostic and Statistical Manual of Psychiatric Disorders* (DSM), edition III, in 1980. In the 1987 revised version (DSM III-R), it was changed to attention deficit hyperactive disorder with three forms: ADHD inattentive type, ADHD hyperactive and impulsive type, and ADHD combined type (traits of the other two occur together). A child gets the label by exhibiting a given number of symptoms, usually decided by adults who observe the child's behavior and complete a questionnaire. Millions of American children are alleged to have ADHD and/or the other currently popular pediatric diagnosis, bipolar disorder. Many mental health professionals and lay people believe neither are valid disorders. I am a member of the International Center for the Study of Psychiatry and Psychology, a large coalition of professionals and citizens from all over the world who embrace the psychosocial theory of emotional distress and believe children's brains should not be tampered with. Many thousands of people internationally, who don't know about us, share our convictions and concerns.

No neurobiological cause of any so-called mental illness has been proved, yet despite the media attention currently paid to ADHD and bipolar, rarely is their validity questioned. The media question the use of psychotropic drugs on children, but pay little homage to the viable psychosocial alternative that eschews both diagnoses and psychotropic drugs.

This chapter continues its historical overview of ADHD; heeds the words of pro-child professionals who challenge dominant neurobiological theories of ADHD; journeys with neurobiological theorists in search of their Holy Grail— the elusive brain disease explanation of ADHD; and heeds scientific rebuttals from researchers who believe that search is a futile one.

The 1998 National Institutes of Health Consensus Conference on ADHD

The National Institutes of Health (NIH) Consensus Conference on ADHD is remembered as the most comprehensive gathering of ADHD specialists to date. During November 16–18, 1998, 31 speakers presented research findings to an audience of over 1,000 and a consensus panel of 13 experts in Bethesda, Maryland. The panel was to reach a consensus regarding the controversy over the diagnosis that had heightened during the 1990s. Little progress was made toward consensus, and little has changed in the field of ADHD since then toward strengthening neurobiological theory, much as its proponents would have us believe otherwise. However, an unintended outcome of their tenacious research seems to narrow the divide between psychosocial theory and neurobiological theory! That is grist for the next topic in this chapter. For now we'll stay in 1998.

Consensus Development Conferences, as they are called, are supposed to include scientists, health professionals, and others with no personal or direct involvement with the controversy. However, most of the presenters at this conference were well-known advocates of neurobiological theory who apply the medical model to the treatment of ADHD. Psychosocial pro-child advocates included psychiatrist Peter R. Breggin,[4] child temperament specialist William B. Carey, and neurologist Fred Baughman.

Contributions of Psychosocial Proponents and One of Their Champions

Breggin pressed his theory of the disabling effects of psychotropic medications. Concerning stimulants, adverse effects include obsessive-compulsive behavior and decreased spontaneity, side effects that drug advocates deem beneficial. They call these adverse effects "focus" and "calming," respectively. Breggin foresaw the tremendously disproportionate representation planned for the conference. In a statement beforehand,[5] he elaborated his stand regarding stimulant medication, underscoring the travesty of the bias toward neurobiological theory evident in the conference agenda. Continuing with side effects of stimulants, he stated that docility, the aim of stimulant medication, is really an adverse effect because it suppresses children's behavioral signals. The four to five million children taking stimulants are deprived of their ability to inform educators and parents of their needs. Moreover, Breggin asserted that while psychostimulants' dulling effects produce compliance, they also dull higher brain function: "That part of the child's brain requiring creativity, freedom, play, energetic activity, consistent discipline, and inspiring educational activities will be blunted," interfering with normal development. Breggin further charged that the conference was primed to promote the medical model while ignoring alternative perspectives, thereby misleading parents and teachers. He censured the conference organizer, Peter Jensen (a staunch Ritalin advocate), for the criteria he used in recruiting panelists, which narrowed the field down to virtually all neurobiological theorists. He encouraged readers of this document to protest the makeup of the conference by writing letters to members of Congress. He even suggested writing to the conference overseer and demanding that he stop the conference.

Breggin sharply criticized Jensen for eliciting the aid of CHADD (Children and Adults with ADHD/ADD) in recruiting conference panelists. The following partially explains his objection. I accessed a Drug Enforcement Administration (DEA) background paper from October 1995, METHYLPHENIDATE, via a Web site.[6] It reveals that CHADD received $748,000 from Ciba-Geigy (now Novartis), maker of Ritalin (methylphenidate), from 1991 to 1994. The DEA expresses concern that "the depth of the financial relationship was not well known to the public, including CHADD members who rely upon CHADD for guidance as it pertains to the diagnosis and treatment of their children." The DEA paper states that the United Nations International Narcotics Control Board has concerns about non-government and parent organizations in the United States that lobby for the use of methylphenidate (a controlled substance) on children. The board states that a financial transfer from a drug company with intent to promote sales of an internationally controlled substance would be a contradiction with provisions of the 1971 Convention. That convention established an international control system for psychotropic substances. It introduced controls over a number of synthetic drugs (like methylphenidate), balancing their abuse potential against their therapeutic value.[7] The document goes on to say "The relationship between Ciba-Geigy and CHADD raises serious concerns about CHADD's motive in proselytizing the use of Ritalin."

The DEA paper reports further that CHADD, in conjunction with the American Academy of Neurology, submitted a petition to have methylphenidate changed from Schedule II to Schedule III (less stringent) under the Controlled Substances Act. CHADD representatives denied this action had anything to do with the $748,000 contribution from Ciba-Geigy. The petitioners claimed methylphenidate has less abuse potential than amphetamines and that Schedule II controls are burdensome to manufacturers of methylphenidate, to physicians who prescribe it, and to consumers who receive it. The petition failed, and methylphenidate remains a Schedule II controlled substance.

Another document by Peter Breggin reported on the Consensus Development Conference following its adjournment.[8] Breggin deplored the absence of members of the International Center for the Study of Psychiatry and Psychology who could have "transformed the meeting from a celebration of psychopharmacology to an examination of the needs of individual children and how to meet them." In summary, he denounced the conference as a betrayal to children, on account of its emphasis on the biomedical approach to ADHD.

William B. Carey asserted that ADHD is a reflection of temperament, not a disorder. In the *American Academy of Pediatrics Newsletter*, he critiqued the overriding opinion about ADHD that was apparent at the ADHD Consensus Conference.[9] He offered alternative opinions missing from the conference: Symptoms of ADHD are not clearly distinguishable from normal behavior; biological causation has not been scientifically proven; brain imaging techniques have not been useful and research in this area has not been rigorous; environmental influences are neglected; the diagnostic questionnaire is highly subjective and impressionistic; adaptive features of ADHD symptoms are neglected; the ADHD label can damage careers; and misapplication of diagnostic criteria causes overdiagnosing. Carey recommended improvement in the diagnostic system, in research, in education of professionals and the public, in evaluations, in treatment with greater reliance on psychosocial and educational interventions, and in insurance reimbursements to allow physicians more time to evaluate. He promoted regulation of medical diagnosing and of teachers' insisting on medication. He wanted better monitoring of the aggressive advertising by drug companies and elimination of unethical conflicts of interest on the part of physicians. Carey wrote this article five years after the convention, but his points are valid today.

Fred Baughman is author of *The ADHD Fraud: How Psychiatry Makes Patients of Normal Children*. Thirty-five years of experience discovering and diagnosing bona fide neurological diseases qualify him as an expert critic of ADHD. His NIH Conference testimony was accessed via the Internet:

> Without an iota of proof or credible science, the National Institute of Mental Health (NIMH) has proclaimed the . . . children "brain-diseased," "abnormal." CHADD, funded by Ciba-Geigy, manufacturer of Ritalin, has spread the "Neuro-biological" lie. The U.S. Department of Education, absolving itself of controlling the children and rendering them literate, coerces the labeling and drugging . . . ADHD is a total, 100% fraud.[10]

According to Lawrence Diller, Nadine Lambert did not represent either side of the controversy at the conference. Without bias regarding the etiology or treatment of ADHD, she presented outcomes of her long-term study of ADHD individuals. Those treated with Ritalin as children were more prone to use illicit drugs as young adults than her untreated control group.[11] We will learn how her presentation was received in chapter 4, where her study is detailed. I include her with the proponents of psychosocial theory because her data supported those proponents. She remains a champion of psychosocial theorists because of her courageous tenacity in sticking by her science in the face of hostile antagonism by the powerful psychopharmaceutical juggernaut.

Judith Bluestone of the HANDLE Institute (which provides non-drug, holistic treatment for learning, behavioral, and other challenges children present with) participated at the convention, although not as an invited speaker. She wrote her impressions of the conference on her organization's Web site.[12] To a consensus panel statement that lack of public information is a major problem in finding appropriate treatment and services for ADHD, Ms. Bluestone countered that there is no lack of information. Instead, she asserted that there *is* a lack of accurate information available to the public due to political and financial funding for a specific agenda only. "We need," she said, "to support the voices of those who have knowledge about more effective and more ethical agendas to help children whose needs are not met." To me, her thoughts are apropos: Only when those voices are heard above the hype of drug advertising and quick fixes will options be available to all who need them.

The outnumbered psychosocial advocates at the convention had an impact. For despite the overemphasis on neurobiological theory and the expected recommendation for continued use of stimulants, the panel's consensus included recognition of the ongoing controversy and unsettled questions. Here are some quotes from their consensus statement, taken from the NIH Web site:

> There are no data to indicate that ADHD is due to a brain malfunction.
>
> Further research to establish the validity of the disorder continues to be a problem. There is no information on the long-term outcomes of medication-treated ADHD individuals in terms of educational and occupational achievements, involvement with the police, or other areas of social functioning. There is little improvement in academic achievement or social skills from stimulant medication.
>
> It is well known that psychostimulants have abuse potential.
>
> Very high doses of psychostimulants, particularly of amphetamines, may cause central nervous system damage, cardiovascular damage, and hypertension. In addition, higher doses have been associated with compulsive behaviors and, in certain vulnerable individuals, movement disorders. A very small percentage of children and adults treated at high doses have had hallucinogenic responses.[13]

PHARMACEUTICAL COMPANY LITERATURE AND A REBUTTAL

Pharmaceutical companies circulate thousands of brochures to public places. Masquerading as informational publications, they use false or misleading information to advertise their products. Sometimes psychologists or psychiatrists collaborate to lend authenticity to the acclaimed "success" of the given drug. One instance of such collaboration between a psychologist and a drug company was challenged by fellow psychologists. The story follows.

A brochure containing myths about ADHD was developed and distributed as a joint project between Division 29 (Psychotherapy) of the American Psychological Association and Celltech Pharmaceuticals, a drug company that produces and markets stimulant drugs for children diagnosed with ADHD. Amazingly, association member Al Galves was apparently the sole constituent of Division 29's 4,000 members who complained about statements in the brochure that were unsupported by adequate scientific evidence. Consequently, in 2002[14] he and fellow psychologist David Walker disputed those myths in a letter signed by 12 members of the American Psychological Association.[15] This letter clearly and comprehensively covers the rebuttals to neurobiological theory. In fact, the first two myths and the rebuttals apply to all the common so-called mental disorders of children. These myths have been used to explain ADHD, bipolar, and other forms of childhood distress.

Let's address one statement at a time.

Myth 1: ADD/ADHD is generally considered a neuro-chemical disorder. The authors' response: Popular opinion maintains this is so, but the evidence to support the statement is equivocal and inconsistent. The truth of the statement requires that the brain physiology of individuals with ADHD is different from non-ADHD individuals. Even if the evidence were more consistent, it still would not prove that the differences were the cause of ADHD, only that there would be an association between the differences and the disorder. If such an association existed, the physiological differences could be the result of behaviors and emotions exhibited by an individual who acts hyperactive. Our authors point out that "the brain is a living, functioning organ constantly responding to its environment with complex neurochemical and other neurofunctional changes, so it is just as likely (perhaps more likely) that the biological dynamics are a **result** of an interplay of emotions, thoughts, intentions and behavior experienced by the diagnosed individual." To support this likelihood, Galves and Walker cite the research of Jeffrey Schwartz and colleagues of the University of California.[16] These scientists found that a group of people suffering with obsessive-compulsive disorder had abnormalities in their brains. Half the group was treated with drugs and the other half with cognitive-behavioral talk therapy. All subjects improved, and when Schwartz and colleagues examined their brains, all had changed in the same way. They concluded that talk therapy and chemical treatment had the same impact on brain physiology.

This is not the only convincing study of its kind. The authors go on to cite seven other research studies in which brain physiology changed in response to environmental stimuli. One showed the relationship between vulnerability to depression and seven psychological variables. For example, suffering trauma at an early age, having a high need for or having lost an important relationship, and having a ruminating style of thinking were shown to correlate with depression. A logical conclusion could be that trauma and personal attributes precipitate depressive episodes, not a congenital chemical imbalance.

The authors continue their rebuttal by citing Baumeister and Hawkins,[17] who performed an exhaustive review of brain studies designed to locate the site of ADHD in the brain. The techniques used by those who allege to have made breakthroughs include structural and functional neuroimaging such as positron emission tomography (PET), single positron scanning, magnetic resonance imaging (MRI), and electrophysiological measurement. Despite popular consensus among experts that ADHD is caused by brain abnormalities, the researchers' review concluded that the neuroimaging literature provides no convincing evidence for the existence of abnormalities in the brains of persons with ADHD. Galves and Walker reiterate that any biological dynamics correlating with ADHD in the brain

> **can be more accurately depicted as a result of psychological and environmental variables** than a neurodevelopmentally damaged, diseased, or dysfunctional brain . . . calling ADHD a "neurochemical disorder" with a "biological cause" implies that it has nothing to do with how a child thinks, feels, reacts, intends, perceives, adjusts and responds. It implies that the behaviors are not under the control of the child or those within the child's world and have nothing to do with how the child finds and makes meaning in that world. That is a fundamental error contradicted by those of us who, like you, also work very closely with children and families every day. (p. 5)

Myth 2: Most people with ADD/ADHD are born with the disorder, though it may not be recognized until adulthood. This myth is so ingrained that the Council of Regional Networks for Genetic Services (CORN) even lists mental illness as a genetic disorder.[18]

Galves and Walker argue cogently against the prevalent assumption that because ADHD seems to run in families, it is genetic in origin. They point out that most of the research on ADHD has been comparisons of monozygotic (identical) with dizygotic (fraternal) twins raised in various socioeconomic circumstances. Researchers almost invariably found higher incidences of both twins having ADHD in identical twins than in fraternal twins; hence, they concluded the genetic theory was correct. Their studies were based on the assumption that both types of twins were raised in equivalent environments. Our authors cite the work of Jay Joseph,[19] who proved this not to be the case. Joseph surveyed the two types of twins using ten variables and concluded that fraternal twins vary little from any other siblings in the family, while identical twins experience a very different relationship with each other. Very close bonding and how others regard them as totally alike comprise the differences found in identical twins. Consequently, they are affected by very different environmental influences than fraternal twins or ordinary siblings. Invalidating the assumption of comparable environments means that correlations between identical twins are just as likely the result of environmental factors as of genetic factors. Galves and Walker's argument against genetic influence on behavior is strengthened when they point out the complicated biochemistry of genes and the role the environment plays in determining how genes express themselves.

Genetic theory proponents have also attempted to prove their case by comparing the incidence of ADHD in the relatives of ADHD children with the incidence of ADHD in relatives of non-ADHD children. But their research has not taken into account all the environmental factors that impinge on family members from generation to generation. Galves and Walker list 13 family and parent characteristics associated with the behavioral traits of ADHD; all reflect unmet needs in childhood. They go on to discuss the work of researchers in attachment and trauma. How successfully parents bond with infants up to age one determines much about the emotional welfare of children later on. Traumatic events early in life have been shown to have a great impact on the ability of victims to modulate their emotions and to deal effectively with stressful or frustrating experiences later on. Galves and Walker assert that the research backing this myth ignores the important variables of trauma and attachment so crucial to early child development, and that such inattention represents a major research deficiency.

The authors concede that common sense and research implicate some genetic influence on the behaviors characterizing ADHD. They add, however, that research indicates genetics is not a major factor. Three psychiatrists—Lewis, Amini, and Lannon—say it best:

> Genetic information lays down the brain's basic macro and microanatomy; experience then narrows still-expansive possibilities into an outcome . . . While

genes are pivotal in establishing some aspects of emotionality, experience plays a central role in turning genes on and off. DNA is not the heart's destiny; the genetic lottery may determine the cards in your deck, but experience deals the hand you can play . . . Like most of their toys, children arrive with considerable assembly required . . . A child's brain cannot develop normally without the coordinating influence that limbic communication furnishes. The coos and burbles that infants and parents exchange, the cuddling, rocking, and joyous peering into each other's faces look innocuous if not inane; one would not suspect a life-shaping process in the offing. But from their first encounter, parents guide the neurodevelopment of the baby they engage with. In his primal years, they mold a child's inherited emotional brain into the neural core of the self.[20]

Myth 3: Poor teaching has no impact on ADHD. Our authors support their opinion that while poor teaching cannot be blamed for the explosion of ADHD diagnoses, public school curricula are not conducive to commanding the attention of students. Consequently, many children are bored or their individual needs are not met. The authors' criticisms include "one-size-fits-all, standardized methodologies, and minimal or no opportunity for active learning." They decry the trend to drop from curricula music, art, and other subjects that appeal to intelligences besides linguistic and mathematical, and cite scholars Holt,[21] Leonard,[22] and Gatto,[23] who testify that typical schools fail to encourage students "to develop into the creative beings they crave to be."

The No Child Left Behind initiative has magnified the very elements of education they criticize.

"Poor teaching" does not mean that teachers are to blame. Many dedicated teachers are equally concerned about curricula they are forced to wield on their students. The blame lies with policy makers who have no expertise in child development or the educational needs of diverse children.

The letter concludes with a request to cease the distribution of the brochure containing all the aforementioned statements. Galves and Walker point out that the statements are not facts, but merely unproven theories. They request that other points of view be given equal exposure with the acknowledgment that psychologists hold a variety of opinions about ADHD and its etiology.

OTHER PUBLICIZED MISINFORMATION

All Americans are exposed to misinformation through periodicals, radio, and television. The United States is the only developed nation that permits direct-to-consumer advertising of pharmaceutical products. Hence, we are inundated with TV advertisements for all sorts of drugs, including psychotropic medications. News releases abound with claims of breakthroughs by brain or gene studies that prove the cause of a disorder, or the efficacy of a new treatment.

An article from *Nami Beginnings*, summer 2003, was circulated through the clinic where I worked. The article introduced Larry Greenhill as "a nationally known" child and adolescent psychiatrist who presented at the 2003 National

Alliance on Mental Illness (NAMI)[24] convention. In his talk "Ask the Doctor: ADHD and Co-occurring Disorders," he contended that ADHD is characterized by abnormalities in two parts of the brain. He explained that transmission of dopamine is lower in both areas. He cited no study to document this statement. We have established there is no medical test for "mental illness," including detection of dopamine in the brain of a living person. Later, he claimed that among three treatment choices, medication-plus-behavior therapy or managed-medication-only are superior to behavior therapy alone. He was apparently alluding to the Multimodal Treatment Study of Children with ADHD (MTA), a controversial study the conclusions of which are still open to criticism. I wondered for a long time who Larry Greenhill was. In her 2008 book, *Our Daily Meds*,[25] Melody Petersen provides the answer. Laurence Greenhill is a professor at Columbia University who presented at a 2005 convention attended by Petersen, at which he disclosed his ties with seven drug companies, including the makers of the biggest-selling medications for ADHD. That information compromises his objectivity.

I picked up two typical ADHD stories in family doctor waiting rooms. The first is the spring 2007 issue of *SUNY Upstate Outlook* that featured "The Young Brain." The article "Attention Deficit Hyperactivity Disorder Collateral Damage," with a subheading that reads "At SUNY Upstate, an extraordinary concentration of ADHD experts warn that—left untreated—the misunderstood condition derails lives and predisposes young patients to mood disorders and even substance abuse." (Remember Nadine Lambert's research that showed people *who had taken Ritalin* were more predisposed to substance abuse than hyperactive people who did not?) The article commences, ". . . an increasing body of neurobiological evidence shows physical differences in the ADHD brain" (p. 10). But the four Ph.D. "experts" do not explain what differences, whether the subjects had taken stimulant medication, or what research revealed them. And they don't bother to add that a brain difference does not mean it's a *cause* of the ADHD. (It could be a result of behavior or an environmental influence, as established earlier.)

Let me digress briefly to explain why scholars like Al Galves, David Walker, and the scientists they cite to support their rebuttals remain less well known than those who perform research designed to support neurobiological theory (like our four Upstate "experts"). Doctors who hold with neurobiological causation prescribe drugs. This pleases the rich pharmaceutical empire, so drug companies fund grants to doctors whose research is aimed at supporting neurobiological theory. Drug companies' largesse finances high profile publicity in prestigious medical journals and mainstream media (journals and media receive lots of money for drug advertising, and drug companies pay researchers to publish studies that appear to support medication as treatment in medical journals). The ubiquitous reach of the pharmaceutical industry dwarfs the influence of scientists who bear witness against the efficacy of medication as treatment for emotional distress. Mainstream psychiatrists embrace neurobiological theory because they prescribe drugs as primary treatment for emotional distress. In most states, only medical doctors (including psychiatrists) can prescribe medication. In the United States, clinical social workers, who cannot prescribe, comprise the largest group of psychotherapists. In public or not-for-profit clinics, psychotherapists usually are required to follow guidelines that include, as routine procedure, referral to psychiatrists for evaluation. Private practitioners enjoy more autonomy than their counterparts in these clinics and may choose not to refer their clients for medication.

The second article, "Out of Step," appears in the September/October 2006 issue of *Web M.D.* It says, regarding the diagnostic outcome for a misbehaving 4-year-old: "A pediatric and neurological specialist independently confirmed that it was ADHD" (p. 50). Later the article refers to "testing" that confirmed another child's diagnosis of ADHD (p. 52). The statement implies that it takes a specialized doctor of medicine to diagnose ADHD. Moreover, it implies there is a medical test to confirm the diagnosis. Readers should understand by now that both implications are totally without merit. They are widely publicized myths. Methods of diagnosing ADHD are very subjective and unreliable.

NEUROBIOLOGISTS SEARCH FOR THE HOLY GRAIL

Let's look deeper now at that topic of intense interest to neurobiological theorists, their search for the indisputable biological markers that prove to cause ADHD and other "brain diseases." Their search has been futile, but I do not expect readers to take my word for it. The media often glorify psychiatrists' claims to be on the brink of cracking the etiology of ADHD or pediatric bipolar disorder. The claims are usually based on various forms of brain imaging. Let's delve into the controversy, giving equal time to the scientists who diminish the relevance of brain imaging research and warn of its potentially harmful effects.

An Early Study Challenges Neurobiologists

"Cortical Atrophy in Young Adults with a History of Hyperactivity" appeared in *Psychiatric Research* in 1986.[26] Henry Nasrallah and colleagues reported atrophy in more than half of 24 young adults. All had been treated with psychostimulants, and the authors hypothesized, "cortical atrophy may be a long-term adverse effect of this treatment." Since that study, many researchers have attempted to disprove the Nasrallah hypothesis. Neurobiological researchers seek to demonstrate that the atrophy is the cause of ADHD, not an effect of psychostimulants. So far they have not done so, but, as we shall see, evidence supporting Nasrallah's hypothesis has emerged. First let's trace some of the well-known studies published since 1986.

Famous (or Infamous) NIMH Study

An early attempt by Alan Zametkin and colleagues at the National Institute of Mental Health (NIMH) to prove the brain disease theory of ADHD is often cited by authors. The following accounts come from Richard DeGrandpre and Thomas Armstrong, who wrote *Ritalin Nation*[27] and *The Myth of the A.D.D. Child*,[28] respectively. DeGrandpre starts with a quote from the November 26, 1990, issue of *Time* magazine: "In a landmark study that could help put to rest decades of confusion and controversy, researchers at the NIMH have traced ADHD . . . to a specific metabolic abnormality in the brain." The research was published in the *New England Journal of Medicine*. While the subjects performed an attention task, Zametkin's group used positron emission tomography (PET) scans to discern levels of glucose metabolism in those areas of the brain associated with control of attention, planning, and motor control. Hyperactive and non-hyperactive adults were examined, and the group found that levels of glucose metabolism were 8.1 percent lower in the ADHD adults than in those without ADHD. Therefore, the researchers proclaimed that ADHD was caused by insufficient glucose metabolism in those areas of the brain that were not working up to par. The news of the study spread like wildfire. Pictures of "ADHD" and "non-ADHD" brains circulated through the media. Parents were ecstatic to learn that they were not the cause of their children being hyperactive—the cause dwelt in the children.

Troubles with the study emerged two and three years later. Major flaws in the study design came to light; for example, the researchers failed to control for gender. Seventy-one percent of subjects in the hyperactive group were men, while only 56 percent were men in the control group. When other researchers compared rates of metabolism between males and females in the control group, they found the men metabolized at a significantly lower rate than the women, which completely discredited the study. Then, when Zametkin and the group tried to replicate the experiment three years later with adolescents, they failed to find significant differences between ADHD and non-ADHD groups. However, these findings were not hailed with the same public enthusiasm; to this day, disease theory proponents sometimes cite Zametkin's research to support their hypothesis. There is unanimous agreement among leading researchers that Zametkin's work was bad science and that brain-imaging techniques even now are only a research tool, not a treatment or diagnostic instrument.

The Breggins, in *The War Against Children of Color*, reveal the callous negligence of Zametkin and his team when they exposed subjects to radiation via PET scans. In fact, his NIMH team claimed the study was successful despite failure to replicate earlier findings because "[t]he feasibility of normal minors participating in radiation research was established."[29] The team apparently was triumphant about being the first to expose normal adolescents to radiation for "research purposes"! The Breggins consulted a radiologist at the National Institutes of Health, who remained anonymous, about the ethical ramifications of this study. He responded that the potential for cancer was unknown, would take many years to manifest, and that such experiments should not have been done. Furthermore, he told them that performing PET scans involves painful injections and lengthy immobilization in a scary machine.

Contemporary Neurobiological Research

At the 1998 National Institutes of Health Consensus Convention on ADHD, Xavier Castellanos and his colleague James Swanson presented their review of studies performed between 1990 and 1998 that used magnetic resonance imaging (MRI). They claimed the scans proved ADHD brains had atrophied features. In a letter to the Portsmouth, Virginia, school board dated October 20, 2007, Fred Baughman[30] countered that virtually all of the studies in their review used subjects who had been on long-term stimulant treatment, which was the likely cause of the atrophies. Reportedly, Swanson responded that he planned to follow up with more studies controlling for this variable. Then Castellanos followed up with just such a study.

Castellanos previewed an ongoing 10-year study on PBS's *Frontline* 2001 program "Medicating Kids," which focused on ADHD.[31] He explained the goal of the study was to determine whether brain atrophy in ADHD children is a feature of the disorder or a side effect of stimulant medications. This study on kids who had never taken stimulants, he claimed, appeared to show that brain atrophy was not related to medication. He claimed the posterior inferior vermis—the small part of the cerebellum—was 12 percent smaller in the 50 or 60 kids with ADHD, compared to the same number of "healthy" (quotation marks denote that ADHD kids are healthy too) kids, and the caudate 6 percent smaller in the ADHD kids. Castellanos continued, "We've scanned children who have ADHD over the past ten years to develop growth curves. Many have had up to four scans. We use MRI to measure the brain, especially the basal ganglia and cerebellum."

At one point in the interview, Castellanos said, "There are some studies that can't be done in children, because the regulations that we work under require that we limit the risk to negligible levels, especially if we're going to be studying healthy children as control subjects." He said children are not supposed to be exposed to radiation. Apparently he deems the powerful magnetic fields used in MRIs to be of "negligible risk."

Sometimes dyes that are not benign are used in scanning procedures. On February 4, 2008, *A Drug Recall*[32] reported that in May 2007 the Food and Drug Administration ordered the makers of gadolinium-based MRI dyes to add a heightened warning to the product's label informing doctors and patients of the risk of nephrogenic systemic fibrosis, or NSF. This kidney disease, linked to the use of these dyes, causes the skin, connective tissues, and sometimes even internal organs to thicken and harden. It can lead to severe debilitation and even death in adults. Children may be at greater risk. In chapter 8, environmental experts explain why children are much more vulnerable to toxins than grown-ups.

The 10-year study on children that Castellanos referred to above was published in the October 9, 2002, *Journal of the American Medical Association*.[33] He was lead author of the study and chief of the National Institute of Mental Health's child psychiatry branch, Judith Rapoport, was among his coauthors. Launched in 1991, this study measured volume in cerebral, total white matter, and cerebellar regions of the brain. Their subjects were 152 ADHD boys and girls, 49 of which had not been treated with stimulants, and 139 non-ADHD children purportedly matched by age and gender. They found that brains of children and adolescents with ADHD were 3 to 4 percent smaller than non-ADHD children. All the children were scanned with MRI at least twice, and some up to four times. Since comparisons were made with ADHD children not exposed to stimulant treatment, the authors concluded that medication was not the cause of brain shrinkage. However, they admitted that even with these differences, the ADHD children's brains developed normally, only somewhat delayed compared to the brains of non-ADHD children.

Pediatrician S. DuBose Ravenel lists several weaknesses in this study.[34] Most importantly, the researchers did not match subjects and controls by age. The ADHD subjects in the study were significantly younger. Ravenel cites Jonathan Leo and David Cohen's[35] observation that the unmedicated subjects, being younger and smaller, would be expected to have smaller brains, based on previous brain research not related to ADHD. Leo and Cohen add that the researchers failed to provide information about dose, duration of treatment, or type of drug used among the ADHD subjects treated with psychostimulants at the time of the first scan. Ravenel concludes, therefore, that the question Castellanos and Rapoport set out to answer—whether brain atrophy is or is not caused by medication—remains unresolved.

Important Implications of the Research

Regardless of its flaws, the study led Castellanos and Rapoport to another significant conclusion: "**Fundamental developmental processes active during late childhood and adolescence are essentially healthy in ADHD**."[36] Still clinging to that neurobiological mindset, they assert, "Symptoms appear to reflect fixed earlier neurobiological insults or abnormalities."

I believe there is great significance in the authors' admission that ADHD children's brains develop normally when not treated with psychostimulants. As to speculation regarding earlier neurological insults or abnormalities, hearken back to Galves and Walker's emphasis on the impact of trauma and attachment in the first year of life. These could explain "neurological insults or abnormalities"!

Equally astounding, recent studies elucidate inferences on the part of neurobiological theorists that some brain differences could be adaptive responses to environmental influences. For example, National Institutes of Health-funded researchers Kerstin Plessen, Bradley Peterson, and colleagues used MRI to scan the brains of 51 ADHD children and 63 "healthy" peers. Their study was published in the July 3, 2006, *Archives of General Psychiatry*.[37] They found the usual differences in size. Their notable statement was in response to the finding that the hippocampus tended to be enlarged in ADHD children, especially the higher functioning ones. **They suggest the changes might be a compensatory response that helps children cope with some of the ADHD traits**. This is tantamount to an admission that brain differences, or changes, could reflect adaptations to environmental stressors!

Nancy Shute interviewed Rapoport for *U.S. News and World Report* regarding still another study published in *Proceedings of the National Academy of Sciences* on November 12, 2007. Coauthor Rapoport explained that the study elucidated exciting new information because this time they examined the thickness of the brain's outer layer, the cortex, instead of just looking at the changes in the volume of gray matter and focusing on the size of the brain's lobes. Thickness was correlated with better outcomes. Four-hundred forty-six children, half ADHD and half controls, were scanned at age 9 and again about six years later. They found that almost half of the ADHD children outgrew their symptoms. Rapoport is quoted as saying this study suggests that **for almost half of ADHD children, their impairment is simply about a three-year delay in maturation and that maturation is, in the end, normal**. She states that the delays were most evident in areas at the front of the brain's outer covering, the cortex, which controls thinking, attention, and planning. She reports that maturation thickness occurred at about age seven in "normals" and age 10 in ADHD children. The authors decide that the nearly 50 percent of ADHD children who outgrow the disorder comprise one of several subtypes of ADHD. Among subgroups, she concedes that **some of these outgrow their symptoms through enlargement of other parts of the brain to "create an alternative intelligence system."**[38]

Here again is recognition that the brain adapts to meet challenges of living. A psychosocial theorist could make the case that this study supports the psychosocial hypothesis that environment and behavior influence brain structure and processes. This is speculative, since we have no information regarding the rigor of the research or whether the children in this study had a history of treatment with stimulants. But when Rapoport refers to subgroups, one could speculate that her research is leading in the direction of normalizing the condition of ADHD—that children come in many forms, along a continuum of motor activity.

The next study almost brings the authors to this same conclusion, although they stop short of reneging the whole disease concept of ADHD. This gene study by Shaw and Rapoport was cited on the *NIMH News* Web site and was published in the August 2007 *Archives of General Psychiatry*. The researchers attempted to correlate genes with subtypes of ADHD. Without detailing the entire study, I quote the startling suggestion by Shaw that "**Since this gene version had similar structural effects in healthy children as in children with the disorder, our findings suggest that ADHD is at the far end of a continuum of normal traits**" (Emphasis added). Shaw also posits that "Some genes have a good side, even though they're linked to disorder." He adds that some traits of ADHD might be advantageous in some settings, and further suggests that "**Evidence suggests that the 7-repeat (gene) may be a relatively new variant that may have been favored through evolution because such traits proved adaptive for survival.**"[39]

Finally—and ironically—Peter Jensen, who has been like a "nemesis" to psychosocial theorists elsewhere in this book, and his fellow authors make an amazing statement.[40] They suggest that evolutionary biology provides a framework for explaining the phenomena of childhood behavioral and emotional disturbances. They say, "Through an evolutionary biological lens, some mental disorders are better viewed as an adaptive response to early pathogenic environments and/or reflect the optimization of brain function to some environments at the cost of poorer response to the demands of other environments." They suggest the attributes of ADHD, like inattention, impulsivity, and hyperactivity, may be potentially adaptive, depending on the nature of a child's environment.

What astonishing suggestions coming from neurobiological theorists—that traits of ADHD may not only be part of a normal spectrum, but might even be advantageous! How, then, could ADHD be an illness? Gene studies may locate sites that house determinants of ADHD traits, but will not prove pathology. Genes determine many traits that are not associated with illness. The good news is that neurobiological theorists' research seems to validate some of the precepts of psychosocial theory. The tragedy remains that probably thousands of children have been and continue to be exposed to potentially hazardous examinations and medications. Now let's hear what a brilliant specialist has to say about all this brain research.

NEUROTOXICOLOGIST GRACE E. JACKSON CRITIQUES BRAIN IMAGING

Psychiatrist and neurotoxicologist (expert in brain toxicology) Grace E. Jackson responds to researchers who claim to have discovered certain anatomical differences or processes in the brain that distinguish a "diseased" (that is, one exhibiting "mental illness") brain from a "normal" brain. Her exquisite explanations appeared in her 2006 article "A Curious Consensus: Brain Scans Prove Disease?"[41] She cites the recent series of appearances by physicians on national television news programs to inform the public that technological advances in brain studies have confirmed the brain disease hypothesis of mental illness. Such appearances have gained momentum since this article was written. Reporters fail to seriously question the validity of their claims. Jackson quotes two doctors who appeared on CNN on June 30, 2005. First, neurosurgeon Sanjay Gupta: "When you don't have enough neurotransmitters firing, making the connections, your brain doesn't act like it should. And you can see what a normal brain should look like. That's an objective measure" (p. 55). She also quotes psychiatrist Nada Stotland: ". . . we can see differences between brain images of someone who is depressed and someone who is not depressed. And if we give medications, the brain of the depressed person goes back to looking like a person not depressed" (p. 55).

First Jackson explains that there are two types of studies. Anatomical differences in the brain are detected with computed tomography (CT) and magnetic resonance imaging (MRI). These capture snapshots of the brain. Functional or physiological processes in the brain, on the other hand, are studied with functional MRI (fMRI), positron emission tomography (PET), and single-photon emission, computed tomography (SPECT). Researchers, by making comparisons between activities of one person or between multiple persons, seek to identify parts of the nervous system that are uniquely involved during certain activities and when persons are at rest. Again Jackson quotes Gupta: "An ADHD brain is on the left side there. You can see, it's mainly on the right side of the brain that things are activating. They should be activating all over and on the left side as well. You see a non-ADHD brain, again, it's different than the ADHD brain. These are measurements that people take. This is the science that people have been talking about and this is what a lot of treatment is predicated on" (p. 56).

Jackson points out that the technologies to which Gupta refers do not directly measure brain activity. Rather, they show temporary changes in blood flow. Second, Gupta fails to mention confounding factors such as age, gender, body size, drug use, medical conditions, physical activity, education, and diet. All these variables that influence the brain's response to stimuli need to be accounted for in research.

Jackson identifies another very important shortfall in using the technologies for the purposes popularized in the media. Blood flow is considered important by the "chosen experts" because they presume that blood flow indicates activity among neurons. This is called neurovascular coupling (blood flow and neural cellular activity occur together). That is, cellular activity in neurons creates a "need" for increased blood flow. However, Jackson informs us that animal and human studies have shown that this is not always the case. For example, in some studies of brain damage survivors, the deprivation of oxygen or sugar in the cerebrum has not been followed by surges of blood flow, as would be predicted by the theory of neurovascular coupling. It follows, then, that until the cause and timing of cerebral blood flow are better understood, the implications of functional imaging technologies remain ambiguous.

Jackson points out still another shortcoming of the technologies described above: there is a time lag between electrical brain events (cellular neural activity) and blood flow. The former happens in a span of hundreds of milliseconds, while the action of blood flow lags by one to three seconds. The imaging scanner and the brain, then, are never synchronized. Therefore, the technologies may provide information about locations of some mental phenomena, but not about the onset or duration of the events that incite the blood flow. Limitations of the technology also include the fact that blood flow does not necessarily indicate neural activity precisely in the underlying regions of the brain. It could be occurring some distance away.

Another interesting feature of Gupta's television presentation was his image of the "ADHD" brain versus the "non-ADHD" brain. Jackson reveals that when an "ADHD" brain is projected, it does not represent any one person's brain. Actually, the variations in one person or between different individuals are so variable that the technique cannot be used in the clinic for diagnostic purposes.

Gupta and others who either describe or perform these techniques take scans of many individuals and make an average composite image. Television presenters do not mention this.

Finally, Jackson reiterates the point made earlier that association (in this case blood flow with neural activity) does not prove causation. She further argues that it is even possible that the changes in or differences between brains could be adaptive, in which case it would be a mistake to administer drugs that interfere with a naturally beneficial process. (Rapoport acknowledged this possibility regarding her genetic research when she stated that enlargement of other parts of the brain creates an alternative intelligence system.)

Another important consideration about brain imaging techniques is their unproven safety. In several animal studies, Jackson tells us, the magnetic fields used in MRI caused contaminants to enter the brain. Serious inflammatory or autoimmune conditions could be initiated should this occur in humans.[42] Another hazard is radiation. Researcher Castellanos, in his interview on *Frontline*, said regulations protect children from certain forms of brain imaging because of radiation. Apparently they are not protected from the potential risks of MRIs.

SCAM "TREATMENTS" BASED ON IMAGING

In the private sector, hazardous SPECT scans that expose patients to radiation are performed on children under the ruse of "treatment." The highly publicized Amen Clinics, founded by Daniel G. Amen, M.D., purport on their Web site[43] to successfully "treat" a variety of mental and emotional conditions, notably ADHD. All their "treatments" are determined through SPECT imaging. Amen claims his diagnoses of ADHD by SPECT are more precise, sometimes avoiding the potential "extreme" side effects of stimulant medication. The Web site prominently displays an ad for CareCredit, an agency that provides a year of interest-free credit for medical procedures, a hint that traditional medical insurance does not cover services (as it shouldn't, since even the neurobiologists admit brain imaging is not a diagnostic tool). Another scheme employing SPECT is discussed later in this chapter.

In Jackson's article and on all the other sites accessed on the topic of SPECT imaging on children, reference is made to *Brain Imaging and Child and Adolescent Psychiatry With Special Emphasis on SPECT,* a position paper drafted in 2005 by the American Psychiatric Association's Council on Children, Adolescent and Their Families. I accessed this document's summary on February 5, 2008, from the APA's Web site.[44] The statement disavows any claims that brain imaging techniques are useful for diagnostic or treatment purposes, and asserts its usefulness is confined to research. It also states, "Particular caveats are indicated with regard to brain imaging involving radioactive nucleotides for children and adolescents because of children's known greater sensitivity to radiation and risk of radiation-induced cancer. The long-term risks of initial and repeated exposure to intravenous radio nucleotides are unknown." Jackson tells us that no dose of radiation from positron emission tomography (PET) or SPECT is ever hazard free, and its effects are cumulative, not fleeting. Potential risks mentioned are cancers, birth defects, and heart disease. When I tried to access this document in March 2009, it had been removed from the APA Web site. We know, for example, from recent statements by "bipolar experts" Kiki Chang and George Bush, M.D.,[45] that the APA has not veered from this position. So the removal of the position paper remains a mystery about which we can only speculate. Jackson assures us that, for philosophical reasons, brain imaging will never be more than a research tool. Her eloquence in an e-mail sent me on March 4, 2009, is inspiring: "No one can demonstrate Human Agency or Volition with a SPECT scan . . . No amount of tampering with new technologies will ever permit psychiatry to move beyond the philosophical question of WHAT a person is in terms of what motivates or controls behavior. Sorry, but there will never be a machine that traps the source of Agency." I think Jackson is saying that we humans are more than computerized automatons. Our beings cannot be quantified (reduced to biological numerics).

Frontline's "The Medicated Child"

Public Television's *Frontline* aired "The Medicated Child" on January 8, 2008. We've established that scientists of any repute agree that brain imaging is useless as a diagnostic tool. But on the *Frontline* program, the television camera zoomed in on social worker Nancy Goodhue, co-founder of a Denver-based organization called Brain Matters, in consultation with her patient, a young boy, and his family. She was interpreting the SPECT images, claiming that the images showed blood flow, and that the colors in one image in the thalo-limbic area of his brain were the wrong colors. "This suggests to our doctor that Matthew has trouble with mood," she explained. "So the recommendation is to prescribe medication that actually stabilizes mood." Matthew's dad said, "Good job explaining. I don't really understand the medical terms used, but I think it's pretty much on target." Matthew's mother asked if Goodhue wasn't raising false hopes. Goodhue replied, "Well, you know, I really hope not. Compared to the diagnostic interview and paper-and-pencil tests we had before, this is so far and away better than what we had so far. Even though it's not conclusive, it's much, much better than what we've had historically." The next scene shows John March, Chief of Child Psychiatry at Duke University, responding: "If it seems too good to be true, it is, unfortunately, too good to be true." Kiki Chang, featured as an expert in pediatric bipolar disorder, followed by stating, "We are five to ten years off from this being a really reliable clinical tool. Now it's strictly a research tool." Nancy Goodhue and her unidentified companion were then shown appearing on *The Dr. Phil Show,* with the narrator saying that Brain Matters had already reached millions of people since its representatives had been invited twice to appear on that show. Apparently the boy seated with his family on the stage was being evaluated. The Brain Matters "experts" were interpreting a brain image. Goodhue's companion stated, "We can see the bipolar pattern much earlier in someone's brain." Goodhue added, "Those areas on top of Fred's head do not receive the right blood flow." (If you wonder what qualifies a social worker to be doing this kind of medical interpretation, you are right to wonder.)

The *Frontline* narrator went on to attest that a cottage industry of diagnostic centers, self-help books, and nutritional programs have burgeoned and have profited from parents' desperate search for answers. He reported that Matthew's brain scan cost $3,000. Dr. Anthony Kane points out that only a few centers in the country use brain imaging for diagnostic purposes. He parrots an unidentified well-known psychiatrist who asks, "If it were really worth it, don't you think that Harvard and Yale would be using it?"[46] Like Amen, Brain Matters uses SPECT imaging, which exposes subjects to radiation. I checked out Brain Matters' Web site and learned that this organization claims to diagnose ADHD, bipolar, autism, traumatic brain injury, and dementia with this tool. Dr. Phil exemplifies how media glorifies a novel diagnostic procedure, however unproven. As a doctoral-level psychologist, he should know better than to promote a sham procedure that may be ruining the lives of countless children. *Frontline*'s exposure of Brain Matters as a sham was subtle, leaving the presentation open to selective listening by people desperate for answers. Vulnerable parents deserve heightened warning to the danger of being exploited for profit.

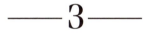

3

The Bipolar Myth

Love depends upon the capacity to reach beneath the surface of persons, to feel and touch the seed of life that is hidden there. And love becomes a power when it is capable of evoking that seed and drawing it forth from its hidden place.

—Ira Progoff

Beholding the child in this way nourishes the seed of the child, even if we cannot fully see what it is or what it is to become.

—Tobin Hart

FIRST MENTION OF PEDIATRIC BIPOLAR DISORDER

Until the 1990s, bipolar disorder, formerly known as manic depression, was considered a mental illness that affected adults. It had never been identified as a pediatric illness. That changed when a team of influential pediatric psychopharmacologists (doctors who specialize in psychiatric medication) at Massachusetts General Hospital published their "discovery" that a significant percentage of their ADHD patients also had a childhood onset form of bipolar disorder (also referred to as "early onset," "juvenile," or "pediatric bipolar disorder"). In the next few years, mainstream psychiatrists and most other mental health professionals jumped aboard the rapidly accelerating bandwagon of clinicians eager to consume the burgeoning literature on the subject and label hordes of children with this "epiphany" of a "disorder." A study by Carmen Moreno and colleagues[1] revealed a 40-fold increase of bipolar diagnoses among individuals aged 0 to 19 between 1994 and 2003 in the United States. Thus, the bandwagon's momentum was at peak in the early 21st century. Then a tragedy launched a cascade of publicity that may have marked its pace.

THE DEATH OF A 4-YEAR-OLD

On December 13, 2006, 4-year-old Rebecca Riley succumbed on the floor next to her parents' bed from overdoses of powerful psychotropic drugs. On February 15, 2007, the *New York Times*[2] released the story of her death. Her parents have been charged with first-degree murder. The family lived in Hull, Massachusetts, an area reportedly known for its excellence in social and medical services. Kayoko Kifuji, Rebecca's psychiatrist at Tufts-New England Medical Center, diagnosed her with ADHD and bipolar illness when she was 2 years old. Since then she had been prescribed a potent cocktail of drugs that, at the time of her death, included Seroquel, an antipsychotic; Depakote, an anticonvulsant prescribed as a mood stabilizer; and clonidine, a blood pressure medication often prescribed to children for its calming effect. The reporters elicited psychiatrists' responses to the tragedy. Gabrielle Carlson, professor of psychiatry and pediatrics at Stony Brook School of Medicine, stated that bipolar is absolutely overdiagnosed, and that parents are led to believe medications are the solution. Carlson added, "Parents very often want a quick fix, and doctors rarely have much time to spend with them, and the great appeal of prescribing a medication is that it's simple." John T. Walkup of Johns Hopkins University School of Medicine and Jean Frazier, psychopharmacology specialist and Harvard professor, defended the diagnosis and its treatment with powerful drugs at early ages. Bessel van der Kolk, professor at Boston University and renowned trauma expert, said, "Most of the patients I see who have been misdiagnosed have been told they have bipolar disorder. The diagnosis is made with no understanding of the context of their life. Then they're put on these devastating medications and condemned to a life as a psychiatry patient."

The *Boston Globe*[3] reported that a medical malpractice suit was filed on April 3, 2008, asserting that Rebecca's psychiatrist, Kayoko Kifuji, is responsible for her death. The lawyer representing the estate of Rebecca Riley blames the death on her diagnosis at the age of 28 months and ensuing treatment for two years with powerful drugs.

Other Media Responses

Anya Bailey

An investigative article about the case of Anya Bailey appeared on the front page of the *New York Times* on May 10, 2007.[4] Anya's story is detailed in chapter 4 in the section on antipsychotic medications. She developed dystonia, a painful, deforming, and often irreversible side effect of Risperdal, the antipsychotic she was taking. The reporters tackled the role of pharmaceutical companies and how their interests intersect with the interests of doctors who diagnose and prescribe. They revealed that the mother's consent to treat Anya was not an informed one (like Mrs. Compton in chapter 1). The doctor did not advise her that Risperdal has side effects to which children are especially vulnerable. He did not mention that Risperdal is not approved by the U.S. Food and Drug Administration (FDA) for Anya's condition, anorexia. The article was one of the first follow-ups to the tragedy of Rebecca Riley, and may have fomented a turning point in the public perception of pediatric psychiatry. Not a dramatic turning of the tide by any means, but many people who read the article were enlightened to the risks of diagnosing and medicating children.

Rebecca Riley's death provoked a multitude of questions in the press. In a March 24, 2007, article[5] Associated Press reporter Denise Lavoie asked rhetorically, "Can children as young as Rebecca be accurately diagnosed with mental illnesses? Are rambunctious youngsters being medicated for their parents' convenience? And should children so young be prescribed powerful psychotropic drugs meant for adults?" I responded with an opinion piece in our local newspaper, based on my clinical experience. My answers were emphatic: "No," "Yes," and "No," respectively, with explanations that did not blame parents. Peter Breggin followed up my piece with a letter to the editor confirming the validity and scientific basis of my statements.

The New Yorker *Article Presents Differing Views of Bipolar Disorder*

The April 9, 2007 issue of *The New Yorker* featured a comprehensive story about bipolar—"What's Normal?" by Jerome Groopman.[6] The author began by underscoring the rise in number of children diagnosed, noting the influence of the Papolos book discussed below, and of the Listserv, BPParents. Groopman reported on a meeting called by then-director of the National Institute of Mental Health (NIMH), Steven Hyman. The goal was to talk about the "newly recognized" children's bipolar disorder. Among the 19 psychologists and psychiatrists in attendance were two of the most publicized bipolar "experts": Joseph Biederman, director of the pediatric psychopharmacology team at Massachusetts General Hospital that first described early onset bipolar disorder, and Barbara Geller of Washington University in St. Louis, another specialist on the bipolar diagnosis. The 19 were to discuss this pediatric bipolar phenomenon. The conclusions of the meeting were published in the August 2001 issue of the *Journal of the American Academy of Child and Adolescent Psychiatry*. Groopman summarized the conclusions: "Bipolar exists and can be diagnosed in prepubertal children." But there was criticism about the lack of diagnostic guidelines. Groopman mentioned the *Time* feature story that soon followed on August 19, 2002, "Young and Bipolar." The 11-page *Time* story lent realism to the diagnosis and included a checklist of symptoms headed by "Is your child bipolar?" (I shuddered to think of the thousands of parents who would now clamor to get their children diagnosed and medicated). Groopman reported on Biederman's research on 4- to 6-year-olds, testing Risperdal and Zyprexa.[7] Despite side effects of weight gain and raised prolactin levels (that could interfere with sexual development), the Biederman team concluded the drugs could be beneficial to bipolar children. The death of Rebecca Riley was mentioned, followed by a quote from Hyman: "The diagnosis has spread too broadly, so that powerful drugs are prescribed too widely. We are going to have hell to pay in terms of side effects."

Nevertheless, Groopman bought the conclusions of the 19, summarizing that "experts now agree that bipolar can occur in children." As in most bipolar stories, Groopman accepted the diagnosis as a "real disease," the only caveat being the overdiagnosing of the "disease." He rationalized that the "dire consequences" of not treating it justify medicating with powerful and dangerous drugs. As in all mainstream media, experts like Peter Breggin, Grace Jackson, Fred Baughman, Daniel Burston, David Stein, and a host of others are conspicuously absent from interviews.

Point Park University Symposium and the Boston Globe

On June 8 and 9, 2007, I attended a symposium at Point Park University titled "Bipolar Children: Cutting Edge Controversy, Insight, and Research." Facilitated by clinical psychologist and associate professor Sharna Olfman, its agenda featured a panel of experts whose attitudes about bipolar ranged from cautious to highly critical. Olfman opened the program with the report of the death of Rebecca Riley. Lawrence Diller closed the program with commentary that laid partial moral responsibility for Rebecca's death on Joseph Biederman. Diller is a longtime critic of the bipolar diagnosis and the Biederman team's promotion of powerful antipsychotics to treat it.[8] A prominent and generally moderate author, he is one opponent of the bipolar movement who was interviewed for a *Boston Globe* article. His outspoken remark at Point Park University appeared in the article, which is detailed below.

Boston Globe author Scott Allen wrote "Backlash on Bipolar Diagnoses in Children: MGH Psychiatrist's Work Stirs Debate," published on June 17, 2007. Allen apparently attended the symposium and interviewed Biederman afterward. He opened his coverage of Biederman's work with "From his perch as one of the world's most influential child psychiatrists, Biederman has spread far and wide his conviction that the emotional roller coaster of bipolar disorder can start 'from the moment the child opened his eyes' at birth." Biederman, Allen continued, likened his work to scientific breakthroughs akin to the discovery of the first vaccinations against disease. He accused his critics of exploiting a tragedy to fan fears about psychiatry, adding that psychiatry has long faced prejudice. Biederman defended his practice by citing his scientific credentials, his authorship of 30 scientific papers a year, and directorship of "a major research program at the psychiatry department that is top-ranked in the *U.S. News and World Report* ratings," according to Allen. Biederman added that his critics "are not on the same level."

Allen also interviewed the lawyer representing Rebecca Riley's doctor, Kayoko Kifuji, who temporarily gave up practicing, with pay, pending ruling by the state medical board. The lawyer, J.W. Carney, defended his client, saying that Biederman's "research and teaching validates Dr. Kifuji's work with patients."

Allen's *Boston Globe* article addressed the extensive financial ties between the pharmaceutical industry and researchers. He reported that Biederman received research funding from 15 drug companies and served as a consultant and paid speaker to seven, including Eli Lilly and Janssen Pharmaceuticals (Janssen and Johnson & Johnson are interchangeable, the latter being the parent company of the former), profiteers of multibillion-dollar antipsychotics Zyprexa and Risperdal, respectively, the drugs that Biederman recommends. Biederman, said Allen, had enjoyed success for his ADHD work previously and had established close ties with companies that manufactured stimulant medications. Biederman refused to disclose how much money he was paid to give speeches, serve on drug advisory boards, and perform other activities on behalf of drug companies, but he claimed that all the income was approved by both his employers, Harvard University and Massachusetts General Hospital. At the time of the interview, Biederman's bosses defended his integrity, denying he would put financial interests ahead of his research.

Those bosses may be having second thoughts. I digress from the Allen article to interject a development in 2008. Biederman made the front page of the *New York Times*[9] in June 2008, followed by a stream of stories in leading newspapers as revelations evolved. A congressional investigation by Senator Charles Grassley of the Senate Finance Committee alleges the failure of Biederman and colleague Timothy Wilens to report income they accepted as consulting fees from makers of the drugs they recommend for juvenile bipolar disorder. The fallout from this explosive news continues in the epilogue.

Despite intense criticism generated by the death of Rebecca Riley, Biederman remains firm in his conviction that bipolar can be diagnosed in infancy, and that the powerful drugs' effectiveness in controlling the intense symptoms of the diagnosis overrides the importance of their safety. In the *Boston Globe* article, Allen reported that Biederman's publication of a paper in the *Journal of Child and Adolescent Psychopharmacology* in 2001, describing treatment of bipolar children with Zyprexa, became one of the most frequently quoted articles in the history of that journal. Despite weight gains of more than 10 pounds in eight weeks among his patients, Biederman claimed that Zyprexa eased outbreaks of aggression. As the bipolar diagnosis gained popularity, Biederman and colleague Janet Wozniak's research was often cited as the scientific rationale for treating bipolar aggressively. These statements explain the burgeoning of bipolar diagnoses nationwide in the early years of this century. Allen cites a national study of community hospitals that found the percentage of inpatient children diagnosed as bipolar quadrupled from 1990 to 2000. Barbara Geller, that other prominent bipolar specialist mentioned earlier, explained to Allen that she adopts a more restrictive view of the diagnosis; she holds off on the label until children demonstrate manic symptoms, such as a reduced need for sleep. The Massachusetts General Hospital team bases the diagnosis on more general behaviors, such as irritability or aggressiveness. Allen interviewed Jon McClellan at the University of Washington, who said in a group of 100 children the Biederman team would come up with five to 20 bipolar disorders, while McClellan might find one or none. McClellan believes no child under 6 can be diagnosed as bipolar.

Steven Hyman, now Harvard provost (director of NIMH in the Groopman article), told Allen, regarding the growing use of antipsychotic drugs: "We don't know the first thing about the safety and efficacy of these drugs even by themselves in these young ages, let alone when they are mixed together." In another noteworthy statement, Allen said numerous psychiatrists reacted to Rebecca Riley's death by suggesting that bipolar had become a fad that left thousands of children on risky medications because of irritability and aggressiveness that could have other causes. He reported that Rebecca's father, for example, had only recently returned to the home after being accused of child abuse, according to police. The *Boston Globe* published a timeline[10] based on information from the Massachusetts Department of Social Services (DSS) and state police. It shows the Riley family's history of alleged child abuse dates back to 2002, when DSS substantiated a complaint that the oldest child was neglected. In the years leading up to Rebecca's death in 2006, there were seven more allegations, with five in 2006 alone. But none of these seven was substantiated. Allen's *Globe* article reported that state officials, since the death, planned to study the 8,343 children taking antipsychotics under the Medicaid program, to determine the appropriateness of the prescriptions. Many other states have followed Massachusetts' example, and readers will find more information about Medicaid investigations and law suits in the epilogue.

Forty-fold Increase in Bipolar Diagnoses in Ten Years

Early in September 2007, the Associated Press released a report on the study mentioned earlier by Carmen Moreno and colleagues at Columbia University that found bipolar diagnoses had increased 40-fold from 1994 to 2003.[11] The report revealed information, both pro and con, related to the surge. Opinions ranged from those who believe bipolar has always affected youngsters, to those who suspect overdiagnosis and believe there is much confusion distinguishing bipolar from ADHD and other childhood diagnoses. Some of the professionals cited do not believe it is diagnosable under the age of 6. **None of the professional experts who challenge the existence of bipolar as a disease was mentioned**.

60 Minutes *Probes Rebecca Riley's Death*

On September 30, 2007, CBS featured a story on *60 Minutes* titled "What Killed Rebecca Riley?" Katie Couric interviewed Rebecca's mother, Carolyn Riley. Riley denied noticing any unusual symptoms in her daughter, while school staff did, according to reports, and made some effort to contact Rebecca's doctor with concerns over her weakness and tremors. Couric noted that Rebecca could barely speak in complete sentences when Kifuji diagnosed her, at age $2^1/_2$, after eight visits. Kifuji was treating two older siblings with similar medications for the same diagnosis. Riley said the night before she died, Rebecca wouldn't go to sleep, so she gave her half a clonidine pill and a pediatric cough-cold remedy. Then she stated that she put her to bed on the floor next to her own bed and went to sleep. Riley said she trusted Kifuji, even though she did think the 10 pills a day that were prescribed were excessive. She said she now knows a lot more about bipolar than she did when Rebecca was living. And now she doesn't think Rebecca really was bipolar—"just maybe a little hyper for her age," she said.

Couric also interviewed Biederman. He stood by his views as described above. Couric asked him if he was concerned that the medications he recommends are mostly not approved for children. Biederman replied that he cannot tell parents to come back in ten years when all the data are collected. He went on ". . . I still need to use medicines that I am assuming that, if they work in adults, with appropriate care and supervision, may also work in children." He said the typical bipolar child's symptoms are so severe as to affect every aspect of his or her life. He talked about extreme irritability along with at least four other criteria, such as recklessness, sleeplessness, and hyperactivity. He said the average age of onset is 4, adding, "It's solidly in the preschool years." The camera switched to Rhys Hampton and his mother. It was reported that Rhys, at age 3, started having violent and explosive outbursts. Couric asked the mother if she deemed Rhys' behavior "extraordinary, severe, dangerous, and affecting every single aspect of his life." The mother responded, "Yeah, every aspect of his life." His doctor diagnosed him as bipolar and placed him on three medications. When the psychiatrist suggested a fourth, the parents thought "enough" and took him to Seattle Children's Hospital, where doctors said he was not bipolar. It was reported that now he takes medication for hyperactivity and a sleep disorder, and is learning to control his explosive moods through a behavioral program.

Jon McClellan, who runs the psychiatric children's hospital in Seattle, said the facility is filled with kids who have been misdiagnosed as bipolar. He added that it has become a catchall for aggressive and troubled children. He derides the practice of diagnosing 3- or 5-year-olds with a major adult psychiatric disorder. He said little kids do things that would be evidence of a mental health problem if an adult did them. He added, "The problem is symptoms like irritability or recklessness or high energy when you're an 8-year-old don't necessarily predict in the long run developing bipolar disorder. Some might. Do you expose all those kids to medications to prevent the one kid that's going to get it?"

The Lamb family was featured on *60 Minutes* regarding the treatment of two children, Annie and Casey, 8 and 9 years old, respectively. Casey recently had been admitted to a psychiatric hospital after he was taken off one of his medications. Most likely, Casey experienced serious withdrawal as the medication left his system, but his mother believed his symptoms indicated that the medication was indispensable. (This is a terribly common misinterpretation on the part of parents and professionals alike.) When Mrs. Lamb became concerned about

Annie's incessant eating, a common side effect of antipsychotic drugs, Biederman team member Wozniak suggested that yet a fourth medication be added to her regimen—one designed to help adults resist alcohol!

FRONTLINE'S "THE MEDICATED CHILD"

On January 8, 2008, PBS's *Frontline* aired "The Medicated Child." This time Biederman declined to be interviewed by producer Marcela Gaviria. Instead, he deferred to a colleague, Kiki Chang, director of the Pediatric Bipolar Disorders Program at Lucile Packard Hospital in Palo Alto, California, and professor at Stanford University School of Medicine. Described as "a rising star in the field of juvenile bipolar research," Chang expressed some of his own unique theories about the diagnosis. He described an elaborate theoretical framework (and I stress *theoretical*) by which children genetically predisposed to bipolar experience their first episode following an environmental stressor. This, he said, initiates a process known as "kindling" in the brain. He maintained that preventive measures taken in early childhood would prevent further serious mood disturbances. He also stated that therapy is a first line of treatment, to minimize environmental triggers. But he added that medication, about which he is "very excited," can protect the brain from further insult of kindling later on. He extrapolated this hypothesis from animal studies, he said, that seem to indicate some of the medicines have "neuroprotective qualities," and may even help with neuronal growth in certain areas. The interviewer pointed out that Chang used "we feel" more than "we know," picking up on the speculative nature of Chang's theories.

Asked about Biederman, Chang responded that Biederman has "pushed the envelope," but he stated, "we need someone to do that." Chang said he thinks the 40-fold increase in bipolar diagnoses is due to a lot of doctors in the community misdiagnosing. His remarks indicated he supports Biederman's protocol of prescribing powerful toxic drugs to hundreds of thousands of children. His notion of medicating very young children as preventive care is explored further when the ominous specter of state-sponsored mental screening of babies is discussed in chapter 5.

Finally, this statement by Chang strikes a familiar chord: "But there should be more time and energy put into understanding the neurobiology, because that is really the future—putting our resources into understanding genetics, neurobiology and any other biological facets of the disorder—**because clearly there is a biological interaction with the environment that causes this kind of disorder.**"[12]

Again, a neurobiologist makes an environmental and biological connection, as discussed earlier. Neurobiological researchers have admitted that environmental stimulation can trigger biological reactions in the brain, as shown in chapter 2. As for genetics, people are born with different temperaments. Some react to stimulation more profoundly than others: Within a family, one member may react to a trauma with great distress, while a more resilient member will "bounce back." Personality characteristics are part of our genetic makeup. I believe symptoms—as described in "early onset bipolar illness"—are expressions of temperament, which can be inherited, but this is a different concept from bipolar as a hereditary "mental illness."

NEWSWEEK'S "GROWING UP BIPOLAR"

My heart sank the day I retrieved my mail to find on *Newsweek*'s May 26, 2008 cover a split photo of 10-year-old Max Blake, upon whom the title "Growing Up Bipolar" was superimposed. The story, as written by Mary Carmichael, would convince any lay person that bipolar is irrefutably a real disease. I was hard pressed to undo its effect on one of my favorite relatives. Most readers would not know that the powerful drug cocktails Max was on all his life had everything to do with his current desperate condition. The story provided clues that could explain Max's emotional problems. But tragically for him, the distressed infant Max was destined to life as a mental patient because his brain was infiltrated with foreign chemicals before he was even a year old.

Peter Breggin responded to the *Newsweek* article in the *Huffington Post*.[13] He identified all the ways that Max was being abused by psychiatrists (for example, "toxic chemicals are impairing and distorting the growth of Max's brain") and feared for Max's prognosis given how long his brain has been "literally bathed in substances like antidepressants, stimulants, mood stabilizers, and antipsychotic drugs that cause severe, and potentially permanent biochemical imbalances."

This concludes a summary of recent developments concerning the bipolar diagnosis. Now we back up to a general discussion of the topic.

WHAT IS PEDIATRIC BIPOLAR DISORDER?

Heretofore, bipolar had been described as strictly an adult illness, marked with periods of deep depression alternating with periods of mania, or euphoria, often attended by psychosis and sleeplessness. Biederman and his group took it upon themselves to alter the symptoms of adult bipolar to fit youngsters who are hard to control, irritable, angry, and unhappy. They maintain that temper tantrums and violent behavior are the "high" of bipolar, and that children so diagnosed cycle several times a day. Biederman is less clear how the low end of the cycle is manifested, as children do not express depression in the same manner as adults. Because pediatric bipolar is a new construct, it does not appear in the current *Diagnostic and Statistical Manual of Mental Disorders* (DSM), published in 1994, which adds to the confusion among clinicians trying to diagnose this newly invented mental illness.

I witnessed firsthand the burgeoning numbers of young children assigned the bipolar label at the turn of the 21st century. The trajectories of these children deeply troubled me, for it seemed they all suffered various traumas early in life that explained their extreme behaviors. But these kids were the ones most likely to be referred to a psychiatrist who invariably identified them as "bipolar" and prescribed powerful antipsychotic and other strong drugs[14] to stem the signs of distress: temper tantrums, irritability, defiance, and other undesirable emotions and behaviors. Then, satisfied with the "quick fix," parents often declined therapy that might resolve the stressors that triggered the distress signals. Even if the child continued therapy, it wasn't successful when parents believed the problem was with the "bipolar child." Soon after their brains were introduced to these chemicals, the children's lives seemed to spiral downward. Symptoms were suppressed, but the children's volitions and personalities got lost. Scores of case histories like the following fueled my odyssey through literature searches and distant destinations to gain more knowledge about the bipolar phenomenon.

WHO ARE THESE CHILDREN?

Robbie was 6 when he was first assigned to my caseload. He seemed happy then; he enjoyed painting lively pictures and playing with my therapy poodle, Solo. I photographed him and Solo doing a fanciful little dance together that thrilled Robbie's parents. The parents' presenting complaint was that they had difficulty managing him, so the clinic psychiatrist started him on drugs. Robbie continuously followed a regimen of various medications. By age 9 he seemed a different boy. He refused to talk, shrugged his shoulders in response to my queries, and in repose his tongue protruded. Robbie's case was typical. The doctor first diagnosed him as hyperactive and started him on stimulant medication, with good results, according to the parents. But after a few weeks, they said the medicine wasn't working anymore. The psychiatrist deduced that since the stimulant didn't help, Robbie must be bipolar rather than hyperactive. So he added strong antipsychotic and mood-altering drugs to Robbie's cocktail. The happy little 6-year-old gradually morphed into the unresponsive 9-year-old. I would have welcomed back the original challenging boy, because we knew who that Robbie was. Despite his challenging behavior, his strengths were intact.

Amy started out at age 3 on stimulants, and by age 12 had been on a steady diet of nearly every psychiatric drug available. Her hands trembled and her movements were jerky. She sustained her wildly unpredictable behavior in spite of (or because of) her drug treatment. This made it difficult to connect with her, yet sometimes her creativity and intelligence emerged, revealing someone I would have liked to know. As with most child clients, Amy's chances for a successful outcome would have been enhanced had her mother been an equal partner in treatment. But her mother's highest priority seemed to be her network of virtual friends on the Internet. Even though she was a stay-at-home mom, relatives reported that she responded cruelly to Amy's pleas for attention.

Tommy's mother shared a little tribute of him she and other family members had written for a first grade project. It conjures up the image of a sweet, intelligent, enthusiastic, much loved little boy. His mother reported that he also was a capable student. The following year, Tommy went into treatment when he disclosed the sexual abuse he had endured as a preschooler at the hands of a family acquaintance. The devastated family entrusted his care to our clinic. His regimen of psychiatric medication started then. Soon Tommy was exhibiting bizarre behavior; he became aggressive toward his mother, and he rebelled at school. His misbehavior escalated to the point of having to be restrained repeatedly while participating in a recreational program at the clinic. Tommy was hospitalized frequently, and with each admission he was prescribed more powerful medications. After his outpatient sessions at our clinic, he would stop by my office to visit Solo. We became friends, and at age 9 he was transferred to me at his behest. My treatment objective was to restore Tommy's identity back to that of just a typical boy. By this time he had a bad case of "learned patienthood," a phenomenon whereby people who are repeatedly hospitalized and treated long term come to identify themselves as permanently dependent upon the mental health system. My efforts to normalize Tommy were thwarted by his school principal, whose adversarial attitude provoked Tommy to misbehave in ways unacceptable to the school. The principal had him adjudicated "a person in need of supervision" (PINS) in family court.

Tommy ended up in the custodial care of the department of social services and was placed in a foster home very far away from family. What followed was a two-year nightmare that entailed illegalities and egregious disrespect to the family by caseworkers and so-called "therapeutic foster care professionals." How the mother finally retrieved Tommy is another story, but through her dogged determination and the help of extended family, the county legislature, a county executive, and a state senator, he came home at last. Reunited with family, Tommy was still a sweet boy at twelve and was behaving well. But he lost the sparkle that so defined him at six in the literary portrayal by his family. He bore an unchanging wistful expression and was way below grade level academically. He seemed somehow to be sedated, which he was. The special educational program he entered has virtually all its students sedated by medication.

THE EMERGENCE OF THE BIPOLAR MYTH

We are now well acquainted with psychiatrist and pediatric psychopharmacologist Joseph Biederman, who has become the icon of "bipolar believers." In 1996, his team published a paper claiming that 23 percent of the ADHD children served in their clinic also had bipolar disorder. Several years ago, before bipolar became well publicized due to the death of Rebecca Riley, I visited Biederman's Web site[15] and was greeted by a photo of this smiling, kindly looking gentleman. Beside the photo is a brief biographical sketch describing his abundant laurels. As I read through the body of information about his work, two things stood out. First, Biederman and his associates work on the presumption that mental disorders are caused by neurological or biological defects. Second, Biederman's research is funded largely by pharmaceutical industry grants. Biederman said in one article that when his team proclaimed bipolar was neurobiologically driven, they freed mothers from any responsibility or guilt about their children's extreme behavior and distress. It's all in the genes and biology. He reveled in this great contribution to motherhood! (Meanwhile, the hapless child is stuck with the problem and the toxic chemical solution.)

Thus, Biederman and his group base their recommendation of powerful antipsychotic medications to treat their "bipolar disorder" on the logic that biochemical cause justifies biochemical remedy. The 40-fold increase of juvenile bipolar diagnoses followed, along with burgeoning pediatric prescriptions for expensive antipsychotic drugs, medications traditionally prescribed for adult psychosis of people diagnosed with schizophrenia or the adult form of bipolar manic episodes.

Psychosocial Proponents Respond

To psychosocial proponents, this theory that bipolar disorder, as well as all other so-called mental illnesses, is neurobiologically based is simplistic thinking. The panoply of difficulties children present with cannot be reduced to a neurobiological brain anomaly. There are just too many variables impacting troubled children to conclude their emotional distress is simply "a brain malfunction." Grace Jackson put it so well when she identified "Human Agency and Volition" as traits far beyond the scope of "a brain."

Furthermore, I would say to Biederman that in neither my training nor my experience have I encountered a treatment model that blames mother or family exclusively for a child's symptoms. Even when parenting styles do explain much of the difficulty, we do not sit in judgment. Parenting styles develop from parents' own experience of being parented. A skillful therapist can facilitate adjustments in parenting styles. And parents who abuse do so because of their own unresolved distress, which often can be relieved with the help of a sensitive therapist. There is enough empathy to extend to all family members. I often helped alleviate pain for all family members by taking a collaborative and supportive role.

Because the medical model, as explained in chapter 1, is the standard treatment for emotional distress, the bipolar diagnosis poses serious risk to the health of children. To reiterate, this is a model of treatment by which the clinician assigns a diagnosis to a patient and then prescribes a remedy. In the case of a bona fide physical ailment, it is appropriate. Conditions of emotional distress (called "mental disorders" by neurobiological proponents) are not physical ailments where a cause-and-effect relationship can usually be identified between germ or anatomical defect and illness. Yet when children are labeled bipolar, most doctors prescribe the standard recommended by that disorder's creators at Harvard: powerful antipsychotic medications. And therein lies the threat to children's health posed by a medical model approach to managing misbehavior. Chapter 4, on psychotropic medications, details the dangerous side effects that antipsychotic drugs exert on children.

Lawrence Diller, as mentioned earlier, was an early critic of the bipolar phenomenon and remains a critic, though he does prescribe stimulant medications to children. In 2002, long before the death of Rebecca Riley, he reacted to Biederman's new pediatric bipolar diagnosis in *Should I Medicate My Child?*[16] He expressed vigorous skepticism of the diagnosis, and especially strong disapproval of the use of the drugs recommended to treat it: antipsychotics, such as Risperdal and Zyprexa; anticonvulsants like Depakote; the antihypertensive clonidine; and the mood stabilizer lithium. Diller quoted an unnamed psychiatrist who stated cynically that "Ritalin is for irritable and irritating children, while lithium is for *very* irritable and *very* irritating children." Diller also disparaged the unproven assumption of neurobiological etiology upon which the use of chemicals is based.

THE PHARMACEUTICAL INDUSTRY SUPPORTS
NEUROBIOLOGICAL THEORY OF BIPOLAR DISORDER

A presumption of neurobiological causation feeds right into the coffers of the pharmaceutical industry. Biological cause would seem to justify the use of biochemicals as treatment, and it certainly creates a lucrative market for the industry that makes them. Trouble is, the presumption is utterly unproven! As explained earlier, no neurobiological explanation of emotional distress has been established. Those who oppose neurobiological theory remain in low profile because we cannot compete with the vastly rich pharmaceutical companies whose reach of influence is staggering. Their massive advertising and marketing are very effective in misinforming the public about their products. Statistics bear this out.

I said earlier that standard treatment for children diagnosed as bipolar are the powerful antipsychotic drugs. the *New York Times* published "Use of Antipsychotics in Children is Criticized" on November 19, 2008.[17] A panel of drug experts reportedly reached a consensus: "Powerful antipsychotic drugs are being used far too cavalierly in children, and federal drug regulators must do more to warn doctors of their substantial risks." More than 389,000 children and teens were treated in 2007 with Risperdal, one of the five so-called atypical antipsychotics. The panel's data showed that of those, 240,000 were 12 or under. When representatives from drug companies that make Risperdal (Johnson & Johnson) and Zyprexa (Eli Lilly) sought the panel's endorsement of the Food and Drug Administration's (FDA) routine monitoring of the safety of the medications, their proposal was unanimously rejected. Panel members said far more must be done to discourage these medicines' growing use in children, especially to treat conditions for which the drugs are not approved. Their concerns extended to the other antipsychotic medications being prescribed to children: Seroquel, Abilify, and Geodon. Data show prescription rates for antipsychotic drugs used on children increased more than fivefold in the past decade and a half, and doctors use these drugs to manage a wide range of behavior problems even though children are especially susceptible to their side effects. In 2007, Risperdal prescriptions to patients 17 and younger increased 10 percent, while prescriptions for adults declined 5 percent. The article reported that 1,207 children who were given Risperdal, from 1993 through the first three months of 2008, suffered serious problems, including 31 who died. At least 11 of the deaths were children whose treatment with Risperdal lacked FDA approval.

Dr. Thomas Laughren of the FDA responded to these concerns by saying medical specialty societies must do a better job of educating doctors about the drugs' side effects. He said there is little the FDA can do to fix these problems.

So long as lucrative alliances prevail between the doctors and the drug companies, I fear nothing will change anytime soon.

THE PAPOLOS EFFECT

The Bipolar Child: The Definitive and Reassuring Guide to Childhood's Most Misunderstood Disorder by Dmitri and Janice Papolos[18] was published in 2000, the same year Steven Hyman called the meeting of 19 psychologists and psychiatrists to talk about the new bipolar diagnosis (critiqued earlier in Groopman's *New Yorker* article). Its timing could not have been better. Groopman[19] reported that 200,000 copies had been sold. He went on to cite Hyman, who told him about the influence the book has had on parents. Many, he said, came to him after reading it, convinced their own children's' difficult behavior was due to undiagnosed bipolar disorder, even when the children were as young as 2 years old. Dmitri Papolos is associated with the Albert Einstein College of Medicine. He is medical advisor for Parents of Bipolar Children, an online support group for parents of children diagnosed as bipolar, and chair of the professional advisory board of the Child and Adolescent Bipolar Foundation.

I found *The Bipolar Child* deeply unsettling. The authors' account of one 10-year-old boy (pp. 133–134) evoked disturbing memories from my practice experience. The boy's parents brought him for treatment due to obsessive-compulsive (OCD) behaviors. Dmitri Papolos' prescription follows: Start with a mood stabilizer (such as Depakote); reassess OCD symptoms and treat with behavioral treatments **plus** an antianxiety agent. (Suggested are Klonopin, a highly addictive benzodiazepine, or Neurontin, an anticonvulsant steeped in controversy.) Then, if that combination isn't doing the trick, **add** an SSRI, such as Luvox. Now the boy, at 10, is on a powerful drug cocktail that is likely to continue to change over his lifetime as his unbalanced brain tries to accommodate this invasion of chemicals. See chapter 4 for the story of Cindylou, a client I saw for OCD. Her mother bought the book I suggested, *Freeing Your Child From Obsessive Compulsive Disorder*. By applying the author's recommendations, she successfully eased her daughter's severe worries.

Electroconvulsive Therapy (ECT) for Bipolar Children?

Others of the Papoloses' solutions were equally chilling. They cited a review by Mark W. Bertagnoli and Carrie M. Borchardt regarding the use of electro-convulsive therapy (ECT) on 151 children and adolescents ages 5 to 19 (pp. 127–128).

Each subject received from 9 to 20 treatments. The Papoloses concluded from this study that ECT was a good choice of treatment for pediatric bipolar. Electroshock therapy remains a highly controversial topic. It is often defended as completely safe and efficacious by mainstream psychiatrists.

Peter Breggin published an article about ECT use in children.[20] He reports that in the 1940s, Lauretta Bender subjected large numbers of children to ECT on the psychiatric ward of Bellevue Hospital in New York City. Her reports on 100 cases were "glowing," while others involved in the projects described the children as terrified and intellectually deteriorated. Breggin reports he assessed two of Bender's survivors. One received 10 ECT treatments in 1949. As far as Breggin could tell from his record, the patient's first instance of aggressive behavior emerged after the treatments. As an adult, he became a convicted multiple murderer. Breggin was an expert witness at his trial and was able to convince a jury the man didn't deserve to be electrocuted after showing the jury old films of ECT being administered in the 1940s. Since society had already electroshocked him as a child, the jury decided on a life sentence. The other survivor of Bender's ECT treatments was Ted Chabasinski, who was taken into custody by city social services and sent to Rockland State Hospital as a small child. He grew up to become a reform-minded attorney in Berkeley, California, where he has actively campaigned against ECT.

Breggin cites others, such as neurologist Fred Friedberg, who refute the safety of ECT. Friedberg describes the effect of the electric current in his 1978 book *Shock Treatment Is Not Good For Your Brain.* He identifies the areas of the brain where the electricity does the greatest cellular damage as the hippocampal formations, so indispensable to memory that their destruction leads to the densest amnesias known to medicine. Breggin also quotes a neurologist and electroencephalographer (expert in electroencephalograms, or EEGs): "In all cases the ECT 'response' is due to the concussion-type, or more serious, effects of ECT. The patient 'forgets' his symptoms because the brain damage destroys memory traces in the brain, and the patient has to pay for this by a reduction in mental capacity of varying degree." Finally, Breggin quotes Lucy Johnstone, author of "Is the Use of ECT a Non-Issue for Psychologists" in *Clinical Psychology Forum,* August 1992. She identified animal studies that demonstrated unequivocal damage by ECT, and psychiatrists admitted that this was the mechanism of improvement (consistent with Breggin's brain-disabling theory of biological treatment); the patient "secures his readaptation to normal life at the expense of a permanent lowering of functional efficiency." With these testimonies in mind, do we want to expose the developing brains of children to ECT? I think not!

Repeated Transcranial Magnetic Stimulation for Bipolar Children?

The other "innovative" treatment described by the Papoloses (pp. 129–130) is repeated transcranial magnetic stimulation (r-TMS): The patient sits in a chair while a small, powerful, coiled electromagnet is placed on the scalp. This creates a strong magnetic field that passes through the skull. When the rapidly changing magnetic field encounters the brain's nerve cells, it causes an electric current that depolarizes them; the nerve cells fire. The patient receives 40 stimulations in two seconds, and this is repeated 20 times. The electromagnetic coil must be water cooled, as the electricity produces heat, and the patient wears ear protection because the procedure is very noisy. The authors cite Mark George of the Medical University of South Carolina, who they say has shown the treatment to be helpful in adult depression. George was planning on presenting data to the FDA so that r-TMS can be used in adolescents and eventually in children. I find that a particularly frightening prospect.

Lobotomy by Any Other Name . . .

As with brain-altering medications, children have no say when exposed to other brain-disabling treatments. Children were involuntarily lobotomized some decades ago too, and one testified on NPR's *All Things Considered* on November 16, 2005. The program centered on the life of Walter Freeman, who performed an estimated 2,500 lobotomies between 1946 and 1967. Howard Dully, now an aging bus driver living in California, is one survivor who endured the ice pick procedure at the age of 12. In this procedure, an ice pick is inserted into the skull through each eye socket and then used to scrape brain matter in the frontal lobes. The results varied from having a calming effect to causing death by hemorrhage. In between, many people suffered drastic personality changes, often for the worse. Howard said he never discussed his lobotomy with his father until just before the program aired. He learned his stepmother talked his father into allowing it. One doctor assessed Howard as a normal boy who interacted typically with a stepmother. But she demonized him. After the surgery he wasn't the obedient, quiet boy she had bargained for, so he was made a ward of the state. He testified that he always wondered what was wrong with him. He felt something was missing from his soul. Now he wonders what he lost during those 10 minutes under the ice pick. He told a very sad story of his life. Could this be the story children of the 21st century will tell 20 years from now? The first antipsychotics were marketed, after all, as lobotomy in a pill.

A VOICE OF REASON: DANIEL BURSTON

Sharna Olfman's anthologies, including *No Child Left Different*, reassure me that reason and sense thrive among professionals, even though their voices remain muted beneath the hype of bipolar enthusiasts. So I close this chapter by presenting contributions of Daniel Burston, associate professor of psychology at Duquesne University, Pittsburgh.[21]

Burston attributes some responsibility for the surge of juvenile bipolar diagnoses to the Child and Adolescent Bipolar Foundation (CABF), which estimates that three-quarters of a million children have bipolar illness and that a great many are undiagnosed. He cites contributors to a book edited by psychiatrists Barbara Geller and Melissa DelBello[22] (we meet her again in the epilogue), who claim that pediatric bipolar disorder may be common in clinically referred children. Statements such as these are self-fulfilling prophecies: They set up an expectation among clinicians that they will encounter many children who are bipolar, but they will be the first to diagnose them. Burston adds, however, that the guidelines of CABF and the American Academy of Child and Adolescent Psychiatry stipulate that bipolar should not, under any circumstances, be diagnosed under the age of 6 (despite what icon Biederman says and does). Burston quotes John McLellan, who said in an editorial of the latter organization's journal, "Labeling severe tantrums in toddlers as major mental illness lacks face validity and undermines the credibility of our profession."[23] The CABF guidelines were a response to the concerns of psychiatrists regarding the proliferation of diagnoses of pediatric bipolar disorder, but they are not binding, explains Burston. Crediting McLellan[24] and Kowatch,[25] he elaborates that many psychiatrists seem to have forgotten how it feels to be a preschooler and declare, "I am Superman!" Or that young children who are hot, tired, and/or hungry can become very distressed and irritable. These characteristics need not fall under a rubric of neurological disease!

Like Breggin,[26] Burston lays some blame for increased awareness of manic symptoms in children on the drugs they are being prescribed for other behaviors (p. 126). Both researchers assert that antidepressants and stimulants trigger or exacerbate behavior disturbances that mimic symptoms of bipolar.

Burston talks a lot about psychiatrist Philip M. Sinaikin,[27] who eloquently discusses the ill effects of a thoughtless diagnosis for a child who may be distressed or poorly socialized, but neurologically intact (p. 130). He believes the plasticity of the youthful mind and spirit can see that child through hard times, given appropriate supports. But he implies that a diagnosis of bipolar forecloses on that possibility, robbing a child of his future. He explains that once diagnosed with a brain disease like bipolar disorder, the child believes he suffers from a lifelong disability and acts accordingly, all the while further impaired by a brain laden with toxic drugs. Harking to the wisdom of sociologists since the 1950s, Burston states, "A diagnosis of a severe mental disorder often constitutes an induction ceremony whereby a child or adolescent is launched on a career as a lifelong mental patient." He sums up by saying of the diagnosis, "It is socially and psychologically disfiguring, a license for immaturity, as well as a potential hazard to the growing child's brain" (p. 130).

Burston grapples with the question of diagnosis. He says we can learn from pediatrician Mel Levine's[28] approach to treating learning disabilities. Levine discovered that even if the problem stems from an organic malady, it is more readily treated when framed as "a different learning style." This encourages an optimistic examination of strengths and weaknesses, rather than assigning a medical disease label that discourages optimism. A medical label sets up the child to believe she cannot measure up to her peers. The result is a global sense of inadequacy that promotes passivity and lowered self-esteem. On the other hand, a "difference" stimulates identification of the child's unique skills and situation, which leads to optimism and a sense of personal agency (p. 137).

Burston does not wholly embrace Sinaikin's philosophy when it comes to serious emotional disturbances. He believes diagnoses, however they proliferate, are necessary because there are many children whose brains are disordered as a result of profound deprivation in infancy and/or exposure to toxic pollutants such as lead or mercury. In such cases, he says, diagnosis sometimes aids in finding the appropriate treatment. My response to Burston at this point would be, "The trouble with this is that most clinicians respond to the diagnosis from a medical model perspective, which means treating with chemicals—not a helpful treatment."

As if to anticipate such a response, Burston continues by deploring the ever-expanding *Diagnostic and Statistical Manual of Mental Disorders* (DSM). He recommends a moratorium on *any* new categories, including pediatric bipolar disorder. He recommends a historical view of how diagnostic categories were determined. He explains by visiting psychoanalytic process (now considered outmoded by mainstream mental health professionals), reminding us how, in psychoanalysis, diagnosis is not established until the end of treatment, after the analyst thoroughly knows the patient. Burston recommends that we adopt the best of psychoanalysis, and that clinicians with ties to pharmaceutical companies be excluded from DSM panels. He believes this is the only way diagnosis can be derived in a humane and thorough manner. Even if these recommendations were adopted (which is unlikely any time soon), I am still left with the question of what Burston considers appropriate treatment. He seems totally averse to polypharmacy (use of multiple drugs) or inappropriate medicating of children, but apparently does not eschew pediatric psychopharmacology altogether.

After reviewing neurobiological research in chapter 2, I concluded that what divides the psychosocial from the neurobiological theorists is choice of treatment. As the brain researchers come closer to recognizing environmental influences on neuro-chemical and genetic changes, and psychosocial theorists agree that stressors stimulate these changes, the question becomes how to restore the natural chemistry of the brain. Neurobiological theorists' choice of treatment is to infuse the ailing brain with various **neurotransmitter blockers or enhancers and/or other chemicals**. Psychosocial theorists recognize that the brain's ailment is exacerbated by the infusion of these toxic substances. Artificially tampering with the brain interferes with its remarkable ability to correct itself in response to **appropriate interpersonal and environmental adjustments**—these are our choices of treatment. The choice of treatment is critical, especially for children, and especially with the prolific rise in bipolar diagnoses: because the dominant medical model of treatment chooses the polypharmacological approach. That is, most mainstream mental health professionals' choice of treatment for distraught, angry, misbehaving children ("bipolar") is a cocktail of two, three, or more of the following: antipsychotic, anticonvulsant, antidepressant, and antihypertensive drugs—a potentially lethal brew for children.

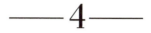

—4—

Pediatric Psychopharmacology and the Psychopharmaceutical Complex[1]

Herein lies the utter travesty, the flagrant inhumanity, of drugging children into behavioral submission . . . It disregards their inborn desire to become whole persons. Given half a chance, the kinds of kids to whom medicalized labels are currently being applied in such wholesale fashion are more than willing and able to learn, grow, and change without someone altering their basic biochemistry. To presume otherwise is to discount the human spirit.
—Chris Mercogliano

Questioning faces dominated by huge dilated pupils gazed up at me daily, as if to ask, "What is happening? Why do I feel like this?" Some saw me as a concerned friend and wondered why their caregivers made them take medicine. Others believed the medicine made them "good" and that without it they were "bad."

REMEMBERING MY CHILD CLIENTS

Lillian[2]

Lillian at 14 was like many children on medications: feisty, smart, and challenging to her parents. Her mother, Donna, eagerly accepted the clinic psychiatrist's diagnosis of bipolar. Pills were easier than evaluating the family dynamics that might be creating conflict between daughter and parents. Indeed, the drugs quelled her spirit and quieted her—results deemed beneficial by doctor and mother. Lillian and Donna came one day to their appointment, and Donna was angry. She told me that Lillian had been dispensing her pills to the wastebasket in her bedroom. Lillian's defense was that she hated to take the pills. When I asked her why, she responded that the pills made her feel shaky, spacey, and not fun to be with. Donna was not interested in excuses or in my explanation of side effects and the potential long-term harm the medication could be inflicting on Lillian. Lillian implored her to listen to me. This only fueled Donna's anger. She left the room and said they would not be back. Lillian wept as I hugged her good-bye.

There were times when I had to defend my child clients who had no say about the psychiatric regimens inflicted on them. I knew that in a few years Lillian would be able to decide for herself about medication, so she deserved to know the truth about their potentially lethal effects. During our visits, I had always highlighted Lillian's strengths: her vivacity, sense of humor, and intelligence. How sad that Donna did not recognize the treasure at her side. I always gave parents credit for good parenting when delightful children captured my heart. Sometimes it worked! At other times, pointing out the positive offended parents, something I tried to avoid. But in extreme circumstances, when I felt the welfare of my young clients was in jeopardy, this would happen. At least the children heard the compliments they never received at home. And sometimes it made a difference at home after caregivers had time to cool down and think about the positive things I said about their skills.

Commentary

Chapter 3 exposed how pediatric bipolar disorder is creating havoc in the lives of millions of youngsters like Lillian. In chapter 3 I mentioned a study that revealed a 40-fold increase of bipolar diagnoses among individuals aged 0 to 19. Over 90 percent of these were on combinations of mood stabilizers (e.g., Depakote), antipsychotics (e.g., Risperdal, Zyprexa), and antidepressants (e.g., Prozac, Lexapro). A widely publicized study by Julie Zito and colleagues at the University of Maryland[3] revealed the skyrocketing increase in psychiatric drugs prescribed to 0 to 19-year-olds from 1987 to 1996: Of the 900,000 children studied, 2.5 percent took psychotropic medications in 1987, compared to 6.2 percent in 1996. The children studied were on either Medicaid or in a private health maintenance organization. In an earlier publication,[4] Zito and colleagues focused on 2- to 4-year-olds among this same study group, and confined the study to years 1991 to 1995. They noted a substantial increase in prescriptions for this age group over this time period. They had observed that methylphenidate and clonidine were the most prescribed in 1991. Prescriptions for clonidine increased the most by 1995, followed by stimulants and antidepressants. Interestingly, neuroleptic (antipsychotic medications) use remained unchanged. That changed dramatically in the mid 1990s, when the Biederman group set off the bipolar explosion with their declaration that bipolar could be diagnosed in very young children. The concomitant rise in antipsychotic medication use among children is documented in chapter 3 and in the antipsychotic medications section of this chapter.

Psychotropic (psychiatric) medication for children, then, is a booming business. The pharmaceutical industry has targeted children as its most promising growth industry. The Zito study attests to the success of this objective, as does a 2008 *New York Times* story: "An analysis of Minnesota data by the *New York*

Times last year found that on average, psychiatrists who received at least $5,000 from makers of newer-generation antipsychotic drugs appear to have written three times as many prescriptions to children for the drugs as psychiatrists who received less money or none."[5]

Using statistics from the U.S. Department of Health and Human Services, Robert Whitaker[6] reports that in 1955, cases of mental illness were recorded at 1,675,352, or 1,028 per 100,000 population. This rose to 10,741,243, or 3,806 per 100,000, in 2000. Whitaker draws a correlation between increasing mental illness and uses of medications: He notes that numbers of people receiving Social Security disability entitlements rose nearly sixfold since Thorazine was introduced. That number has also increased dramatically since 1987, when Prozac, the first of the selective serotonin reuptake inhibitors (SSRIs), came on the market. Both these drugs were touted as panaceas for the mentally ill. But Whitaker asks the obvious question: Can psychiatric drugs be causing mental illness?

Hildy

Four-year-old Hildy was a beautiful child with shiny black braids and a sweet face. Her mother, Rita, complained that Hildy was violent toward her older sisters. Rita said she was here at the clinic to find out "what is wrong with my daughter?" While she was talking, Hildy was at play with the toys in my office. I noticed that she had lined up little cars along the streets of the "magic city" rug on my floor. No other child had thought to use the illustrated rug in this manner. Talking softly to herself, she was deep into fantasyland. Even as Hildy did so, Rita was telling me that her daughter wasn't like other children; she never played constructively or imaginatively. Rita did seem to register my positive comments about Hildy. At the same time, I acknowledged that the violent behavior she was describing was unacceptable and empathized with her frustration over Hildy's defiant attitude. I urged Rita to attend my parents' class, an interactive forum in which I instructed parents to use Howard Glasser's *Nurtured Heart Approach* to transform the behavior of "difficult" children. Rita said she wasn't interested and didn't have the time, and besides, "something was terribly wrong with Hildy that only a doctor could help by prescribing something." She mentioned relatives with mental illness. I had no choice but to set up an appointment for Hildy with our psychiatrist. Her continued presence at the clinic among kids waiting for the doctor told me she was on drugs, and her mother told me the family chose not to pursue therapy. I wondered how she was faring. I didn't have time to follow the course of treatment of all the children who left my caseload after starting medication. But I watched many over the years become chronic consumers of mental health services and unnecessary medications.

Commentary

Washington Post staff writer Shankar Vedantam commented on the Zito study mentioned above.[7] He quoted Michael Jellinek, Chief of Child Psychiatry at

Massachusetts General Hospital, who reviewed the study: "The insurance system gave an incentive for medications and a disincentive for therapy." Vedantam went on to say that insurers have increased their profits by decreasing the use of psychotherapy. Pamela Greenberg, Executive Director of American Managed Behavioral Healthcare Association, which represents companies that cover mental health services, denies Jellinek's suggestion that insurers are only looking out for their profit margins.[8] Based on my own experience, I do not believe her.

Cindylou

Cindylou at age 8 presented with classic symptoms of obsessive-compulsive disorder (OCD). Her emaciated body reflected her fear of choking, which diminished her food intake. Convinced something was in her throat, she constantly asked her mother to check and be sure nothing was there. She imagined her father was going to have a fatal car crash on his way to work, so she begged all day to check up on him. She worried that her little sister would be kidnapped, which spoiled many family outings. Cindylou's mother, Iris, brought her to therapy. She responded with gratitude when I endorsed her wish to avoid medication. I recommended Tamar Chansky's *Freeing Your Child from Obsessive-Compulsive Disorder.*[9] Iris went right out and bought the book. She embraced the author's recommendations, which shed an entirely different light on how to respond to her daughter's constant demands for reassurance.

Cindylou's managed care insurance company required me to submit a treatment plan. I did so, noting the book and program the parents were implementing with my help as coach. A "specialist" from the insurance company phoned me to go over the plan. She asked had I spoken with Cindylou's pediatrician. I responded I had not thought that necessary at this time, since he had not attempted to treat the problem. The "specialist" reluctantly agreed to go along with this treatment plan for a month with the stipulation that I would consult with our staff psychiatrist if no improvement occurred within that time frame. She clearly wanted Cindylou on drugs. But significant improvement occurred, which surprised even me, as I had not before encountered this kind of condition with a child. I took substantial pride in reporting success to the "specialist" the next time she called me. This was not an isolated case of a "specialist" aggressively pushing psychotropic medication during treatment plan reviews. I stubbornly resisted the drug option every time, always to the consternation of the "specialist," who claimed to know better than I what would benefit my child clients. In Cindylou's case, treatment without drugs was not only much more beneficial, it was also more expedient. There was no need for continued visits to the psychiatrist or a lifelong expensive drug regimen that the psychiatrist likely would have recommended.

Commentary

At the symposium I attended at Point Park University, Robert Whitaker was an invited speaker on June 9, 2007. He used statistics from the public record to document that the explosion of psychotropic drugging of children has not stemmed the so-called surge of pediatric mental illness. He reported that in 1987 only 19,000 children received Supplemental Security Income (SSI), a benefit to which children with documented disability are entitled. Of these, 7.3 percent were diagnosed with mental disorders. In 2005 the number of children receiving SSI had grown to 483,000, and 47 percent had mental illness. The explosion of bipolar diagnoses accounts for much of the increase. The next case illustrates how this occurs.

Many of the families who came to our mental health clinic were economically, educationally, and intellectually limited—not in intelligence, but in opportunity. Some people's lives have been ravaged by poverty, substance abuse, and/or domestic violence, which suppresses their innate capability to make healthy choices. Many eventually found their way to the mental health clinic. I knew many of these clients had potential because some of their children were as delightful and bright as any I encountered.

Ivy

Ivy was only 3 years old. Her mother, Trudy, informed me that Ivy's three siblings were in the custody of social services. Ivy's curiosity and energy propelled her around my office, investigating various toys and objects. I observed that Trudy was overwhelmed by Ivy's continuous motion. But eventually Ivy settled into coloring vivacious images and cleverly constructing objects out of Play Dough and construction paper. She was incredibly talented, and her lucid verbal communication revealed intelligence and precocity. This was part of the problem. Trudy just didn't have matching ability to satisfy Ivy's inquiring mind or to channel her energy into positive activities. Consequently, Ivy screamed a lot out of frustration and boredom. To her credit, Trudy did attend my *Nurtured Heart* parent class. She was unable or unwilling to *consistently* apply the techniques of the model and did not complete the program. She stopped counseling and continued to bring Ivy in to renew medications and occasionally to see other therapists. I intervened on Ivy's behalf at case conferences when her name came up, to vouch for her sound mental health and precocity. But our child psychiatrist, like many, was highly influenced by the bipolar diagnosis icon, Joseph Biederman. And he embraced the Biederman treatment protocol of prescribing powerful antipsychotics. Ivy was one of many casualties added to the surge of this alleged disorder. These cases explain the massive increase of children eligible for SSI that Robert Whitaker reported above.

CHILDREN IN FOSTER CARE

Children placed in foster care are by far the most chemically abused children in our nation. Rima Laibow, Medical Director of the Natural Solutions Foundation,[10] decried the practice of family courts mandating parents to medicate their children or risk losing custody. She stated, "Children in foster care are, sadly, all too frequently abusively medicated, sexually and physically molested/abused and emotionally damaged, sometimes to horrifying degrees." She based her remarks on her experience as child psychiatrist for the Westchester County, New York, department dealing with foster children. She asserts that children in other states also endure abysmal conditions.

My observations support Laibow's statements. When parents lose their rights to consent to or refuse treatment for their children in foster care, those children are at the mercy of custodians who have no training in mental health. The youngsters have no loving party to monitor their care. In foster care, children often spiral downward, not only because of losing their family, but because they are forced to ingest powerful psychotropic drugs to quell their natural expressions of distress. Children descend into serious mental illness after years of multiple labels and medications, and their lives are often irreversibly damaged. These children may end up in institutional care through no fault of their own.

Texas State Comptroller Carole Keeton Strayhorn conducted a two-year investigation into allegations that Texas foster kids were overmedicated.[11] She tracked all medications prescribed to foster children for the year 2004. An e-mail message to me from Mind Freedom reported that CBS News ran a story on the subject of medicating children in foster care on October 18, 2006, and quoted Ms. Strayhorn: "I found babies, 2-year-olds, 3-year-olds being given mind-altering drugs . . . Children in foster care in Texas are dying. Children in foster care are being drugged." The CBS story included a typical narrative concerning a Texas boy, Colby Holcomb. CBS reporter Byron Pitts characterized his experience as a "travesty."

Colby was taken into custody by social services when he was 7 after his mother's ex-husband alleged sexual abuse was occurring in the home. It turned out to be a false allegation, but Colby was in foster care for 18 months, in five foster homes. His expressions of distress earned him the bipolar label. He was on at least 20 different drugs in the 18 months, sometimes taking as many as four medications at a time. While on the four, he suffered seizures and woke up in the hospital with a needle in his arm. His mother, Andrea, was never consulted or told why he was put on the drugs.

Colby's is not an isolated unusual case. Many children like him passed through our clinic. No matter they are in custody unnecessarily. It still takes up to 18 months or more to reunite them with their families.

Pitts revealed that the same allegations of overmedicating foster children were being reported in California, Ohio, and Florida. Investigators in Florida found that foster children younger than 5 were treated with psychiatric medications at a rate nearly four times higher than the general population of children receiving Medicaid.

On February 14, 2008, Congressman Jim McDermott, Democrat from Washington and chair of the Subcommittee on Income Security and Family Support, introduced the Investment in Kids Act, calling for the most comprehensive reform of child welfare in nearly 30 years.[12] Four titles of the act provide all-around improvements in the foster care system with a statement in Title 4 to "[r]equire States to develop plans to oversee and coordinate health care for foster children." On May 8, 2008, Congressman McDermott held hearings regarding the psychiatric drugging of children in foster care. Several professionals and one "alumnus" of foster care served as witnesses.[13]

Hopefully, McDermott is following up with that selection from Title 4 so that children in foster care will be protected from chemical abuse, something they surely do not deserve on top of all their other suffering.

SCHOOL COERCION TO MEDICATE STUDENTS AND LAWS CURBING THE PRACTICE

I received many referrals of child clients from their teachers or other school staff. Some years ago it was not unusual to receive calls from the schools pressing aggressively for psychiatric assessments for the purpose of putting a child on stimulant medication. Sometimes it took weeks for a child to get an appointment with the staff psychiatrist, and I would take heat for the wait from impatient teachers who believed their classroom would benefit from my client being drugged. It was even possible to report parents to social services for medical neglect if parents did not follow a recommendation to have their children evaluated by a psychiatrist or to refuse to give psychotropic medication to their children. Some states, including New York, have passed laws prohibiting school personnel from coercing parents in this manner, or from suggesting diagnoses such as ADHD or recommending medication. School staff I encountered subsequently took care to heed the letter of the law but found alternative language that still accomplished the objective of getting students on medication. Now they recommend "medical solutions," a euphemism for psychoactive drugs. At one Individual Educational Plan (IEP) meeting that I attended, the school nurse pressured the student's caregiver by predicting dire consequences in later years without the help of "medical solutions." Their tactics became more sophisticated, if less specific, about diagnoses and medication. Yet not all school personnel condone such practices. Over time, more teachers were hesitant to seek "medical solutions" because they, too, became concerned about the overuse of drugs and frequency of psychiatric referrals. Some innovative teachers knew how to engage and manage children who didn't fit the typical student profile. Others, including some principals, went "head to head" with these children and became stuck in lose-lose power struggles.

Some other states have enacted legislation to protect students and parents from coercive measures. Colorado passed such a law in the wake of the Columbine school shooting. It was reported that Eric Harris, lead shooter in the tragedy, had been taking Zoloft for depression during the year before the murders.[14] The report said Eric complained of having obsessive homicidal and suicidal thoughts six weeks after starting the medication. Weaned off Zoloft, he said he felt better. His psychiatrist then started him on Luvox, another SSRI known to cause mania in one out of 25 patients taking it (according to the drug label).

Several bills have been introduced in the U.S. Congress titled "The Child Medication Safety Act," intended to curb schools' interference with student mental health. On May 21, 2003, the House passed H.R. 1170 with a vote of 425 to one. It died before getting to the Senate floor. The 2005 version, H.R. 1790, passed overwhelmingly in the House, but also did not make it to the Senate floor. However, Senate bill 891, introduced in March 2007, would require all states to enact policies prohibiting schools from coercing parents to drug their children with stimulants and other psychotropic medications as a condition of staying in school. It also protects parents from being charged with abuse or neglect for refusing to administer these drugs to their children. Federal funding would be contingent on states complying with the law. Last action was recorded March 15, 2007, when the bill was read twice and referred to the Committee on Health, Education, Labor and Pension.[15] In the next chapter, laws prohibiting schools from screening children for mental illness without parental consent are discussed.

THE TOXICITY OF PSYCHOTROPIC DRUGS

Neurologist Fred Baughman stated that humans recognize the potential harm by the many chemicals in our environment and "hasten to sweep from the mouths of our toddlers, dirt, pebbles, drinks, or volatile (gaseous) liquids and any pill they come upon." Yet, he points out, adults believe anything packaged by "Big Pharma" and said to be safe by the FDA is safe to ingest. Baughman underscores his point with a quote from John Griffith of Vanderbilt University when Griffith was testifying at a congressional hearing in 1970, when funding for psychostimulant therapy for school problems was being debated:

> I would like to point out that every drug, however innocuous, has some degree of toxicity. A drug, therefore, is a type of poison and its poisonous qualities must be carefully weighed against its therapeutic usefulness. A problem, now being considered in most of the capitols of the Free World, is whether the benefits derived from amphetamines outweigh their toxicity. It is the consensus of the world scientific literature that the amphetamines are of little benefit to mankind. They are, however, quite toxic.[16]

Peter Breggin's Brain Disabling Theory

Brain-Disabling Treatments in Psychiatry by Peter Breggin explains how drugs work on the brain. Breggin's theory is nicely summarized by Joanna Moncrieff.[17] Psychiatric drugs, like electroconvulsive therapy (ECT) and lobotomy, are a type of physical intervention that work by disabling brain function. The desired therapeutic effects of drugs are achieved by impairing higher mental functions. The same disabling function occurs in all people, not only in people labeled as mentally ill, although there is individual variation among people in the way they respond to a given drug, physically and emotionally. Psychiatric drugs can create their own psychiatric or physical problems. The foreign substance (drug) causes the brain to adapt to chemical changes; it is perturbed, and chemically imbalanced, as a result of the foreign substance. These adaptations can cause adverse side effects and withdrawal. The people taking the drug may have poor judgment regarding the effect of the drug. Breggin talks about a "spellbinding" effect, similar to euphoria, that makes people feel the drug is helping. This is like a person intoxicated by alcohol who believes that alcohol improves his or her functioning.

Physicians who prescribe the drugs also often have unrealistic judgments about the risks and benefits of the drugs. For example, when my client, Bradley, started taking Ritalin, he sat still in class and seemed to be attending to his lessons instead of getting out of his seat and fidgeting. His doctor concluded by the teacher's report that the Ritalin "was working." Actually, to Bradley, the drug "working" may have meant he was drugged into platitude. He may have been obsessing more than focusing on his lessons. Bradley's subjective report to me was that he felt "weird" on Ritalin and didn't feel he was able to enjoy friends and activities like he used to. He didn't like taking the drug, even though it did improve his school performance.

Chemobrain

Grace Jackson reveals another aspect of psychiatric drug toxicity.[18] She related the life history of a boy who was treated with chemotherapy for leukemia as a toddler. Jackson said that in this case, the chemotherapy successfully treated the leukemia, but the neurotoxicity of the multiple therapies resulted in a delayed but persistent seizure condition and mental handicaps. The patient developed a serious neurological condition known as Lennox-Gastaut syndrome. By his early teens, he was placed on multiple medications that ultimately included Depakote (an anticonvulsant) and Risperdal (an antipsychotic). He worsened progressively on these two drugs. Following the successful withdrawal from Risperdal and Depakote, the boy's condition has improved considerably, although severe mental handicaps and occasional seizures continue.

The point of Jackson's lecture was to introduce the properties of many psychiatric drugs that duplicate the toxicities of cancer therapies, especially the toxic effects on the cells of the brain. Many psychiatric drugs currently in use for "neurobehavioral" conditions are being explored as adjuvant (enhancing) therapies for various cancers, due to their cytotoxic effects. In other words, just as cancer chemotherapies can and do destroy the cells of the brain, so too do psychiatric medications, especially drugs like Depakote.

METHODS OF RESEARCH ON PSYCHOTROPIC MEDICATION

Drug makers usually perform their own clinical trials on safety and efficacy of the drugs they market. The companies can perform any number of studies, but it only takes two "successful" ones to earn approval, or licensing, from the U.S. Food and Drug Administration (FDA) to market the drug. The quotation marks indicate the suspect nature of studies done by the companies on their own drugs, due to conflicting interests. I asked our clinic psychiatrist about the safety of the many drugs he prescribed to children "off label" (not approved for children). He responded, "We just go by the 'five-year rule.'" He explained that if a drug is still on the market after five years, it must be okay. Lawrence Diller[19] puts a different slant on the "five-year rule." He quotes an unnamed colleague: "Prescribe a new medication in the first five years, before the full extent of side effects are known. In the second five years, you'll become more cautious because the drug's effectiveness and safety will start to look similar to the older drugs available for the condition. But by the third five years, you won't be pre-scribing the drug at all because its patent will have expired and a new drug pro-moting better effectiveness and fewer side effects will be offered."

In contrast, the gold standard of clinical trials accepted by many researchers is the double-blind randomized controlled study (DBRCS).[20] Some profes-sionals agree that the DBRCS represents the most rigorous, valid, and reliable research possible. In a DBRCS, no one involved with the study, such as family, subject, and doctor, know whether the child is taking the medication or the pla-cebo (inactive substance). Potential subjects are carefully screened for the condi-tion being studied and then randomly chosen to participate in the study. Parents, the doctor, and sometimes others observe the children for benefits or side effects. Sometimes subjects display beneficial effects or complain of stomach-aches or headaches when taking placebos. (Some placebos have built-in side effects so the subjects won't guess they're on placebo.) Only at the conclusion of the study are all informed who took the drug and who did not. At this time the "real" versus the "believed" effects of the drug can be known. For example, in the only DBRCS of Prozac on children, 60 percent of the improvement in depressive symptoms was attributed to the placebo effect. The placebo effect is improvement based on the subject's belief or expectation that he will improve because of the treatment.

The DBRCS is the most difficult study to undertake with human subjects and mental health conditions, and many social scientists believe the DBRCS method has significant shortcomings. To explain these shortcomings, Grace Jackson[21] takes us back to the first century A.D., when two camps were first identified among medical practitioners: the evidence based and the reason based. The first held that the effects of treatment and experimentation were of primary impor-tance; the second placed highest importance on understanding the theoretical mechanisms responsible for disease. The two became integrated as modern medi-cine evolved, yet tensions remain between the two camps. The evidence-based believers contend that all human experience can be explained in terms of brain activity, while the reason based believe the human experience cannot be explained by science alone. The evidence-based group attained prominence in 1991 when the *Journal of the American Medical Association* (*JAMA*) published an article that announced the arrival of "Evidence Based Medicine" (EBM). In clinical judgments, EBM de-emphasizes intuition and "unsystematic clinical experience"; instead it stresses the examination of evidence from clinical research. Neurobiological theorists embrace EBM and think in terms of populations, experiments, and appropriate medication. Psychosocial theorists, like the reason-based camp, believe those are insufficient. We emphasize individuals' and families' strengths to overcome distress and encourage a placebo effect, negating the need for medication.

I explained this dichotomy to a group while speaking about treating children (and adults) through empathic listening, which would lead to "heart-to-heart" connection, or joining. This "shared wavelength" opened a path for communication that truly made a difference in the lives of both of us. I told my audience, "That is what doing therapy is about; it's not 'best practices' or 'evidence-based research.'"

We'll now proceed with discussion of common psychotropic medications prescribed for children, starting with the earliest: the psychostimulants.

PSYCHOSTIMULANT MEDICATIONS

The History of Psychostimulant Medications

Jackson provides a historical account of the use of stimulant drugs to treat ADHD.[22] Even in ancient times, people used a variety of stimulants in their natural forms to alter stamina and mood. However, not until the 20th century were they recognized as useful in treating asthma and the respiratory effects of surgical anesthetics. Jackson cites the work of chemists at Eli Lilly in the 1920s. They isolated Ephedra from the botanical stimulant ma huang. It was effective in opening constricted airways and thus became a common treatment for asthma. During the same time period, other scientists were producing forms of amphetamines such as Benzedrine and Dexedrine. Benzedrine became a common over-the-counter inhalant to reduce nasal secretions, and Dexedrine was used for narcolepsy and weight control. It wasn't long before the alerting and euphoric qualities of these drugs became known. Jackson credits Solomon Snyder[23] for the revelation that college students were disassembling inhalers and swallowing the Benzedrine to stay awake and cram for exams.

During World War II, amphetamines were distributed to soldiers in Europe and Japan and to industrial workers. The addictive potential became evident when an epidemic of amphetamine abuse occurred in postwar times. Hence the sale of Benzedrine inhalants was banned in 1959 and amphetamines were restricted to prescription use only.

Jackson reports that in 1937 American physician Charles Bradley discovered by accident the potential of Benzedrine to aid in learning.[24] His use of spinal taps to assess children caused severe headaches in his patients, so he gave them Benzedrine tablets as a pain reliever. Benzedrine didn't help with the pain, but some of the children noted that it increased their ability to learn. They called the Benzedrine tablets "math pills." This discovery went without recognition by other physicians for over a decade.

Jackson continues that in 1944 Ciba (now Novartis) synthesized methylphenidate (Ritalin), but not until 1963 did the first clinical trials with children take place at Johns Hopkins University. This landmark study evaluated the efficacy of Ritalin and Dexedrine in managing difficult behavior of institutionalized children. Four years later, the same researchers took their studies into classrooms to see how these drugs worked with students identified as talking loudly, giggling, daydreaming, leaving their seats, and other typical "hyperactive" behaviors. By the time stimulants came into common use for controlling difficult childhood behavior in the 1960s, this practice gained the support of the National Institute of Mental Health (NIMH) and major universities. When stimulants also became the drug of choice to treat adult maladies such as nervousness and fatigue, concerns developed over the potential for abuse of the drugs and some of their side effects. We return to the abuse potential later in the chapter.

Types of Stimulants and Their Properties

Millions of children have been treated for ADHD with the generic drugs methylphenidate and amphetamine. Common brand names for methylphenidate are Ritalin, Focalin, Metadate, and Concerta. The 2008 methylphenidate labels carry the Food and Drug Administration's (FDA) strictest warning, known as "Black Box." The warnings indicate that methylphenidate has potential for drug dependence; that it should be given cautiously to patients with a history of substance dependence; that chronic use can lead to marked tolerance and psychological dependence with varying degrees of abnormal behavior; that psychotic episodes can occur, especially with parental (injection) use; that careful supervision is required during withdrawal from abusive use since severe depression may occur; and that withdrawal following chronic therapeutic use may unmask symptoms of the underlying disorder that may require follow-up. There is no warning regarding cardiovascular risks. Later in this chapter we will see that many experts strongly recommended one.

Some brand names for amphetamine are Adderall, Adderall XR (d-amphetamine and amphetamine mixture), Dexedrine and DextroStat (dextroamphetamine or d-amphetamine), and Desoxyn (methamphetamine). A new brand of stimulant, Vyvanse (lisdexamfetamine dimesylate), was approved by the FDA in February 2007 for use in children. Daniel Carlat suggests that manufacturer Shire's use of "f" instead of "ph" in the generic form is a clever attempt to "make it less obvious that Vyvanse is simply a fancified version of good old Dexedrine."[25] All the amphetamine labels carry the Black Box warning: high potential for abuse; prolonged use could lead to drug dependence and must be avoided; particular attention need be paid to the possibility of subjects obtaining amphetamines for non-therapeutic use or distribution to others; and misuse may cause sudden death and serious cardiovascular adverse events. Yet oddly enough, Adderall doses are recommended for children as young as 3, but not under. This is the drug considered so dangerous it was banned in Canada!

Often people ask for Strattera (atomoxetine) as an alternative to stimulants because it has been marketed as a non-stimulant. Jackson[26] explains that it is actually a derivative of the stimulant phenylpropanolamine, or PPA. In November 2000, the FDA required PPA to be removed from over-the-counter cold remedies and other products due to risk of hemorrhagic stroke (bleeding into the brain or surrounding tissues). It has many of the same side effects as methylphenidate and amphetamine (classified as stimulants): increased blood pressure and heart rate, dry mouth, pupillary dilation, and urinary retention. Its behavioral effects are the same: enhanced alertness, insomnia, loss of appetite, nervousness, suicidality, hostility, akathisia (urgent need to move about), and mania. Jackson explains that Strattera has been marketed as a non-stimulant because it does not appear to enhance dopamine transmission in parts of the brain. However, she notes that rats, pigeons, and monkeys failed to distinguish between Strattera and low doses of cocaine or methamphetamine on drug discrimination tasks. Moreover, the potential for Strattera to induce psychological dependence has not been disproved.

Strattera is classified as a psychostimulant by the World Health Organization. Because of its stimulant effects, it has been used to treat narcolepsy, and has been investigated as a treatment for obesity. Jackson reports that in January 2006, the Office of the Chief Medical Examiner in North Carolina reported discovery of ventricular abnormalities in the hearts of two young people who died while on therapeutic doses of Strattera. Jackson wants the FDA to appropriately characterize Strattera as a stimulant and, as with other stimulants, to issue warnings about its potential cardiovascular risks. The current revised label for Strattera does indeed bear the same warnings regarding cardiovascular risks as the stimulants. While the label does not identify Strattera as a stimulant, it cautions about increased heart rate and blood pressure, and it warns of side effects of potential manic symptoms and aggressive or hostile behavior—all effects of stimulant medications—just as Jackson documented above! Strattera is the only ADHD medication that carries a Black Box warning for suicidal ideation and the need for close monitoring for suicidality. It also warns, although not in the Black Box, of potential liver damage.

Jackson explains that the World Health Organization characterizes pharmaceutical substances according to three properties: chemical, pharmacological, and therapeutic, or behavioral. Behavioral properties of stimulants include heightened arousal, enhanced stamina (decreased need for sleep), feelings of well-being, and appetite suppression. Other behavioral effects are nervousness, insomnia, agitation, mania, paranoia, hallucinations, and movement abnormalities such as tics and other involuntary body movements.

Efficacy: Do They Work?

ADHD specialist Lawrence Diller[27] reports that thousands of studies have researched the short-term efficacy of stimulant medications on thousands of children, mostly young boys. Most professionals agree that stimulant drugs are effective in improving concentration, academic grades, productivity, impulse control, and relations with family and peers. Diller and others add, however, that no studies have demonstrated any long-term benefit. Jackson[28] cites studies that show a waning of drug benefits over time, possibly due to tolerance of the drug, physical changes of the body such as brain maturation, situational changes, or toxic effects of the drugs on brain physiology and behavior. In my practice, it was almost inevitable that, especially with the stimulant medications, caregivers would return in a matter of weeks complaining that the drug was not working anymore and/or the child's behavior was worse. David Stein[29] talks about "cognitive toxicity" as a notable side effect. This means that the drugs improve learning for simpler skills like addition or subtraction, but impair more complex cognitive skills such as deeper understanding of concepts, appreciating literature, or writing creatively. Stein reports 40 percent of children who take stimulants experience this phenomenon. This corroborates Breggin's observation that stimulants inhibit the kinds of activity crucial to the development of the part of the brain responsible for higher functioning.[30]

How Do We Know if Stimulants Are Safe?

The safety of all stimulant medications has been challenged. Methylphenidate, amphetamine, methamphetamine, along with cocaine and morphine, are all Schedule II controlled substances. As explained in chapter 2, the Department of Health and Human Services implemented the Controlled Substances Act in 1971. It classifies drugs into Schedules I–V, according to their potential for abuse. The act set strict guidelines for record-keeping and storage of the drugs.

Peter Breggin told a *Frontline*[31] interviewer that the makers of Ritalin and other ADHD medicines are breaking international law when they advertise directly to the public. He cites international law that prohibits advertising of Schedule II drugs due to their highly addictive qualities. Other developed countries outlaw direct-to-consumer advertising of medications. The overdosing of Americans described by writers Melody Petersen (*Our Daily Meds*), John Abramson (*Overdosed America: The Broken Promise of American Medicine*), and others is largely attributed to this daily bombardment of advertising on television and in other media.

Xavier Castellanos, on the same *Frontline* program, speculated about the cause of ADHD. He adheres to the dominant theory that the brain doesn't keep its dopamine and said two studies with adults suggest this is true in the basal ganglia. He cited a study in which individuals never treated before were given Ritalin. He said the study seemed to confirm his hypothesis that Ritalin, since it boosts dopamine, should increase the size of the parts of the brain that are smaller in ADHD individuals. Apparently the adults' basal ganglia enlarged with the medication.

But suppose the smaller size of some parts of the brain is an adaptive response to some previous behavior or experience? Artificially boosting dopamine perturbs the brain. Perturbations disrupt the brain's natural tendency to regain balance, known as homeostasis. So introducing a foreign chemical (Ritalin) into the brain could create havoc in this exquisitely sensitive organ. The result could be one of those undesirable side effects usually mistaken for a worsening of the original condition or the emergence of "an underlying condition" such as bipolar. Typically, the doctor then increases or changes the medication, which further perturbs the brain.

Cardiovascular Side Effects

It is not uncommon for cocaine abusers to develop cardiovascular problems. The *Drugs-Forum* Web site[32] posted a report on December 8, 2004, that cocaine use has been associated with a number of cardiovascular complications, such as artery blockages and heart attacks. No wonder, then, that methylphenidate and amphetamines, in the same class of drugs as cocaine, have been associated with similar heart ailments. Only in 2007 were warnings added to the labels of stimulants regarding potential serious adverse cardiovascular events, including sudden death in children with existing heart problems. Later in this chapter, one of our experts speculates that the stimulants can cause heart damage even in people who have no history of cardiac problems.

Nick's Heart

The new warnings came too late for my client, Nick, who started his regimen of stimulant medications in 1996. Labeled both ADHD and bipolar, he was 12 when his mother told me about his heart condition. Looking back through his records, I found an electrocardiogram (ECG) that his former psychiatrist had ordered three years prior. The test showed Nick had a "right bundle branch block," and it was labeled "abnormal test." I recalled a former cocaine addict client who told me he had right bundle branch block due to his cocaine use. Nick had been taking stimulants for the three years **since** his ECG and had already been on them for three years **prior** to the ECG. Why his former clinic psychiatrist continued prescribing stimulants following this abnormal ECG was unknown! I brought this information to the attention of Nick's current psychiatrist. Our clinical director followed up with a referral to a cardiac specialist. Nick continued seeing the clinic psychiatrist but terminated counseling, so I do not know what was done about his medications. Like many of my clients, Nick was constantly targeted as trouble-maker at school, and all the diagnoses and medications only exacerbated his problems. School staff perceived his labels "proof" of his incorrigibility and his need for medications. His mother held fast to what she called his "bipolar medicine" and "ADHD medicine." She cared deeply, but couldn't fathom challenging the judgment of a doctor even when his treatment put her child's health, even his life, seriously at risk. Nick suffered another common side effect of stimulant use. He developed a tic in the form of rolling his eyes repeatedly in the space of a few minutes. Many of my clients developed tics while on stimulants.

The Abuse Potential of Stimulants

It is well documented that children and especially adolescents have distributed their Ritalin and other ADHD stimulant medications to peers, either for recreation or for profit. The effects of methylphenadate (Ritalin) on the brain are virtually identical to those of cocaine. Drug sales representatives visited our clinic regularly, laden with containers of delicious food and gifts. In addition to a lavish lunch, we were fed propaganda. A favorite pitch claimed their studies showed a lower incidence of stimulant abuse in later years among children taking Concerta (a long-acting form of Ritalin). I asked one drug representative how long these subjects were on the drug. She responded, "They stay on it indefinitely." I countered that as long as individuals are taking Concerta, they are not tempted to use cocaine because they are already on a cocaine-like drug! This raises the question of what happens with individuals who discontinue Ritalin use before adulthood.

Nadine Lambert's Work

Much of Nadine Lambert's life was devoted to studies of just such individuals. Her research is frequently cited as the most comprehensive of its kind in terms of length and number of subjects. I take the following account from an article by Lawrence Diller[33] in which he describes the work of Nadine Lambert, Ph.D. She started with a special education study in the 1970s to determine how many children in the San Francisco Bay area were hyperactive or handicapped. She set out to follow the same children diagnosed with ADHD from the 1970s until adulthood. In 1998 she presented the results of her 20-year study to the National Institutes of Health Consensus Conference on ADHD described in chapter 2. Her long-term study of nearly 400 children concluded that those who previously were treated with Ritalin had double the rates of cocaine abuse and cigarette smoking as young adults who had not taken Ritalin in childhood. This news was a bombshell to her audience, since most conference attendees had high stakes in the production and application of Ritalin. The implications of Lambert's research posed a grave threat to proponents of stimulant therapy, especially when the media picked up the story and publicly questioned the advisability of Ritalin treatment. High-profile ADHD specialists decided to do their own studies. Joseph Biederman and Timothy Wilens of Harvard bipolar notoriety claimed their meta-analysis (a compilation of previous studies) demonstrated that Ritalin created a protective effect against stimulant abuse. Russell Barkley performed a study that was compromised by too small a sample size, so the differences between subjects and controls were not statistically significant. But the differences agreed with those of Lambert. Yet Barkley claimed, along with the others, to have discredited her work.

S. DuBose Ravenel[34] wrote that Lambert's study had advantages over Biederman and Wilen's. It had a larger untreated ADHD control group, was community based, and used non-clinic-referred samples. Despite their shortcomings, the pharmaceutical companies that produce stimulants circulated reprints of those later studies to every pediatrician and child psychiatrist in the country.

Lambert's experience is grievous testament to the potential of the psycho-pharmaceutical complex to ruin careers of prestigious scientists whose work runs counter to prevailing neurobiological theory. Lambert had no vested interest in the outcome of her careful, scientific life's work, but she was professionally ostracized because of the unpopular outcome of her study. The National Institute of Drug Abuse terminated her funding, her research proposals were unfairly criticized, and no American medical journal would publish her work. When she presented to the 2004 convention of the International Center for the Study of Psychiatry and Psychology, she informed the audience, of which I was part, that she was looking to Great Britain to publish her latest findings. Tragically, she died in a traffic accident two years later, leaving her work unfinished.

The Multimodal Treatment Study of Children with ADHD (MTA)

Proponents of stimulant medications often cite the Multimodal Treatment Study of Children with ADHD (MTA), the largest study of its kind. Its objective was to determine the best treatment for children diagnosed with ADHD. The researchers compared four groups. One group's treatment was stimulant medication alone; another had behavior therapy alone; another had the two combined; and the last had the usual community treatment. The National Institute of Mental Health undertook the study in 1991. It randomized 579 children diagnosed with ADHD into the four groups above, and concluded in 14 months. At that point results favored the group on medication only or the combined group. But at the three-year point, the behavioral group appeared to be overtaking the other groups on success measures.

Jackson[35] identified four methodological deficiencies that weaken the study even further. It wasn't blinded, so all involved knew which treatment each child was receiving; over one-third of the children in the study had previous stimulant treatment; behavioral treatment phased out early, while drug treatment continued the whole 14 months; and compliance with treatment protocols was spotty in all groups.

The puzzling three-year outcomes spurred further research with the study participants. Kathleen Doheny discussed the research in *WebMD Health News*. Results were published in the August 2007 issue of the *Journal of the American Academy of Child and Adolescent Psychiatry*. Overall, the conclusion reached was that at the three-year mark, all the children had improved, no matter which group they were in. However, there were some differences.

A study led by Brooke Molina at the University of Pittsburgh showed that despite treatment, the ADHD children showed significantly higher-than-normal rates of delinquency and substance abuse than the non-ADHD kids in the study: 27.1 percent versus 7.4 percent engaged in delinquent behavior; 17.4 percent versus 7.8 percent used substances. Molina said they weren't addicts, but they were more prone to experiment.[36]

Daniel DeNoon discussed another study in WebMD that[37] documented the suppression of growth in children on stimulant medication. James Swanson, at the University of California, reported that after three years on Ritalin, children were shorter and lighter than their peers. Children who never took medication grew larger by about three-fourths of an inch and 6 pounds, on average. The medicated children resumed normal growth by the third year, but they did not make up for the earlier slowing in growth. A surprising finding was that kids with ADHD who never took stimulant medication were actually much bigger than kids who don't have ADHD. And without medication, they continue to grow larger than their non-ADHD peers. The issue of whether stimulants stunt growth had been disputed for years. It was assumed that if growth were indeed stunted, there would be a growth spurt when medication was discontinued. Swanson reported there is no evidence of any growth spurt; the long range outcomes remain to be seen. Researchers plan to continue follow-up with the MTA children as they pass through adolescence and enter adulthood.

A Drug Representative's Visit

A representative of the Concerta drug maker brought lunch to our clinic along with a "featured speaker," a Ph.D. researcher apparently in the employ of the drug's manufacturer. Like most presenters who favor medication, she cited the MTA study and its results that favored stimulant medication as treatment. Granted, this was before the follow-up studies were published in 2007, but the fact remains that drug proponents still like to quote those original findings, claiming that the famous MTA study proved medication or medication combined with behavior therapy brought superior outcomes compared to behavior therapy alone. I challenged this claim and cited Howard Glasser's Nurtured Heart Approach (NHA) non-drug school program.[38] I told how Maria Figueroa, the principal of Tolson Elementary School in Tucson, presented to our group while we were in training with Howard Glasser in Tucson. Her school was failing and doomed for closure until Howard trained her staff in the NHA for teachers. Figueroa showed data documenting that it has made dramatic differences in student academic achievement and staff morale, and testified that no child in this school was started on medication since the program was initiated. Our presenter countered, "Training school staff is expensive." I argued, "Not as expensive as buying medication for all those children." Our presenter blanched and said lamely, "Well, insurance doesn't pay for training." As if the millions of dollars taxpayers pay (through Medicaid) for stimulant drugs was okay. Even worse, this speaker made one of the most irresponsible and insensitive selling points I have ever heard. She told us about a boy whose parents took him off Concerta during the summer. Tragically, he was killed on his bicycle when hit by a car. The presenter blamed his death on the fact he had been taken off the drug, claiming, "He lost his ability to focus."

The Question of Safety Looms Larger

Events Leading Up to the FDA Stimulant Medications Label Changes

On January 3, 2005, National Public Radio's *Morning Edition* announced new information about Ritalin use in youngsters under 5.5 years of age. The FDA had approved the drug for children, but a National Institute of Mental Health study showed the drug to be less effective for children younger than 5.5 years and even to have negative effects such as agitation, emotional outbursts, and sleep disturbances. A third of the children experienced growth retardation. Therefore, NIMH was recommending that Ritalin be prescribed only to children aged 6 and above.

Stimulant Adderall XR, a combination of amphetamines and dextroamphetamines, was banned in Canada in February 2005,[39] following reports of sudden cardiac death in 20 patients, more than two-thirds of them children, and strokes in 12 patients, one-sixth of them children. But the U.S. FDA chose only to add a warning to the Adderall XR label not to use the drug on anyone with structural cardiac abnormalities. Adderall XR is a longer-acting form of Adderall, also marketed in the United States, but not sold in Canada.

News reports[40, 41] on June 29, 2005, indicated the FDA was adding new warnings to the methylphenidate products (Ritalin, Concerta), but not about cardiovascular risks. The FDA would not warn of these because it believed no causal link was proven between the drugs and cardiovascular events. Its concerns at this time were about psychiatric symptoms that did seem to be caused by the methylphenidates. (Adderall and Adderall XR would be examined in 2006.) Then on June 30, 2005,[42] the FDA announced its own review of Concerta's use in children revealed psychiatric reactions not previously known: suicidal thoughts, hallucinations, and violent behavior. Similar effects were reported from use of all methylphenidate products. Previously labels had warned of possible side effects of agitation, psychosis, or transient depression. According to this news story, FDA drug safety evaluator Kathleen Phelan stated, "Indeed, stimulant drugs may exacerbate symptoms and reveal them for the first time in children with previously unrecognized psychiatric illnesses." This statement is alarming.

Kathleen Phelan contradicts previous statements asserting a causal relationship between the psychiatric side effects and the drugs. Side effects are not "previously unrecognized psychiatric illnesses." This is a dangerous misinterpretation. If the prescribing physician starts a child on stimulant medication followed by the parents' description of "off the wall" behavior, that doctor is likely to tell parents the ADHD has "transmuted"[43] to bipolar and switch from stimulant to antipsychotic medication. Diller calls this "diagnosis by pharmacological dissection."[44] Parents and doctors also often misinterpret "rebound" as symptomatic of "a previously unknown disorder." Rebound is actually withdrawal: the child's body reacting to the absence of the drug when either it has been discontinued or it wears off. Rebound is another cause of "off the wall" behavior.

Returning to cardiovascular adverse events and the FDA's uncertainty that stimulant medications *caused* them, let's go back to 1977. Vernon Fischer and

Hendrick Barmer reported in a letter to the editor at the *Journal of the American Medical Association*[45] that they had discovered the presence of structural alterations in the left ventricular myocardium of a patient who had been treated with methylphenidate for about four years. The abnormality was revealed during bypass surgery, when a biopsy was examined. The cellular changes are associated with cardiomyopathy (enlarged heart). The abnormal membrane accumulations in the left ventricle are known as lamellated bodies.

Fischer joined Theodore Henderson to see if a causal effect could be confirmed by duplicating these changes in rodents. They published their results in 1994.[46] Ritalin in mice and rats produced the same kinds of membrane proliferation observed earlier in the human subject. The authors noted other cardiovascular side effects of Ritalin: arrhythmia, tachycardia, and changes in blood pressure. A result of Ritalin being administered, wrote the authors, is that it induces the cardiac alterations that lead to the presence of lamellar bodies. The changes wrought in mice on therapeutic doses of Ritalin appeared only three weeks after the drug was administered and persisted, suggesting irreversibility. In my personal communication with Grace Jackson on July 7, 2008, she informed me that studies on these cardiac alterations continue and, fortunately, further animal studies demonstrated that the changes producing lamellar bodies in the original study do reverse when the drug is removed.

A 1994 Brookhaven Laboratory[47] study replicated Nasrallah's research from 1986,[48] which led to Nasrallah's hypothesis that Ritalin caused shrinkage of brain tissue. Brookhaven scientists injected Ritalin into healthy volunteers who then experienced a 20 to 30 percent global reduction in cerebral blood flow. The investigators hypothesized the reduction of blood flow was caused by constricted blood vessels, related to Ritalin's impact on dopamine.[49] They warned that oral doses of Ritalin might produce similar, but even longer lasting, decrements. Jackson believes the neuroscientific evidence clearly demonstrates that Ritalin, like cocaine and other street drugs, impedes neurodevelopment and shrinks the brain.

Swanson's follow-up study[50] to the MTA experiment documented that methylphenidate stunts the growth of children. Jackson says we should consider the importance of concomitant stunting of craniofacial development. She points out that the human skull undergoes significant growth through age 7, along with important remodeling well into adolescence. Impairments in this process could have dire consequences for normal brain development.[51] Peter Breggin agrees. Stein[52] reiterates Breggin's concern that Ritalin interferes with normal growth during years when important developmental events in the brain are unfolding, such as neural pathways, and establishment of receptor sites on neurons. Beyond that, Breggin mentions other important events such as development of secondary sexual characteristics and overall body development, which has its own natural timetable. Breggin notes that the resumption of growth is assumed to follow cessation of Ritalin. (Swanson, cited above, documented that Ritalin stunted growth, that there was no evidence of "growth spurt," and that the long-term outcomes remain unknown pending further studies.[53]) Breggin ponders what will happen to children who continue the drug for years into adolescence, or beyond. That is the question Swanson hopes to answer in a few years when the MTA subjects attain maturity.

The FDA Is Advised to Require Black Box Warnings on Stimulants

The Drug Safety and Risk Management Drugs Advisory Committee's job is to keep abreast of reports regarding drugs and other products for which the FDA has regulatory responsibility, and to advise the FDA about any risks. Responding to continuing reports of adverse cardiac and psychiatric events associated with stimulant medications, it convened in February 2006 and recommended by an 8 to 7 vote to place Black Box warnings on labels of stimulants. Black Box warnings, outlined in a conspicuous black box at the top of the label, describe potential risks of the drug. They alert prescribers of the risks and require them to inform patients of these risks before prescribing. The Black Box is the most serious warning next to banning the drug altogether. The FDA responded with two days of hearings in March 2006.

Fred Baughman was among professionals recommending the Black Box warning to the committee. He quoted Karch's *Pathology of Drug Abuse* to sum up some of the strong evidence presented to the FDA:

> Amphetamine's adverse effects on the heart are well established . . . (sharing) common mechanisms with cocaine toxicity . . . cardiomyopathy seems to be a complication of amphetamine abuse more often than cocaine abuse . . . The clinical history in most of these cases is consistent with arrhythmic sudden death . . . Reports of amphetamine-related sudden death were first published shortly after amphetamine became commercially available (late 1930s, about the same time Bradley discovered the paradoxical calming effect of amphetamines that has led to today's Ritalin epidemic) . . . Stimulant-related cardiomyopathy has occurred in association with amphetamine, methamphetamine . . . and methylphenidate (Ritalin) . . . In all cases there was acute onset of heart failure associated with decreased cardiac output. . . .[54]

Despite testimony such as this and from other experts, including Breggin, Jackson, and reliable watchdog groups—long aware of the serious cardiologic and psychiatric risks posed by stimulants—the committees did not uphold the Black Box recommendation for warnings about suicidality or cardiovascular risks. It recommended that a Medication Guide describing the risks, benefits, and adverse effects of the stimulant medications be developed for parents. This change is reflected in 2008 package inserts. Each label contains a section with a heading "Medication Guide."

Stimulants made news again in May 2006, when the U.S. Centers for Disease Control and Prevention estimated that problems with stimulant drugs send nearly 3,100 children and adults to emergency rooms annually.[55] The report said two-thirds of cases—overdoses and accidental use—could be prevented if parents locked up the drugs. Other emergencies involve potential cardiac problems: chest pain, fast pulse, stroke, and high blood pressure. The report prompted doctors to write letters to the *New England Journal of Medicine*, once again calling for Black Box warnings on stimulants.

Cardiovascular Warnings and the American Heart Association

In April 2008, the American Heart Association (AHA) recommended that all children should have a thorough medical exam and be screened for potential heart problems before taking stimulant medication.[56] The AHA's Congenital Cardiac Defects Committee and Council on Cardiovascular Nursing compiled a lengthy report. They responded to the following concerns: an increasing number of children prescribed stimulants, including children with preexisting heart conditions; public concerns regarding the side effects and toxicity of psychotropic drugs; and regulatory factors and warnings issued by the FDA and the pharmaceutical industry. The report also mentions an editorial published in the *New England Journal of Medicine* in 2006, "ADHD and Cardiovascular Risk" by eminent cardiologist Steven E. Nissen. He recommended Black Box warnings. But psychiatrists who wrote rebuttals to the journal diminished Nissen's influence. It is troubling that a cardiologist of such import as Nissen, Chairman of the Department of Cardiovascular Medicine, immediate past president of the American College of Cardiology in Washington, D.C., and author of hundreds of articles related to his profession, was undercut by psychiatrists who *should instead* be heeding his professional advice! Even more troubling is that those psychiatrists seem to place the protection of their financial arrangements with pharmaceutical companies ahead of their responsibility for the medical care of their child patients.

The AHA report reviewed studies from 1980 through August 2007. It mentions the Risk Management Advisory Committee of the FDA that recommended Black Box warnings on stimulant medications. It reviews all reports of adverse cardiac events associated with stimulant medications, including the deaths of children. It explains that the available data do not provide sufficient information about preexisting heart conditions in the children who died, because of the uneven manner in which the adverse events are reported to the MedWatch database. The AHA investigators were looking for evidence that deaths occurred among children who had no history of cardiac problems. Purportedly, because of the insufficient information about that, the AHA did not recommend Black Box cardiac warnings. They instead issued detailed recommendations. I reiterate them here for caregivers who might be considering stimulant medication for children.

After a diagnosis of ADHD is established and before the administration of any medication the child should have a thorough evaluation with special attention to symptoms that can indicate a cardiac condition. All medications used, including over-the-counter products, should be listed. A complete family history should be obtained especially for conditions associated with sudden cardiac death. The detection of any such symptoms or history warrants an evaluation by a pediatric cardiologist before initiating treatment. This includes a thorough physical examination for hypertension, cardiac murmurs, physical findings associated with Marfan syndrome, and signs of irregular rhythms. Since some of these cannot be detected on a routine examination, an electrocardiogram (ECG) is recommended to detect hard-to-identify conditions. ECGs should be read by a pediatric cardiologist or a cardiologist or physician with expertise in reading pediatric ECGs. Once medication has been started, the child should have a repeat ECG after age 12 if the first was done prior to that age. The same is recommended if the family history should change. The association suggests a central registry of children, adolescents, and young adults who experience sudden cardiac death. Future studies to assess the true risk of sudden cardiac death associated with stimulant drugs would be facilitated by such a registry by collecting data in a more organized way on a large scale. While acknowledging the difficulty of randomized, double-blind, placebo-controlled studies, these are recommended. The association stresses the need for better research on this topic.

The authors of the AHA report were apparently influenced by the neurobiological perspective on ADHD. They supported the dangerous conclusions of the FDA Committee Hearings that also declined Black Box warnings despite the recommendations of the Drug Safety and Risk Management Drugs Advisory Committee. The AHA report stated, "ADHD is a serious illness with dire consequences if left untreated," and they never mention psychosocial treatments as an alternative that would altogether avoid the risk of iatrogenic (caused by the treatment) sudden cardiac death. And they fail to mention the studies discussed in this chapter that appear to demonstrate a causal relationship between stimulant drugs and abnormal changes in heart tissue.

A 2008 Update

The FDA 2008 stimulant medications labels are appearing on the drugs listed on the FDA Web site. I noted that the following statement is included: ". . . [The stimulant drug name] is indicated as an integral part of a total treatment program for ADHD that may include other measures (psychological, educational, social)." Even more notably, "[s]timulants are **not** intended for use in patients who exhibit symptoms **secondary to environmental factors** and/or other primary psychiatric disorders including psychosis" (Emphasis added). It goes on to assign critical importance to appropriate educational placement. Then, "[p]sychosocial intervention is often helpful. **When remedial measures alone are insufficient, the decision to prescribe drug treatment will depend upon the physician's assessment**. . . ." (Emphasis added). In other words, medication should be only part of the treatment, along with psychological, educational, and social interventions. **And** stimulants are not indicated when the disturbance can be attributed to something in the environment. Appropriate educational placement and **psychosocial intervention** are recommended, with stimulant medication more of a last resort.

This labeling reflects a conservative posture toward medication rarely seen in mainstream mental health care. If prescribers actually heeded these recommendations, thousands of children would be spared chemical abuse.

ANTIDEPRESSANT MEDICATIONS

History of Antidepressants

Again, Jackson is our historian. People used unregulated substances for depression in the 19th and early 20th centuries. Early on, these included cocaine, alcohol, and opiates. By the 1930s, amphetamines like Benzedrine and other stimulants were commonly used. Then in the 1940s and 1950s, sedatives became vogue: barbiturates, bromides, and paraldehyde. The treatments changed with the evolving views of what was considered depression. There was melancholia, neurosis, and a condition of weakness and fatigue known as neurasthenia.[57] In the 1950s depression was mainly treated with inpatient electro-convulsive therapy (ECT). Through a series of combining reserpine with other drugs, the class of antidepressants known as monoamine oxidase inhibitors (MAOIs) was developed. These were popular until it became apparent that they sometimes caused dangerously high blood pressure. At the same time, a Swiss psychiatrist developed imipramine (Tofranil), which gave rise to the class of antidepressants known as tricyclics (TCAs). These remained popular until concerns were raised about the lethality of overdoses, complex dosing, and worrisome side effects.[58]

The Selective Serotonin Reuptake Inhibitors (SSRIs) Arrive

The early 1980s saw the introduction of the SSRIs as we know them today. Jackson summarizes the views of researchers: "Far from being selective for the serotonin reuptake transporter, the SSRIs have been found to interact with a complex variety of receptor subtypes."[59] She explains that an antidepressant cannot be specific for one type of chemical (serotonin), as scientists have discovered the very complex interactions that exist among and between the neurotransmitter systems of the brain.

The experts' insight notwithstanding, SSRIs remain the most popular of the antidepressants. They include Prozac (fluoxetine), Paxil (paroxetine), Celexa (citalopram), Zoloft (sertraline), Lexapro (escitalopram), and Fluvoxamine (or Luvox). Symbyax (olanzapine/fluoxetine) is a combination SSRI and antipsychotic. The labels of all these medications were updated in January or March 2009. All have Black Box warnings regarding increased risk of suicidal thinking and behavior in children, adolescents, and young adults taking the drug for major depression and other psychiatric disorders. None except Prozac are approved for treating depression in children. Prozac is approved for major depression in youth ages 8 to 18 and for obsessive-compulsive disorder in patients ages 7 to 17. Luvox and Zoloft are approved for treatment of obsessive-compulsive disorder in children ages 8 to 17 and ages 6 to 17, respectively.

Other Classes of Antidepressants

Other classes of antidepressants have been described: Effexor (venlafaxine) and Cymbalta (duloxetine) are known as "serotonin noradrenaline reuptake inhibitors" (SNRIs). They carry the same Black Box warnings as the SSRIs and are not approved for pediatric use. Classified as "other" is Remeron (mirtazapine), which carries the same Black Box warning and is not approved for pediatric use. Wellbutrin (bupropion hydrochloride) is in a class of its own, an aminoketone. It carries the same Black Box warning and is not approved for children.

Prevalence of Use

Zito et al.[60] compiled statistics from three primary care sites in the United States. Data revealed antidepressant use among youth ages 2 to 19, between years 1988 and 1994. The authors noted that even without evidence of efficacy for children, increases were far greater for youths over those years than for adults. The average increase across the three sites was 3.6-fold. Despite the rapid rise in SSRI utilization, in 1994 more than half the antidepressants prescribed for children were tricyclics, to treat ADHD. The prevalence was mostly among 10- to 14-year-old boys and 15- to 19-year-old girls. Second to ADHD, the antidepressants were prescribed for depression.

In 1994, Express Scripts researchers published a prevalence of antidepressant use in children study covering years 1998 to 2002.[61] Approximately 2 million commercially insured pediatric beneficiaries 18 years old and younger were examined. Researchers revealed an increase from 1.6 per 100 to 2.4 per 100 prevalence, or an adjusted annual increase of 9.2 percent. The increase was greatest among preschoolers aged 0 to 5 years. Use among girls doubled and use increased 64 percent for boys. Now the SSRIs were the most commonly prescribed antidepressants, replacing the tricyclics.

After the risks associated with suicidality were publicized and the labeling of the SSRIs changed in 2004 to alert prescribers and consumers of the risks, Express Scripts researchers evaluated antidepressant prescription claims for 2003 and 2004. They found that antidepressant use continued to rise through 2004 for children and youth ages 10 to 19 years. But for children 9 and under, use declined in 2004, starting with the 0- to 4-year-olds. During the second quarter of 2004, researchers saw a moderation in increase for all ages.

I suspect this decline could be only partially explained by the new awareness of risk and new labeling regarding the need to monitor for suicidal thinking and behavior, especially with pediatric use. In my workplace I saw a dramatic escalation of antipsychotic drug prescriptions around 2002, along with the surge of juvenile bipolar diagnoses. As antipsychotics became the drugs of choice for bipolar, they seemed to supplant the widespread use of antidepressants. My hunch is documented in a study[62] published in 2006. Researchers examined data for outpatient prescriptions for antipsychotic drugs for years 1993 to 2002 among people ages 20 and younger. Their data revealed that antipsychotic drug treatment increased from approximately 201,000 in 1993 to 1,224,000 in 2002. Most were treated for disruptive behavior disorders and mood disorders. The study showed greater antipsychotic use among youth on Medicaid. This emerged as a major scandal, as we'll see in the section on antipsychotic drugs; there came a backlash against using taxpayer funds to pay for drugs that are not FDA approved (none of the antipsychotic drugs was approved for pediatric use at that time). The researchers also noted the trend toward using multiple drugs. They saw the increasing use of an antidepressant and mood stabilizer in combination with the antipsychotic. This became the norm for the treatment of the increasingly popular bipolar diagnosis in the early years of the century.

Safety Concerns

SSRIs are designed to overstimulate the serotonin nerves in the brain, causing the nerves to become less sensitive, a phenomenon known as "downregulation."[63] Breggin and Cohen explain this unnatural perturbation of the brain, and warn that it is unknown whether it can be reversed. In any event, the brain remains "unbalanced" for some time. This can have negative effects on mood and behavior. From their own practices, the authors document that patients can become very disturbed and violent when dosage is changed or when the drug is stopped. Prozac can cause akathisia, that tortuous restlessness that makes the person have to move constantly. People have been driven to violence to self or others due to this unrelenting discomfort. Baum Hedlund investigators learned that 20 years ago German regulators refused to approve Prozac without stronger suicide warning.[64]

Breggin[65] writes extensively on the dangerous side effects of the antidepressants, including all the SSRIs, and Luvox, Effexor, Wellbutrin, and Remeron. In a 2004 report to the FDA, he said the FDA warns of anxiety, agitation, panic attacks, insomnia, irritability, hostility, impulsivity, akathisia, and mania, but fails to emphasize their significance as precursors to violence. Breggin likens the behaviors induced by these effects to those produced by PCP, methamphetamine, and cocaine, drugs associated with violence. He documents out-of-control reactions to these stimulant effects of the new generation of antidepressants.[66] His examples demonstrate the more frequent and severe adverse behavioral effects of drugs on children and youth compared to adults. A 16-year-old became manic with angry outbursts after three weeks on paroxetine (Paxil). A 17-year-old mildly mentally retarded boy started on fluvoxamine (Luvox) for depression and anxiety. After a single dose, he developed increasing agitation and insomnia, followed in the next 24 hours by severe psychotic symptoms requiring hospitalization. In all the cases portrayed in the article, symptoms receded when the SSRIs were discontinued.

Of seven empirical studies, I mention three cited by Breggin that proved SSRIs caused aberrant behavior. First,[67] three controlled clinical trials for paroxetine (Paxil) submitted for FDA approval for children under 18 yielded three times more self-harm and suicidal behavior among the medicated group than among the placebo group. Because of this, in 2003 the British Committee on Medicines prohibited the use of paroxetine in children and the FDA issued a warning. Second, like previous authors, Breggin cites the Emslie[68] controlled trial of fluoxetine (Prozac) in depressed pediatric patients. The drug caused mania in 6 percent of the children ages 7 to 17, severe enough that these youngsters had to be removed from the study. None of the placebo group developed mania. In the third study,[69] 6 of 42 youngsters being treated with fluoxetine (Prozac) became aggressive and violent. The researchers hypothesized a drug-induced stimulation (a specific serotonergic-mediated effect) caused the behavior. This report is significant as it provides insight into the development of obsessive violence and a school-shooter mentality. A 12-year-old boy taking Prozac developed nightmares about shooting classmates and getting shot himself. He had been having increasingly "bad dreams" about such events that included shooting himself and his parents dying. The boy became agitated and anxious and refused to go to school. He reported marked suicidal ideation that made him feel unsafe. Since this was a controlled clinical trial in progress, the investigators did not know the boy was on Prozac. He was hospitalized briefly, discharged, and then readmitted for 17 days. Prozac was discontinued. Three weeks after discharge, his physician (not one of the investigators) put him back on Prozac and he became acutely suicidal until the Prozac was stopped again. This experiment preceded any of the school shootings, so this was not copycat behavior. Stressing the scientific rigor of this study, Breggin underscores its important implications regarding drug-induced violence among youth.

Jackson[70] warns that serotonin, the neurotransmitter whose reuptake is inhibited with the SSRIs, stimulates the production of prolactin in the pituitary gland. This results in a condition known as "hyperprolactinemia." Its consequences include decreased sexual appetite, lactation (breast milk production), breast enlargement in males, and other hormonal pathologies.

Withdrawal

Doctors and patients have documented severe withdrawal reactions when antidepressants, especially Paxil and Effexor, are discontinued.[71] Gina O'Brien told a reporter she tapered off Paxil, per her doctor's orders, only to be overwhelmed by nausea and uncontrollable crying. She had to go back on the drug and a year later was still on it. She fears she will never be able to stop it. Psychiatrist Richard Shelton of Vanderbilt University School of Medicine said he now rarely prescribes Paxil or Wellbutrin. He explained his patients coming off these drugs have experienced flu-like nausea, muscle aches, uncontrollable crying, dizziness, diarrhea, and "brain zaps." The latter are bizarre, brief, but overwhelming electrical sensations that come from the back of the head. A well-known anonymous entertainer said he has taken a small dose of Wellbutrin for eight years rather than suffer through the withdrawal experience. Critics of the drug companies say the companies downplay the severity of withdrawal, calling it euphemistically "antidepressant discontinuation syndrome," and failing to place adequate precautions on their labeling.

Efficacy: Do They Work?

Researchers conducted a study (meta-analysis) of 47 clinical trials, published and unpublished, of six of the best known antidepressant drugs. The studies were submitted to the FDA in application for approval to market the drugs. Included were the studies of Prozac, Paxil, and Effexor. The results showed the drugs to be effective in only a very small group of the most extremely depressed people. A British newspaper[72] reported that in response to this study, health secretary Alan Johnson announced that 3,600 therapists were to be trained in the next three years in "talk therapy" for depression. He said the training program signaled a decisive shift away from drugs and toward non-drug treatments. Mentioned were exercise, friends, cognitive-behavioral therapy, interpersonal therapy, and counseling, with antidepressants the choice of last resort.

Jackson[73] explains the placebo effect, which has proven to be very nearly as effective as the antidepressants. Placebos are inert substances used in clinical trials in place of the real drug. Subjects don't know whether they are getting a placebo or the drug. The effectiveness of the drug is proved only if the subjects experience a significantly greater benefit from the drug than from the placebo. In the meta-analysis study mentioned above, the difference in benefit between the placebo and the drugs was not significant. Jackson explains that patient expectations of improvement have physiological effects that indeed are salutary. These physiological effects have been detected with imaging technologies, like the famous research cited in chapter 2,[74] in which imaging technology showed the same resolution of abnormalities in the brains of subjects treated with drugs and subjects treated with therapy alone for obsessive-compulsive disorder.

Discrepancies in Drug Trial Reports Lead to Hearings of 2004

According to Jonathan Leo,[75] the first studies on children emerged in the late 1990s. Discrepancies were noted between the studies published in academic journals and those submitted to the FDA for approval. It takes only two "successful" studies to get approval from the FDA, no matter how many studies were unfavorable to the drug in question. The published studies exaggerated the benefits of the drugs and minimized the risks. Eventually the unpublished version submitted to the FDA becomes public; this version contains much more information than the published academic studies. Because of the negative information in the version provided to the FDA, only Prozac was approved for children, out of seven drugs for which approval was sought (Prozac, Paxil, Zoloft, Celexa, Remeron, Effexor, Serzone). Serzone has been discontinued. Zoloft was approved only for obsessive-compulsive disorder. When academics demonstrated the discrepancies between the FDA versions and the published versions of about 12 studies over a span of 10 years, the FDA was forced to reconsider its directives. Two days of hearings were convened in February, and again in September, 2004 in order for the FDA Advisory Committee to hear from witnesses and experts about the issue. In October 2004 the FDA reached its decision to require Black Box warnings of the risk of suicidal thoughts and behavior boldly printed at the top of product labels, not only for the nine antidepressants examined during the hearings, but for all classes of antidepressants. Yet more reports keep coming to light regarding discrepancies between published and unpublished research submitted to the FDA. The malfeasance apparently continues.

2004 Hearings Were the Tip of the Iceberg: Shocking Revelations of Antidepressant-induced Suicides

Discrepancies between published and unpublished studies became news in 2008.[76] Lisa Bero and colleagues at the University of California evaluated 164 efficacy trials submitted to the FDA for 33 medicines approved in 2001 and 2002. They found in most cases, the journal-reported findings were more favorable to the study drug because unfavorable data were omitted and never published—large amounts, since the FDA requires only two "successful" studies. As Leo's paper reveals, these discrepancies have been noted before. In fact, the following report alleges that the danger of SSRIs was known long ago and kept undercover.

The Citizens Commission on Human Rights (CCHR),[77] an international psychiatric watchdog group, reported that documents obtained through the Freedom of Information Act in 1989 revealed that over 500 deaths had been linked to Prozac and that 83 children between the ages of 4 and 18 had attempted suicide. Two children aged 5 completed suicides, and 77 experienced hostility, agitation, and intentional injury. CCHR and medical experts presented this information to the FDA's psychopharmacological drugs advisory committee in 1991. According to this report, nine psychiatrists and a psychologist who comprised the panel ignored family members' testimonies about the violent and suicidal effects of Prozac. The CCHR president had strong words following the 2004 FDA hearings that finally required Black Box warnings: "The FDA may be accountable for failing to warn the public, but psychiatrists were their advisors with a vested interest in maintaining a multibillion-dollar child drugging industry. Now, in the wake of international controversy over the antidepressant drugs' great risk to children's lives, psychiatrists claim they were unaware of the potential harm to children. This is a lie and they should be held accountable."

In 2004, Vera Sharav[78] posted an analysis of prescription sales data and suicidality for the SSRIs for years 1988 to 2002. She reported, "The results show that the number of people taking an SSRI, and the number of suicides by those taking an SSRI are staggering." Sharav cited the research of Arif Khan and colleagues on the unpublished clinical trial data submitted to the FDA for application to license all the antidepressants (SSRIs) from 1985 to 2002. At a meeting of the New Clinical Drug Evaluation Unit of the National Institutes of Health in

August 2002, where Kahn reported his findings, he stated, "In the case of trials for depression and anxiety disorders, suicide rates were in fact higher among those who received the investigational drugs than the placebo . . . We have to ask if medication is the only way to approach the prevention of suicide." They discovered the suicide rate in SSRI antidepressant trials to be 718 per 100,000 (718 patients out of 100,000 patients per year). Compare this to the national average of 11 out of 100,000. Khan noted that it is especially surprising, since in most clinical trials, attempts are made to screen out any actively suicidal subjects.

A colleague of Kahn's, Graham Alfred, followed up the Kahn study. Alfred developed a computer program with which he could calculate antidepressant drug-induced suicides from 1988, when the SSRIs hit the market, to 2002. First he calculated the number of people on each drug by tracking prescription sales. Then he calculated the number who committed suicide while on each drug. He used conservative rates, not the 718 per 100,000 of Kahn's study. Instead, he based his calculations on rates of 34 per 100,000 to 104 per 100,000. When calculated at a suicide rate of 34 per 100,000, his results showed the number of SSRI users who committed suicide totaled 21,900. At a suicide rate of 104 per 100,000, the number of SSRI users who committed suicide rose to 70,297. It may be estimated, then, that 28,119 suicides could have been caused by Prozac; 19,271 by Zoloft; and 22,907 by Paxil.

Kahn et al. also studied the same trial data for the atypical antipsychotic medications. Carl Sherman[79] reported on the results: The trial data on the antipsychotic drugs showed the suicide rate for patients on placebo had higher suicide rates than those on the study drugs. "But," Kahn cautioned, "because participants were exposed to placebo for far less time than to the drugs, 33 versus 148 days respectively, this could not be assumed to indicate an anti-suicidal effect of medication." Sherman quoted psychologist Ann Blake Tracy: "The most likely reason researchers saw an even higher rate of suicide in placebo with the antipsychotics is that these patients were likely being abruptly discontinued from their older anti-psychotics for the clinical trials. This abrupt withdrawal can cause suicidal depression."

In the debate regarding Black Box warnings, the SSRI data presented to the FDA Advisory Committee in 2004 were these: Out of 4,400 children participating in several studies, those taking antidepressants experienced twice the number (3 to 4 percent) of suicidal symptoms as those on placebo (1 to 2 percent). None of the subjects completed suicide. Our child and adolescent psychiatrist discussed the Black Box warnings with staff. When he stated, "No one died," it sounded like he was saying no one has ever died from SSRIs. Considering the data I just outlined above, such minimization is breathtaking.

One Tragedy

The committee heard from parents of children who did die, and the evidence is compelling that the tragedies were caused by the drugs.

Candace's mother, Mathy, spoke at the International Center for the Study of Psychiatry and Psychology Annual Conference in 2006. She detailed the tragic death of her daughter, who initially expressed symptoms of mild anxiety. She had no history of depression and had always been a happy youngster. Her doctor put her on a low dose of Zoloft. When she was very excited about starting seventh grade, her doctor doubled the dose to help her cope with the transition. In January 2004, she accidentally took two tablets instead of one and was advised to go to the emergency room. There she was injected with sedatives, which caused her to become so seriously psychotic that she was placed in pediatric intensive care. The parents learned that sedatives mixed with antidepressants are apt to cause a reaction like Candace's. Home again, Candace and all her friends were thrilled she was back in school. Even when her teacher allowed her to take a test she had missed, she scored well and was fine. She felt no anxiety or other adverse symptoms at that time. Still too weak to play basketball, she cheered her team on to win. Later at home, her mother reported she was curled up in her father's arms watching *Animal Planet*. When left alone briefly, she called a friend and was reported to be laughing. Yet later that day she was found to have hanged herself and could not be revived. The parents reported that at no time did any doctor mention the risk of suicidality, psychosis, or other serious side effect associated with the drugs Candace was prescribed. Candace's sister still struggles with the loss and the adjustment of being an only child. Candace's story and those of five other children are told in a documentary film, *Prescription: Suicide?* by Robert Manciero. All suffered life-threatening consequences of antidepressant use and some, like Candace, tragically ended their lives.

The recurrent argument by drug enthusiasts is that suicidality is not caused by the SSRI, but by the depression itself. But Candace was not being treated for depression: She was being treated for mild anxiety. Child psychiatrist Michael Brody[80] cites case studies by Riddly King and associates at the Yale Child Study Center. The Yale authors reported that children treated with SSRIs for obsessive-compulsive-disorder who were not depressed became actively suicidal on the antidepressants.

Brody echoes the query of so many: Without evidence of efficacy and with the documented dangerous side effects, why are antidepressants so widely distributed to children? He finds the answer in David Healy's book, *Let Them Eat Prozac*, where Healy, referring to a 1997 Emslie study, concludes that distressed children show extremely high placebo response rates. (Healy apparently cited the same Emslie study[81] as Breggin, above, but to demonstrate a different phenomenon.) The researchers excluded from the study children who showed placebo responses to Prozac in order to control for that effect. The Prozac group did better, but not dramatically so, than the placebo group (consisting of non-placebo responders). Healy, who is also the former secretary of the British Association for Psychopharmacology, concluded, "The finding does not legitimize widespread prescribing in this age group. Indeed, this trial demonstrated that many children—perhaps a majority—did no better on Prozac than they would have done simply seeing a sympathetic clinician."[82]

Conflicts of Interest among Academics

The above information evokes a disturbing question. Since the FDA gave the stamp of approval to the makers of antidepressants when that agency *had the unpublished data* at their perusal, is there collusion between the pharmaceutical industry and the FDA? Jonathan Leo[83] takes the query further, questioning the role of academics in the FDA's approval of antidepressants. Leo's article is rife with disturbing associations. Two studies submitted to the FDA as part of Eli Lilly's successful bid for approval of Prozac for children again call forth Professor Emslie! And his first study—the same one cited twice earlier, "A Double-blind, Randomized, Placebo-controlled Trial of Fluoxetine in Children and Adolescents with Depression"—appeared in the *Archives of General Psychiatry* in 1997. It was funded by the National Institute of Mental Health (NIMH). This published study reported minimal side effects, findings considered insufficient to discontinue use of the drug. There was no mention of two children attempting suicide. But in the FDA's "Medical Review of Prozac," written in 2001 but not made public until 2003, there was a discussion of the two children out of 48 on Prozac who attempted suicide. Between 1997 and 2003, doctors lacked this important information, and even after 2003 would not have it unless they consulted the FDA Web site. Leo probes: The NIMH has not explained the discrepancy between its published version of the first study in 1997 and the unpublished version submitted to the FDA. He also questions NIMH-funded research being used as part of Eli Lilly's submission to obtain approval for Prozac. Leo has a lot of questions about monetary transactions that may have occurred among these associations, but regardless, by the time a second Prozac study was published in 2002,[84] Emslie and his coauthors were either Lilly employees or consultants. Leo explains the conflict of interest when an investigator like Emslie simultaneously receives funds from a nonprofit organization like the NIMH and a for-profit pharmaceutical company. Leo also wonders how Eli Lilly, maker of Prozac, had access to a NIMH study not yet in the public realm, and how that unpublished information became part of the package submitted to the FDA for licensure. He wonders if Lilly paid the researchers or NIMH for this information.

My query is, if this study provoked two attempted suicides, as Leo points out; stimulated mania in 6 percent of the children ages 7 to 17, severe enough that these youngsters had to be removed from the study, as Breggin points out; and demonstrated very little benefit from Prozac, as Healy points out; then why was Prozac approved for children?

Litigation for Victims of Paxil-induced Suicide or Injury

The Baum Hedlund Corporation of attorneys announced on March 23, 2006, that it was representing plaintiffs, the mother of an 11-year-old Kansas boy who committed suicide while on Paxil and a teen from Texas who attempted suicide while taking Paxil. The national class action suit theoretically represents all individuals under the age of 18 in the United States who attempted suicide or the families of individuals who killed themselves as a result of an adverse reaction to Paxil. The complaint charges the maker of Paxil, GlaxoSmithKline (GSK), with fraud, negligence, strict liability, and breach of warranty. Trevor Blain had "separation anxiety" in October 2000, for which he was prescribed Paxil. He developed insomnia and had angry outbursts, but his family did not connect the behaviors with the drug and he kept taking it. In November 2000 he hanged himself with his dog's leash in the family laundry room. He was comatose for several weeks and died on December 7, 2000. Tonya Brooks, a shy 17-year-old, was diagnosed with "social anxiety disorder." She was prescribed Paxil in 2004. She too developed insomnia as well as agitated and aggressive behavior. She attempted suicide by overdosing on Paxil and a sleep medication, Ambien. She survived but two days later gouged a huge hole in her leg with a pair of scissors. She was hospitalized for several days. Tonya's mother describes the horror of the event in the film *Prescription: Suicide?* Baum Hedlund partner Karen Barth Menzies stated:

> Through our Paxil litigation, we've obtained documents that show a seriously troubling mentality of profit over safety and a callous disregard for the welfare of children. That's about as reprehensible as you can get. Governmental regulators around the world have now analyzed the actual data from the clinical trials, not GSK's version of it, and have found an increased risk of suicidality. Yet the drug companies and their hired mouthpieces in the medical academic community, including the pediatric arm of the APA [American Psychiatric Association], continue to downplay the Black Box warnings as an "over-reaction" by FDA. They continue to try to hide this risk from parents for the sake of profits. We wanted to make sure the rights of all of these kids are protected by filing this lawsuit.[85]

Since 1990, Baum Hedlund has represented more than 100 individuals across the country in suicide and suicide attempt cases involving SSRI antidepressants, including Paxil, Zoloft, and Prozac. On October 2, 2008, a federal judge in Pennsylvania ruled that a lawsuit filed by the parents of a 16-year-old New Jersey boy who committed suicide while taking Paxil can proceed to a jury trial. Baum Hedlund expects other cases to be approved to go to trial in 2009.

In still another matter, on October 1, 2008, a federal judge approved a final $40 million settlement in the second phase of Baum Hedlund's national pediatric class action against GlaxoSmithKline. Class members are all insurance companies who can prove they paid for Paxil prescriptions for persons under the age of 18 between January 1, 1998, and December 31, 2004 (when the suicide warnings were put in Black Box labeling for SSRIs). They are to be reimbursed up to 40 percent of their actual cost for prescriptions, providing a diagnosis of major depression was given. The rationale was that Paxil prescriptions were written "off label"—Paxil is not approved for pediatric use. And there were no conspicuous suicide warnings on the labeling of the SSRIs.[86]

This concludes the topic of antidepressant medications. We now move on to the antipsychotic drugs.

ANTIPSYCHOTIC MEDICATIONS

Ella

Sue, the adolescent psychiatric ward social worker, was speaking to me on the phone about my 11-year-old client, Ella, recently admitted. Sue's voice vibrated at a fast clip with a nuance of collegial elitism. She demonstrated her polished grasp of Ella's bipolar diagnosis by explaining the behaviors Ella exhibited that defined the disorder. She assured me that Ella was being treated with the standard fare for her diagnosis, the antipsychotic Risperdal (Ella was acting a little crazy), the anticonvulsant Depakote (used as a mood stabilizer), and the antihypertensive clonidine to keep her calm. I wondered if Sue knew that none of these medications was approved for pediatric use.[87] She went on to report that Ella's mother had strong objections to medication, but the staff had responded that the only alternative was long-term admission to a state hospital. My criticism of this kind of coercion quelled Sue's exuberance. I suspected this was a common tactic, since most psychiatric wards accommodate only short-term stays during which the patient is simply "stabilized," usually meaning sedated to a point of indifference.

Prevalence of Use

The most recent data I found were in a 2008 *New York Times* story,[88] which quoted a member of a panel of drug experts: "Powerful antipsychotic drugs are being used far too cavalierly in children, and federal drug regulators must do more to warn doctors of their substantial risks." It was reported that more than 389,000 children and teens were treated in 2007 with Risperdal (risperidone), one of the five so-called atypical antipsychotics. The panel's data showed that of those, 240,000 were 12 or under. When the makers of Risperdal and Zyprexa (olanzapine), Johnson & Johnson and Eli Lilly, respectively, sought the panel's endorsement as FDA routine monitoring of the safety of the medications, their proposal was unanimously rejected. Panel members said far more must be done to discourage these medicines' growing use in children, especially to treat conditions for which the drugs are not approved. Their concerns extended to the other antipsychotic medications being prescribed to children: Seroquel (quetiapine), Abilify (aripiprazole), and Geodon (ziprasidone). **Data show that prescription rates for antipsychotic drugs used on children increased more than fivefold in the past decade and a half** (since 1993) and that doctors use these drugs to manage a wide range of behavior problems, even though children are especially susceptible to their side effects. In 2007, Risperdal prescriptions to patients 17 and younger increased 10 percent, while prescriptions for adults declined 5 percent. The article reported that from 1993 through the first three months of 2008, 1,207 children given Risperdal suffered serious problems, including 31 who died. At least 11 of the deaths were children whose treatment with Risperdal was unapproved by the FDA.

The dramatic increase in pediatric antipsychotic prescriptions is documented in another study.[89] Reporting on trends between 1993 and 2002, this research revealed that in 2002 antipsychotics were prescribed to 1,438 children per 100,000, up from 275 per 100,000 between 1993 and 1995. More youngsters covered by Medicaid received antipsychotic prescriptions than those on commercial insurance plans. The study included only doctors' office visits, not community mental health centers and outpatient clinics, where most visits are covered by Medicaid. Most likely, the data drastically underestimate actual antipsychotic use among children and youth under age 21 at that time. Patients taking antipsychotics were evenly divided diagnostically between behavioral problems, those with psychotic symptoms or developmental disabilities, and mood disorders, which would include bipolar. More than 40 percent of these were on more than one antipsychotic drug, and 90 percent were prescribed the newer atypicals rather than the older traditional brands.

In still another prevalence study, Salynn Boyles[90] reported in 2006 that children continued to represent the fastest growing group of antipsychotic drug users. Between 2001 and 2005, pediatric (up to age 19) prescriptions for these drugs increased by 80 percent, compared to an increase of 40 percent for adults. By 2005, close to 97 percent of all antipsychotic prescriptions in the United States were for the atypicals. These data came from Medco Health Solutions, Inc. Studies at Vanderbilt Medical Center suggest prescriptions targeted children diagnosed as ADHD. But Medco official Lon Castle refutes the studies, claiming the increase is due to a growing conviction that children suffer from psychotic illnesses and other psychiatric conditions, referring to schizophrenia and bipolar. Pediatrician William Cooper of Vanderbilt Medical Center told Boyles, "We are seeing a huge increase in the use of these medications among children, and we are not sure if they work or if they are safe. These drugs have not been tested for many of the indications they are being used for."

The Atypicals

What is meant by "atypical" antipsychotics? Sometimes called "second generation" antipsychotics, their use commenced in the 1990s with great fanfare, as they were marketed to be safer than "first generation" or typical antipsychotics. Notably, their introduction followed the expired patents on the latter, which meant that the "first generation" antipsychotics became available as generics, greatly diminishing the profits of the brand name drug makers. In March 2009, I perused the following at the Web site: Clozaril (clozapine), Zyprexa (olanzapine), Risperdal (risperidone), Seroquel (quetiapine), Geodon (ziprasidone), Abilify (aripiprazole), and Invega (paliperidone). Only Risperdal and Abilify appear to be approved for pediatric use. Some of the latest labeling is not available. In October 2006, Risperdal was approved to treat irritability, aggression, self-injury, temper tantrums, and changing moods in children ages 5 to 16 diagnosed with autism. In June 2007, it was approved for adolescents diagnosed with schizophrenia ages 13 to 17, but clinical studies did not go beyond 8 weeks. It was also approved for short-term treatment of bipolar in children aged 10 to 17, with the caveat "there is no body of evidence available from controlled studies to guide clinicians in longer-term management beyond 3 weeks." Abilify is approved for adolescents ages 13 to 17 for schizophrenia, and children and youth ages 10 to 17 for bipolar, again with the caveat that no bodies of evidence or efficacy are available to guide clinicians in long-term or maintenance therapy with this age group. All antipsychotic drugs bear Black Box warnings that the drugs pose the risk of increased mortality among elderly patients with dementia. Clozaril's Black Box warns of side effects so deadly that the drug is only approved for the most serious of conditions that have failed to respond to other treatment. Black Box warnings on Seroquel and Abilify add "[i]ncreased risk of suicidal thinking and behavior in children, adolescents and young adults taking antidepressants for major depressive disorder and other psychiatric disorders." The Seroquel Black Box previously warned, "Not approved for pediatric use," but the May 13, 2008, revised label omits this warning in the Black Box. It only states inconspicuously, and well below the Black Box, "[s]afety and effectiveness have not been established for pediatric use."

Typical Antipsychotics

The first generation antipsychotics prevailed from the 1960s through the 1980s, and were referred to as "major tranquilizers." Both the old and the new are also called "neuroleptics." Common ones included Thorazine (chlorpromazine), Haldol (haloperidol), Prolixin (fluphenazine), Mellaril (thioridazine), Trilafon (perphenazine), and Navane (thiothixene). Thorazine came first and was heralded as "lobotomy in a pill" because of its sedating effects that were deemed helpful back when psychotic patients were institutionalized. Other forms of typical antipsychotics followed, but unpleasant and dangerous side effects of these drugs became apparent. A movement disorder known as tardive dyskinesia (TD) was common and permanently debilitating. People suffered involuntary jerky, spasmodic, and often painful motions that affected various parts of the body. Science writer Robert Whitaker[91] explains how the drugs dampened down the dopamine system of the brain, producing an immediate pathology (consistent with Breggin's brain-disabling theory). Since dopamine systems are also involved in intellectual and behavioral functions, these people also suffered impairment in learning, memory, speech, and a host of other cognitive tasks. Whitaker reports that 5 percent of people on the older neuroleptics developed TD during their first year on the drug, 10 percent during their second year, and an additional 5 percent with each succeeding year.

Are Atypicals Safer?

The main newspaper for Eugene, Oregon, published a guest column by longtime mental health worker Chuck Areford that seriously challenged the claims of safety made by the makers of the atypical antipsychotics. Areford is on the Advisory Committee for MindFreedom International. He states that the life expectancy of patients treated in community mental health centers has decreased at an appalling rate—possibly by as much as 15 years since 1986. He attributes the untimely deaths mainly to cardiovascular disease caused by the antipsychotic drugs. He acknowledges the high rates of cigarette smoking, poor nutrition, homelessness, and poor access to health care among people treated in mental health centers, and says giving them atypical antipsychotic drugs "pours gasoline on fire."[92] Areford does not cite a source for his information, but does mention "deplorable conditions at the Oregon State Hospital." When the following well-documented information about the atypicals is taken into account, Areford's life expectancy figures are believable.

When the atypical antipsychotics appeared in the 1990s, they were marketed as "safe" when compared to the typicals. Breggin and Cohen[93] assert that such claims are untrue. Their account of the very serious side effects of neuroleptics makes no distinction between the old and the new antipsychotics. Tardive dyskinesia, described above, is one. Another, neuroleptic malignant syndrome (NMS), is a potentially fatal condition similar to viral brain inflammation associated with encephalitis. Reports confirm that irreversible psychosis and/or dementia can result during withdrawal from antipsychotics. As with other classes of psychiatric drugs, withdrawal symptoms are often mistaken for relapse, even in cases of transient adverse effects. Consequently, most people diagnosed with schizophrenia become drug dependent for life. Other harmful effects of neuroleptics include sudden death, especially among long-term hospitalized patients, which may be caused by convulsions, impaired swallow reflex, or heart arrhythmias. The drugs desensitize the body to signals of illness, so people may not respond to serious symptoms in a timely manner. All the antipsychotics cause parkinsonian syndrome, characterized by flattened emotions, stiff facial features, tremors, and a stooped, shuffling gait. The syndrome includes a slowing of emotions and movements. These adverse reactions that impair thinking and moving are sometimes called "extrapyramidal" side effects. Jackson[94] explains that extrapyramidal symptoms are caused by basal ganglia dysfunction. Basal ganglia are interconnected gray masses deep in the cerebral hemispheres and in the upper brain stem that are involved in motor coordination. Jackson agrees with Breggin and Cohen that these side effects have not been eradicated in the newer antipsychotics. Investigators have reported these side effects in as many as 20 to 50 percent of the patients exposed to atypical antipsychotics. All three authors agree that all the antipsychotics can cause that tortuous inner anxiousness, akathisia, a condition that can become irreversible.

Extrapyramidal side effects explain why a number of consumers at our local mental health clinic have shuffling walks and vacant expressions. Most observers mistakenly attribute their peculiarities to a primary mental illness, instead of to the drugs ingested.

I treated middle-aged Lena, who was prescribed Haldol for years when she was diagnosed in her twenties with schizophrenia. Lena was a highly intelligent, gifted person who told me about her myriad accomplishments as a teen. She was still a fine artist. But she had debilitating TD and cognitive disintegration that made intelligible speech difficult, even though abstract concepts still interested her. Comprehending her speech required a kind of "reading between the lines." I was struck by the enormity of Lena's loss: a direct consequence of previous long-term Haldol use.

Other serious side effects are acute, painful, often irreversible spasms called dystonias. This segues to the next account about Anya Bailey.

Side Effects on Children

The *New York Times*[95] ran a story about Anya Bailey, who developed an eating disorder at age 12. George M. Realmuto, a psychiatrist at the University of Minnesota, prescribed Risperdal, noted for its side effect of weight gain. For two years she gained weight, but developed a painful, persistent, crippling dystonia in her back, necessitating regular injections of Botox to unclench her back muscles. We revisit Anya's psychiatrist later in the chapter.

Researchers[96] from the Johns Hopkins Children's Center warned that the atypical antipsychotics might trigger insulin resistance, a condition that increases the risk of developing type 2 diabetes, heart disease, and stroke later in life. The study's lead investigator, Mark Riddle, said the study included children who gained significant amounts of weight while taking Zyprexa, Seroquel, or Risperdal. All children who were on moderate or high doses of the drugs and 3 out of 5 on low doses exhibited hypertension, high levels of triglycerides, low levels of "good" cholesterol, and increased levels of protein in the urine. These are symptoms of insulin resistance, and were reported to be greater than would be expected by weight gain alone. Insulin resistance means muscle, fat, and liver cells do not properly use insulin. Eventually the pancreas fails to keep up with the body's demand for insulin and excess glucose builds up in the bloodstream, causing diabetes. In light of these findings, Riddle suggested that monitoring of metabolic side effects might become standard practice among clinicians prescribing atypical antipsychotic medications to children.

USA Today[97] reported that research on the safety of antipsychotic drugs is lacking, and that deaths and dangerous side effects are mounting all the time. The most common is weight gain. The article named 13-year-old Alexa, who gained 100 pounds in a year, putting her at risk of a host of other health problems. Rex's parents believe their 13-year-old son was permanently harmed by an atypical antipsychotic drug. He has tardive dyskinesia and suffers daily episodes of involuntary jerking movements and grimacing. Stephen, now 15 years of age, was diagnosed as bipolar at the age of 6 and placed on antipsychotic medications. He developed liver abnormalities and obesity. Since then, his mother told the reporter, he has been on a variety of drug cocktails, and none has worked for long. Now she thinks he never had bipolar, and he is being weaned off all medications. She is worried about the effects of all the drugs that might manifest later.

The article revealed there were at least 45 unexplained child deaths between 2000 and 2004 in which the FDA listed an atypical antipsychotic drug as the "primary suspect." Other side effects common among young people under age 18 were listed. Dystonia, the malady Anya Bailey suffers with, was reported 103 times. Tremors, sedation, and tardive dyskinesia were mentioned. Forty-one cases of neuroleptic malignant syndrome were reported over five years. A child psychiatrist from Brown University School of Medicine was quoted as saying this was the most troubling side effect, as it is life threatening and can kill within 24 hours of onset.

Ben Hansen[98] reported some disturbing statistics from Michigan. His data cover the 10 months of January through October, 2006. They showed a 100 percent increase in children under age 18 on three or more mood stabilizers; a 100 percent increase in children ages 6 to 17 on four or more psychiatric drugs; a 45 percent increase in children under age 18 on two or more antipsychotics; and a 45 percent increase in children under 18 on a benzodiazepine for at least 60 days. Perhaps most alarming, the data show the second most frequently prescribed class of psychiatric drugs to children under age 5 were antidyskinetics (also called antiparkinsonians). These are for relief of movement disorders such as dystonia, dyskinesia, tics, and tremors. Hansen warns we could be facing a monumental health disaster if young children are suffering drug-induced movement disorders at such an astonishing rate.

NIMH-directed researchers compared two of the atypical antipsychotics to an older generation antipsychotic.[99] They found no differences in outcomes, but for youngsters, there was a big difference in side effects. Children and teens who took Zyprexa and Risperdal gained about 13 pounds and 8 pounds, respectively, during the two-month study. Those who took Zyprexa also experienced increases in total cholesterol, including "bad" cholesterol, and increases in liver enzymes. The researchers noted that these metabolic side effects, in addition to the weight gain, "generate considerable long-term risks for diabetes and cardio-vascular disease." Young patients on the older antipsychotic experienced no weight gain, but did have more akathisia (driving restlessness making a person need to constantly move). Participants in the study numbered 116 children and teens ages 8 to 19, diagnosed with early onset schizophrenia. There was no sta-tistically significant difference in outcomes. However, at best, only half of the patients responded to either type of medication. Medco officials Lon Castle and Robert Epstein agreed that very real concerns exist regarding the safety of the atypical drugs. The latter stated in a news release, "There is evidence that the risk of diabetes and metabolic disorders from using atypical antipsychotics could be much more severe for pediatric patients than adults, and there is a need for more studies to understand the long-term effects of these drugs on children." NIMH director Thomas Insel responded to the study, "We really need a new era of drug development for psychotic illness, both in children and adults. These studies remind us that we are not where we want to be in the treatment of psychosis. There are just too many people who aren't getting better."

I believe we have the solution in chapter 7. Loren Mosher, former chief of schizophrenia studies at NIMH, treated patients in a small setting with as little medication as possible, and they got better!

Prolactin Imbalances

Jackson[100] explains why some of my child clients experienced lactation (milk leaking from breasts) while on Risperdal and why some boys on the drug developed enlarged breasts. Antipsychotic drugs have the capacity to produce prolactin imbalances by blocking D2 receptors on cells of the anterior pituitary gland. These are associated with rapid hormonal shifts at the time of each dose of medication. She notes that children and adolescents are at particularly high risk for these effects. Jackson stresses the hazards of these fluctuations. She quotes researchers in obstetrics and gynecology who acknowledge that even intermittent, subthreshold (normal but elevated) changes in prolactin can be sufficient to cause infertility.

"Mood Stabilizers" Used in Combination with Atypical Antipsychotics

Bipolar is the diagnosis for which antipsychotic medications are most commonly used on children. But a "mood stabilizer" (and sometimes other drugs) is almost always prescribed concomitantly. Depakote (valproate or divalproex sodium) is a standard "mood stabilizer" for pediatric use, despite its lack of FDA approval for this age group. The label states that its safety and efficacy for acute mania have not been studied in people under age 18. The drug has an exhaustive Black Box warning.[101] First, hepatic (liver) failure resulting in fatalities has occurred in patients receiving valproic acid and its derivatives (all forms of Depakote). Second, children under age 2 are at considerably increased risk for fatal hepatotoxicity. Third, there is a risk of teratogenicity (fetus malformations such as spinal bifida). Fourth, cases of life-threatening pancreatitis have been reported in both children and adults. Some cases have been fatal. Depakote was developed as an anticonvulsive medication. Its labeling indicates use in stabilizing acute manic phases in adults, even though its safety and efficacy have not been established through controlled trials for longer than three weeks. "Mood stabilizer" has no precise clinical or neurological meaning, but the term has been a successful selling gimmick.

Jake

Jake was placed in foster care without due cause at age 9. He had been heavily medicated since age 6 with a changing regimen of drug cocktails that included stimulants, antipsychotics, and adjunctive drugs. In his first foster home of many, out of ignorance or carelessness, he was overdosed with Depakote. Jake had almost continuous vomiting for days, and he was accused of inducing it himself. He endured ridicule and denigration by teachers and caseworkers. Then the clinic psychiatrist documented his dangerously high blood level of Depakote. I used this information in court in one of my attempts to bring Jake home. The judge and social services lawyer coldly demanded proof, which I gave them in the form of the doctor's note. Still, Jake and his family suffered physically and emotionally for over another year before we succeeded in reuniting them.

Clonidine

Many children carry diagnoses of both bipolar and ADHD. Stimulants often make it difficult for children to settle down at bedtime. It is common for psychiatrists to prescribe Catapres (clonidine hydrochloride) as a sedative, even though it is only approved to treat hypertension in adults. Although the drug label does not carry a Black Box warning, it does warn of some serious side effects. It reports body weakness in about 10 of 100 people, and heart arrhythmias and other cardiovascular events in about 5 of 100 people. It states that the safety and effectiveness for people under age 12 have not been established.[102]

The death of 4-year-old Rebecca Riley in December 2006, discussed in chapter 3, was attributed to overdoses of clonidine. Staff at her school described her as a "floppy doll," so weak she had to be helped onto the school bus. According to news releases, her psychiatrist had been prescribing antipsychotics, clonidine, and Depakote for Rebecca since the age of $2^1/_2$, when she diagnosed her as bipolar.

BIRTH OF THE PSYCHOPHARMACEUTICAL COMPLEX

With all this bad news about antipsychotics, how could it be they are still touted as the first line of treatment for bipolar and other so-called pediatric disorders? Marcia Angell[103] offers a convincing explanation. It was extremely fortuitous for academia and the pharmaceutical industry that the atypicals came along early in the Reagan administration. Angell concedes that other economic considerations, besides bestowing riches upon these two heretofore quite differently motivated domains, inspired the Bayh-Dole Act early in the 1980s. The act enabled universities and small businesses to patent discoveries emanating out of research funded by the National Institutes of Health (NIH). Previously, taxpayer-financed discoveries remained in the public domain. Now academic researchers could grant exclusive licenses to drug companies and charge royalties. Other legislation even allowed the NIH to enter into deals with drug companies that would transfer NIH discoveries to industry. Bayh-Dole was a boon for academia, drug companies, and small biotech companies. All parties cashed in on the public investment in research. Angell reports that at least a third of drugs marketed by the major drug companies are now licensed from universities or small biotech companies. She points out that this arrangement changed the ethos of medical schools and teaching hospitals. They became very entrepreneurial in seizing opportunities to turn their discoveries into financial gain.

In 1984, the Hatch-Waxman Act provided another series of laws just as lucrative for the pharmaceutical industry. Coupled with a series of subsequent laws, it enabled drug companies to lengthen the patent life for brand name drugs from 8 years to 14! For a blockbuster drug like Zoloft—one that earns over a billion dollars a year—six more years of exclusivity are pure gold! Now we can understand the power of big pharma, as it has become known. The companies hired "armies of attorneys," as Angell put it, to look after their interests. Whitaker[104] explains that prior to this, academic scientists performed clinical trials on new drugs and kept the pharmaceutical industry in line, as these academics had the upper hand in the approval process. The laws passed during the Reagan administration removed most of the checks and balances provided by independent research, and a new industry emerged: a for-profit clinical trials model that served the pharmaceutical companies. It developed gradually. Community physicians, feeling the squeeze of health maintenance organizations and managed care, discovered they could profit by running clinical trials. Drug companies would pay them for doing the trials and publishing in medical journals as academic authors. Some doctors formed groups that solely performed clinical trials. The movement burgeoned for over a decade and by 1997 had become big business, with ventures consolidating to provide services nationwide. The pharmaceutical companies poured money into these enterprises: In 1990 they spent under $1 billion; in 2000 they spent $3.5 billion. In 1997 community physicians reported earning an average of $331,500 for their research services. Clinical trials moved out of academia into a for-profit setting. Even academic departments revised their research tactics to attract funding from the pharmaceutical industry. Academic researchers no longer had either the upper hand in the relationship with drug companies or the previous disdain for them. It was quite the reverse. Now the drug companies had it very good. They could use the for-profit research sites to perform their studies and hire academic doctors to publish, creating an illusion of intellectual prestige and independence.

Many academic doctors are corrupted by this revolution, as they strive to produce results favorable to the medication being tested. The researchers are not independent; their income depends upon results that promise profit for the companies. The drug companies can and do design trials they know will not be challenged by the researchers, and the designs are often set up to make the competitor or the placebo group appear inferior. Details of how they accomplish this are abundant in Whitaker's *Mad in America* and Angell's *The Truth About the Drug Companies*. Obscene profits have empowered the pharmaceutical industry, which, in collaboration with the "bought" psychiatric and psychopharmacological researchers, form the juggernaut dubbed "psychopharmaceutical complex" by Peter Breggin. No longer is the playing field even between members of that complex and the *truly* independent doctors, scientists, and other mental health professionals. The latter cannot compete with the constant hyperbole that impacts citizens about new drugs, as they are marketed directly to the public via the media. And many of the most influential academic doctors are collaborators in the psychopharmaceutical complex.

Reporter Gardiner Harris of the *New York Times* provided statistics in 2007 to show how this collaboration of psychiatry and the drug industry has impacted the prescribing trends of doctors. He noted a pattern that has emerged:

> As states begin to require that drug companies disclose their payments to doctors for lectures and other services, a pattern has emerged: Psychiatrists earn more money from drug makers than doctors in any other specialty. How this money may be influencing psychiatrists and other doctors has become one of the most contentious issues in health care. For instance, the more psychiatrists have earned from drug makers, the more they have prescribed a new class of powerful medicines known as atypical antipsychotics to children, for whom the drugs are especially risky and mostly unapproved.[105]

This article discusses payments to doctors in Vermont and Minnesota, where disclosure is the law. In Vermont, drug company payments to psychiatrists more than doubled to an average of $45,692 in 2006, up from $20,835 in 2005. But the companies spent $2.25 million on marketing, fees, and travel expenses, just in Vermont. Even that is a small fraction of marketing, as it doesn't include free drug samples, gifts, or salaries of sales representatives. Payments to psychiatrists in Minnesota ranged from $51 to $689,000, and the doctors who received the highest payments from makers of antipsychotic drugs tended to prescribe those drugs to children. This article mentions Senator Grassley's interest in legislation requiring public disclosure of payments to doctors. We hear more from the senator in the epilogue.

This discussion's objective was to elucidate how the conglomerate of academia and industry has exploited our most vulnerable and cherished resource— our children. There are signs that the tide is turning regarding this exploitation of children. Law firms are becoming savvy about the pharmaceutical complex and are available to represent individuals who have been harmed by the devolution of the pharmaceutical industry and its collaborators. Additionally, some legislators are unveiling lack of transparency among physicians who are so generously remunerated for their parts in the devolution.

Jim Gottstein and Eli Lilly

Attorney Jim Gottstein lives and practices in Anchorage, Alaska. Known to me through the International Center for the Study of Psychiatry and Psychology, he is a tireless advocate for people caught in the mental health system against their will. In 1988 he co-founded the Alaska Mental Health Consumer Web that provides peer support and a drop-in center. He co-founded a number of other organizations that provide services to people who struggle with mental health issues.

He devotes most of his time doing pro bono work for others who have been victimized by pharmaceutical companies and the mental health system.

Jim won a landmark case, Myers vs. the Alaska Psychiatric Institute, in June 2006.[106] Faith Myers had been forcefully hospitalized and medicated with Zyprexa, a drug that had previously caused her serious side effects. The Alaska Supreme Court decided Ms. Myers' constitutional rights had been violated when the state forced her to take psychiatric medication without proving it to be in her best interest.

Jim's heroic efforts in this case exposed the deceptive practices of Eli Lilly, maker of Zyprexa. In the course of representing Ms. Myers, Jim followed protocol to obtain documents from Eli Lilly in December 2006.[107] The documents, which covered the years 1995 through 2004, were under a protective order as part of a large liability case. A class action suit against Eli Lilly was filed representing people who became ill using Zyprexa, and Lilly had to pay about $700 million to 8,000 plaintiffs. Dr. David Egilman was a professional witness for the plaintiffs in the class action suit and was in possession of these documents. Knowing they would be of interest to Jim, he contacted Jim, who responded with a subpoena for the documents. The documents revealed that Lilly had deliberately concealed knowledge it had as early as 1999 about the dangerous side effects of Zyprexa that might have spoiled sales. Zyprexa's side effects of obesity and high blood sugar placed thousands of people at risk of serious illness and death. Lilly's own data showed that 30 percent of people taking the drug gain 22 or more pounds a year. Some gained as much as 100 pounds. Its own doctors warned the company that they should come clean about the data or they could get in deep trouble. Yet Lilly's drug representatives were instructed to downplay the serious risks posed by the drug. Consequently, Zyprexa became known as the best drug to treat schizophrenia and was Lilly's best-selling product, with sales of $4.2 billion in 2005. Jim weighed his knowledge that Lilly may have already caused the deaths of hundreds of people, while continuing to place patients at risk, against his own risk of retaliation by Lilly, which could ruin him financially and threaten his career. He chose to make the documents public and sent them to a reporter at the *New York Times*. The newspaper published the first of five scathing articles about the documents on December 17, 2006. Two appeared on the front page, and one was an editorial.

Lilly took Jim to court along with others with whom he had shared the documents: Peter Breggin, Vera Sharav, David Cohen, Will Hall, and Robert Whitaker. Lilly claimed the documents had been improperly obtained and that they contained "trade secrets" the company didn't want to fall into the hands of its competitors. Sharav reportedly was eloquent on the stand, characterizing Lilly's failure to inform doctors and the public about its drug's dangerous risk to patients. Others had their say as well. But the judge decided in favor of Eli Lilly on February 13, 2007. Judge Weinstein decided Jim had acted improperly and had been a co-conspirator with Egilman, who sent him the documents, and Berenson, the *New York Times* reporter who wrote the articles. Worst of all, he declared that Lilly had been irreparably harmed by their actions. Jim's response? "I vigorously dispute this." He continues the fight for justice against the monolith, Lilly. The trial, with its moving testimonies, and the *New York Times* articles did not go unnoticed. The editorial called for congressional investigations into the drug companies. As we'll see in the epilogue, this is not the end of the story for Zyprexa and Eli Lilly.

Meanwhile, Jim has undertaken another enormous challenge. In the name of the Law Project for Psychiatric Rights, he is suing the state of Alaska, its governor, the Alaska Department of Health and Social Services and its director, the Office of Children's Services and its director, the director of the Division of Juvenile Justice, the director of the Division of Behavioral Health, the director/CEO of the Alaska Psychiatric Institute, and the deputy commissioner and director of the Division of Health Care Services.[108] Jim underscores the constitutional right of children and youth not to be administered psychotropic drugs involuntarily, unless it is in their best interest and no viable alternative exists. He demands a process of informed decision-making regarding the administration of psychotropic medications to children and youth in custody of the state of Alaska. He also underscores the unlawful practice of the state paying for psychotropic medications that have not obtained approval by the FDA and certain other compendia. (As detailed in the epilogue, many states have initiated lawsuits around this unlawful practice.) His lengthy, detailed case includes a "CriticalThinkRX" curriculum specifically for non-mental health workers, with an exhaustive set of questions to be answered before the administration of a psychotropic drug to a child or youth.

Jim Gottstein's relentless efforts of behalf of Alaska's children may be empowering those youngsters in state custody. The *Anchorage Daily News* reported on November 15, 2008,[109] that a group of Alaska's foster kids and graduates of the system advocated for less medicating and more opportunity to participate in normal activities while in foster care. They spoke before influential people at a legislative meeting that included the director of the state Office of Children's Services, one of the defendants in Jim's lawsuit. The kids belong to an advocacy group, Facing Foster Care in Alaska, that numbers about 140 young people statewide.

Conflicts of Interest Make for Bad Science

I promised I would return to Anya Bailey's psychiatrist, George M. Realmuto. the *New York Times*[110] exposed the story on May 10, 2007. Complaining that his university salary of $196,310 shows that academics don't get paid much, Realmuto said he accepted $5,000 from Johnson & Johnson for giving three talks about Concerta. He said a study by Melissa DelBello, a psychiatrist at the University of Cincinnati, influenced him to use combinations of Depakote and atypicals in bipolar children. DelBello's study, financed by Seroquel maker AstraZeneca, tracked the moods of 30 adolescents labeled bipolar for six weeks. Half received Depakote and the others received Depakote with Seroquel. Both groups did about equally well until the last few days of the study, when the Seroquel group showed slightly better improvement. **But half of the subjects in the study had dropped out by this time, so it was a study of 8 subjects**. Even though DelBello admitted it was not conclusive, when the study was published in 2002, she and her co-authors declared that Seroquel in combination with Depakote was more effective for the treatment of adolescent bipolar mania than Depakote alone. To compound the outrage, in 2005 a panel of prominent experts from across the country decided that DelBello's study was the only one regarding the use of atypicals for bipolar children that ranked high for scientific rigor! The panel recommended that doctors should consider atypicals as a first line of treatment for some children and published their guidelines in the *Journal of the American Academy of Child and Adolescent Psychiatry*. Disclosures in the guidelines revealed that three of the four panel members served as speakers for or consultants to makers of atypicals. Robert A. Kowatch of Cincinnati's Children's Hospital was lead author. He and DelBello were hired by AstraZeneca to give sponsored talks. DelBello claimed she doesn't make much from the drug companies, but declined to reveal how much. She admitted receiving marketing or consulting income from eight drug companies, including all five makers of atypicals. The "inaccuracy" of influential doctors regarding how much money they receive is now being exposed.

DelBello's saga is continued in the epilogue, but the crux of this lengthy account is that the fate of children rests on bad science and deteriorating morality.

As for Anya Bailey, in 2005 her mother took her to the Mayo Clinic, where doctors discontinued the Risperdal. (Unlike most universities and hospitals, the Mayo Clinic restricts doctors from giving drug marketing lectures.) Anya still has to take medicine for the pain of her dystonia. Mrs. Bailey said she wished she had waited to see whether counseling would help Anya before trying drugs.

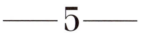

5

Screening Children for Mental Illness and the New Freedom Initiative: Freedom or Coercion?

Families are really what stands between individuals and impersonal corporate and government structures . . . Experts with good intentions can do harm. We need to be as scrupulous about the effects as about the intentions of our behavior.

—Mary Pipher

TWO YOUNGSTERS

Chelsea

Fifteen-year-old Chelsea Rhoades was coping well with her typical teeter-totter teen life, blossoming independence at one end and parental authority at the other. She was confident in her ability to fulfill her dreams for the future. But one day in 2003 her healthy self-image was shattered. She returned home from her public Indiana high school that day visibly upset. She asked her parents what OCD (obsessive-compulsive disorder) and social anxiety were. The parents answered to the best of their ability and asked if Chelsea was working on an assignment for school. She told them she wasn't, but the people at her school had informed her that she had these two mental illnesses. Chelsea had always been a normal, happy child and was raised to take her responsibilities seriously. Now she expressed dire concern about her mental stability. Outraged, the parents called their local mental health association and inquired who at the school had diagnosed their child based on a brief computer test. Chelsea's mother reports she could not get a straight answer from them or from the school. Eventually they were able to discover the people were from TeenScreen, a nationwide program developed at Columbia University, ostensibly to curb the rate of teen suicide. They also discovered that David Shaffer, the program's author, and others associated with it had close ties with the pharmaceutical industry.

With the help of the Rutherford Institute, a prominent advocate for human rights and civil liberties, the Rhoades family is in litigation to hold account-able the school district, certain school personnel, and the center that performed the TeenScreen for the injurious act perpetrated on Chelsea, the *New York Times* on April 13, 2005, quoted Vera Sharav, president of the Alliance for Human Research Protection and expert on citizens' rights in the mental health arena. She said, "When you label people as having a mental problem, such a label stays with them for their entire lives, whether or not it's accurate."[1] Not only are they stigmatized for life, the labels can be obstacles to career choices. The Rhoadeses aim to have these bogus diagnoses expunged from Chelsea's record.

When they obtained a copy of the test given to Chelsea, her parents learned that TeenScreen was a ten-minute computer questionnaire. She received the label of OCD because she answered "yes" to the question of whether she per-formed repeated actions over and over that she wished she could stop. Chelsea explained she answered affirmatively because she was required to do chores every day when she completed her homework and she didn't like doing them. As for social anxiety, she responded affirmatively to the question of whether she felt anxious in front of her peers. She explained that when she had to deliver book reports to her class she felt nervous. And asked if she went out with friends much, she responded "no," meaning that she was not allowed to go out all the time because she had responsibilities at home. The test did not allow for any explanations, and the children did not know they were being tested for mental illness. Moreover, parents' permission was not required. Mrs. Rhoades learned that at another Indiana school, parental permission was required and only nine students received that permission. The mental health association approached the authorities at Chelsea's school and said not enough children were being tested, so they suggested "passive consent" as a better option. Consequently, more than 750 students at Chelsea's school were tested. Notices were sent home with students about screening, which had to be returned to the school if parents did not consent. This, of course, drastically reduced the number of non-consents. Children often lose slips of paper or for-get to give notices to parents. Many parents quickly glance at such notices and figure the school is just doing another routine test like vision or hearing screen-ing. Failure to return the slip represents passive consent. This form of "con-sent" is not uncommon.

On August 6, 2008, the Rutherford Institute announced that a federal court judge ruled the lawsuit may proceed to trial. In his ruling, Judge James T. Moody upheld claims that the local school district deprived the Rhoades family of their federal constitutional rights to family integrity and privacy when it sub-jected Chelsea to the TeenScreen examination.

Update

On June 5, 2006, TeenScreen director Leslie McGuire wrote a letter to TeenScreen colleagues informing them that effective August 1, 2006, all school-based sites will be required to obtain written ("active") consent from the parents or guardians of minor students.[2] A fact sheet was released on August 1, 2006, stating that TeenScreen's consent forms were meant to conform to consent requirements of the federal Protection of Pupil Rights Amendment (PPRA).[3] The PPRA has been in effect since 1978! It took six years for TeenScreen's directors to decide they could not afford to ignore this federal law. The drawback is that the law applies only to agencies that are recipients of funding from the Department of Education. This does not protect children in youth facilities such as detention centers or homeless shelters.

Aliah

Aliah Gleason's experience in seventh grade at a middle school near Austin, Texas, was even more nightmarish. A lively girl who sometimes spoke out impertinently, she was placed in special education and labeled oppositional defiant (another diagnosis given to kids who misbehave). Texas has a screening system for youngsters similar to the model developed there for adults, which will be discussed shortly. Psychologists from the University of Texas (UT) performed mental screening to sixth- and seventh-graders. Aliah's parents first received a letter from UT saying Aliah was not experiencing any significant level of stress. Before long, however, they received a phone call from a UT psychologist claiming that Aliah scored high on suicide risk and needed further evaluation. The parents complied, albeit reluctantly. Six weeks later, in January 2004, a child protective worker ordered Mr. Gleason to take Aliah to a state hospital because she was deemed suicidal, apparently on the basis of the evaluation.[4] When he refused, Aliah was placed in "protective" custody by social services and taken to the hospital. She was not allowed to see her parents for five months, was forcibly drugged, and was repeatedly placed in restraints. All this was without her parents' permission. Aliah was given various vague diagnoses and deemed psychotic. She was prescribed multiple drugs: four antidepressants, an anti-anxiety, three antipsychotics, and two anticonvulsives, some of them simultaneously, and an anti-Parkinson's medication to treat the side effects of the others. When transferred to a residential facility, she was on six different drugs.

All told, she was wrenched from her family for nine months. Back home again, she secured aftercare with Texas psychologist John Breeding, pro-child mental health activist and author of books, including *The Wildest Colts Make the Best Horses*. In cooperation with the family doctor, they tapered Aliah off all the drugs. The ordeal was a year in duration, and Dr. Breeding said their job after that was to help Aliah recover from the emotional wounds caused by the trauma to which she was exposed at the hands of social services and the state mental health system. He added that she also needed help to lose all the weight she gained due to the antipsychotic drugs. Aliah returned to a normal life at home and school. She is one of the fortunate children who appears to be recovering from extreme psychotropic drug use, unlike many who do not. However, long-term effects of the toxic drugs forced on Aliah remain unknown.

PARENTS OPPOSE SCREENING

Of all parents of children currently being screened, the Rhoadeses and the Gleasons are among the exceptional ones who refuse to submit to the abuses of an intrusive state system. The majority of parents trust the "experts," especially when high government officials such as the surgeon general and the president promote programs. Consequently, thousands of children have been unnecessarily labeled, drugged, and hijacked into the mental health system for life. Teresa Rhoades, Chelsea's mother, has posted a petition addressed to school board members at large and state and federal legislators at www.petitiononline.com. This well-written document contains additional information about TeenScreen, and anyone can sign it.

Not all school districts are sanguine about TeenScreen. A Web site, *TeenScreen Locations Across the U.S.*,[5] lists 30 school districts in 15 states, representing every geographical section of the country, where TeenScreen was discontinued. Ten of these cite unfavorable results as their reason; some of the comments are very caustic. The list was last updated June 15, 2007. Protesting citizens and parents are rare, but unfortunately the methods that threaten our children's mental health and the sanctity of our families are not. Our government plans to screen everyone in the country, starting with the youngest, for mental illness. To find out how this plan came about, we journey back a few years to trace its development.

BIRTH OF THE NEW FREEDOM INITIATIVE

The 1990s saw a surge of interest in mental health. Congress declared those years "The Decade of the Brain." The first White House Conference on Mental Health was held in 1999, and two federal agencies, the Substance Abuse and Mental Health Services Administration (SAMHSA) and the National Institutes of Health (NIH), collaborated to release *Mental Health, A Report of the Surgeon General.* The report contained a comprehensive overview of current perspectives on children's mental health. Surgeon General David Satcher called for an action plan to address the perceived unmet mental health needs of children. Consequently, *Report of the Surgeon General's Conference on Children's Mental Health: A National Action Agenda* was released January 3, 2001. This report contained the seed that grew into universal mental screening of American children. Satcher began his foreword to the report with "The burden of suffering experienced by children with mental health needs and their families has created a health crisis in this country."[6] On January 3, 2001, a press release of the U.S.

Department of Health and Human Services interpreted Satcher's statement as "According to the report, the nation is facing a public crisis in mental health for children and adolescents."[7] Hence grew the compelling myth that toddlers, children, and youth are so afflicted with mental health problems as to constitute a public health crisis.

That same month President Bush, in his inaugural address, pledged to address inequalities that prevented people with disabilities from enjoying full participation in terms of employment and community integration. He quickly followed up on February 1 by appointing his New Freedom Commission on Mental Health, whose mission it was to study the U.S. mental health care delivery system and to advise him how to improve that system so that adults with serious mental illness and children with serious emotional disturbances can fully participate in their communities. As of early 2009, indications are that Bush's successor, President Barack Obama, shares similar attitudes and intentions regarding mental health. Unless Obama can be persuaded to revise the onerous strategies affecting children that are recommended by the New Freedom Commission on Mental Health, we can expect to see a continuation of its programs that are already implemented, and continually expanding.

NEW FREEDOM COMMISSION ON MENTAL HEALTH

Final Report: Achieving the Promise

In July 2004, President Bush released the New Freedom Commission's final report, entitled *Achieving the Promise: Transforming Mental Health Care in America* (hereafter referred to as *Achieving the Promise*). The task of developing a blueprint to implement the goals of *Achieving the Promise* was delegated to the SAMHSA, which released *Transforming Mental Health Care in America. The Federal Action Agenda: First Steps* in 2005 (hereafter referred to as the *Federal Action Agenda of 2005*). "New Freedom Initiative" is a general term referring to the mission and intentions of the New Freedom Commission on Mental Health since its inception.

The New Freedom Commission's *Achieving the Promise* remains the document of substance, while the *Federal Action Agenda of 2005*, a much more condensed document, lends specificity and some minor alterations to the very weighty commission's final report. Let's proceed with a close look at *Achieving the Promise*. The commission concluded that the mental health system was not observing its most important function, that of fostering recovery. The commission aims to transform the system by setting six goals that would prevent or cure mental illness, detect mental illness early, and provide everyone at any stage in life access to effective treatment and supports. The goals are:

- Americans Understand That Mental Health Is Essential to Overall Health.
- Mental Health Care Is Consumer and Family Driven.
- Disparities in Mental Health Care Are Eliminated.

- Early Mental Health Screening, Assessment, and Referral to Services Are Common Practice.
- Excellent Mental Health Care Is Delivered and Research Is Accelerated.
- Technology Is Used to Access Mental Health Care and Information.[8]

Goal 4: Early Mental Health Screening

Can you discern the "Trojan Horse"? Goal 4, "Early Mental Health Screening, Assessment, and Referral to Services Are Common Practice," is nestled smugly among some very noble-sounding objectives. The first time I read the whole document my reaction to the goals, except for numbers 2 and 4, was "These are not new. Those commissioners must be far removed from the real world of mental health trench work and social work education." Social workers, who comprise the largest group of mental health clinicians in the country, are taught well the importance of those other goals and have long pursued them in the field. I believe they are window dressing for the "Trojan Horse," Goal 4. Goal 2, the other exception, recommends a Recovery Model. This innovative alternative to the medical model is discussed later in this chapter.

Schools as Mental Screening Collaborators?

Within the 12 pages of Goal 4 in *Achieving the Promise*, the commissioners extol partnership with schools in attaining the goal. They say, "Schools are where children spend most of each day . . . schools must be partners in the mental health care of our children. Schools are in a key position to identify mental health problems early and to provide a link to appropriate services." They add that focusing on schools provides the opportunity to screen 52 million students and 6 million adults working at schools.[9]

As we saw above, many parents do not believe schools should interfere in the private affairs of their children. Aside from this ethical issue, they may have other concerns. The mother of a child she described as autistic phoned me about the difficulty she was having receiving appropriate support from her daughter's school. She referred me to a Web site, *Wrightslaw*, to find an article, "School Problems: It's the Kids' Fault!"[10] Author Pamela Darr Wright, licensed clinical social worker, described a study undertaken by Galen Alessi, professor of psychology at Western Michigan University. He published its results, "Diagnosis Diagnosed: A Systemic Reaction," in *Professional School Psychology*, Vol. 3, number 2. Dr. Alessi identified five causes that could explain students' learning or behavior problems: 1) child may be misplaced in the curriculum, or curriculum may include faulty teaching routines; 2) teacher may not be implementing effective teaching and/or behavioral management practices; 3) principal and/or other school administrators may not be implementing effective school management practices; 4) parents may not be providing home-based support; and 5) the child may have physical and/or psychological problems that contribute to learning problems. Alessi interviewed 50 school psychologists from around the country, and rounded off the number of children evaluated each year to 100 cases for each psychologist, for a total of 5,000 cases. All those contacted agreed that the five factors listed above played a prominent role in school learning or behavioral problems. Then the psychologists responded to the number of cases they believed corresponded to each of the five categories. To the first three, all responded that in no case was the problem traced to factors related to the school. All the psychologists responded they were fortunate to have "the best" curricula, teachers, and administrators. To the fourth factor, 10 to 20 percent responded that parents were at fault for various reasons. And to the fifth, responses were 100 percent that the problem resided in the child.

Granted, it might be that these psychologists felt beholden to defend their schools and administrators. Even if this were the case, it is still tough for the child and family, who feel betrayed or misunderstood by teachers and administrators at their child's school. I observed the phenomenon repeatedly at Individual Educational Plan (IEP) meetings I attended to advocate for my child clients and their caregivers. During these meetings, behavior and learning problems were attributed to the child, and medication was the preferred solution. Occasionally an individual teacher would express differing opinions to me in private: criticism of the widespread use of medications, and genuine concern for the child's circumstances. She was apt to confide to me her frustration as a relatively powerless agent in the larger school arena.

Goal 4 as a Conundrum

Pro-child psychosocial advocates recognize a diabolical conundrum in Goal 4. It **precludes** the attainment of that central aim of *Achieving the Promise*, "preventing or curing mental illness"; in fact, it promotes mental illness! Here's how. First, screening for mental illness sprang from the misconception that we have an epidemic of mentally ill children, so screeners are set up to expect high numbers of disordered children. Expectation becomes a self-fulfilling prophecy. Second, the labeled child takes on the characteristics of the label, as his caregivers and all those in his environment treat him according to how a child so diagnosed is expected to behave. And third, medication perturbs brains, creating mental illness where originally there was none.

Others saw the flaws of Goal 4. Daniel Fisher, M.D., Ph.D., heads the National Empowerment Center, Inc. He was a member of the New Freedom Commission on Mental Health, and he courageously took exception to the majority opinion of commissioners during the formulation of *Achieving the Promise*. Investigative journalist Jeanne Lenzer, in the August 14, 2004, *British Medical Journal* Web edition, quoted him as follows.

> Widespread screening at a time when medical education is geared to the biomedical model and teachers want to get kids fixed could result in greater numbers of children being given a label, a diagnosis, and a medication . . . What

troubles me a little bit is that mental health will continue to be used as a substitute for addressing the social, cultural, and economic needs of children. Addressing those needs and heeding the recommendation of the plan to transform the system to one based on fostering recovery and resilience could solve many behavioral problems . . . but widespread screening before systems are transformed could undermine some very positive elements of the plan, including its focus on care that is driven by patients and on housing support, educational rights, and employment.[11]

Fisher, in his wisdom, seems to be saying that "transforming the system" would foster attainment of the goals of *Achieving the Promise* that repair America's infrastructure, which would ultimately meet the social, cultural, and economic needs of children. He implies that Goal 4 (screening) might preclude the attainment of **transformation,** the centerpiece of *Achieving the Promise*. This statement underscores the conundrum I am talking about. Fisher's fears were realized years later.

In 2007, when the State of Massachusetts was debating mandated mental screening of all children on Medicaid, Fisher wrote a letter to the *Boston Globe* in response to an editorial supporting this screening. He pointed out that overworked pediatricians would likely score many false positives with devastating consequences for the children and their families. Quick-fix screening tests, he said, would end up with quick "fixes" of kids by placing them on medication without the benefit of thorough psychosocial assessments. Psychosocial evaluations often identify interpersonal or environmental stressors that can be resolved without medication. He added that even though parents could opt out of the screening, often they wouldn't for fear of loss of custody for noncompliance with mental health treatment.[12] Unfortunately, Fisher's statements did not thwart the state's decision to go ahead with the screening mandate. On December 27, 2007, *Boston Globe* journalist Carey Goldberg reported that Massachusetts doctors were facing a mandate to offer simple questionnaires to the state's half million children and youth on Medicaid during annual checkups. They were to watch for warning signs of possible mental health problems.[13]

Opposition Mounts

The public release of *Achieving the Promise* provoked outcries from many quarters. Critics foresaw that Goal 4 would lead to labeling many more millions of children and referring them for treatment with psychotropic drugs. A *WebMD-Health* article reported that children are the fastest growing group of antipsychotic drug users, even though most of these medications are not approved for children. The article reported that between 2001 and 2005 (the period during which mental screening proliferated), prescriptions for atypical antipsychotic drugs increased by 80 percent among children and teens, compared to an increase of 46 percent among adults.[14] This same time period saw the dramatic rise of pediatric bipolar diagnoses, as discussed in chapter 3. It seems appalling that screening is the centerpiece of *Achieving the Promise*, given the abundance of caveats in all the reports leading up to *Achieving the Promise*. All stressed the unreliability of diagnosing very young children and a lack of scientific studies to determine the safety of any psychotropic drugs for this age group. That the pharmaceutical industry stands to profit enormously from universal screening is another source of outrage.

Other opponents discerned the specter of government intrusion on the rights of parents and the violation of privacy rights. Goal 4 states that screening will be "common practice." Implementation of this goal has established programs that screen *every* child in targeted areas starting at birth. Later in this chapter I describe one that is a model of state invasion on family. One of its tactics involves home visits to first-time mothers to check up on their parenting skills and the potential for mental illness in their infants.

The New Freedom Commission calls for nothing short of *fundamental transformation* of the mental health care delivery system of the United States—from **"one dictated by outmoded bureaucratic and financial incentives to one driven by consumer and family needs that focuses on building resilience and facilitating recovery"** (Emphasis added). Goal 4 actually *enhances* bureaucratic and financial incentives. Government-sponsored early intervention and screening represents bureaucratic intrusion into families, and screening for mental illness lines the pockets of pharmaceutical companies and the psychiatrists who collaborate with them by labeling and medicating millions of children.

A true transformation of mental health care in America would eliminate the requirement of diagnosis via the *Diagnostic and Statistical Manual of Mental Disorders* (DSM). It would promote the psychosocial model and devalue diagnosis. Instead, *Achieving the Promise* lends legitimacy to the theory of mental disorder as "chemical imbalance" and maintains the status quo of the mental health system. Goal 4 does nothing to build resilience and facilitate recovery. But in examining all the reports leading up to *Achieving the Promise*, some foundation was laid for doing so. Unfortunately, neurobiological influence shot holes through this foundation. The next section explores how it all went so wrong.

HEGEMONY OF NEUROBIOLOGICAL THEORY IN RETROSPECT

Federal Policy Makers: Does Theory Trickle Down or Trickle Up?

I studied all reports from meetings and conferences, from 1999 to the final SAMHSA action agenda of 2005. In so doing, the neurobiological theme became apparent. It started with Surgeon General David Satcher. In his preface to the 1999 *Mental Health, A Report of the Surgeon General*, he wrote that the contributions of mental health research ("neuroscience") have mended the "destructive split between 'mental' and 'physical' health."[15] This perception sets the stage for the opinion that there is no distinction between physical and mental illness. In the same report, Secretary of Health and Human Services Donna Shalala was even clearer. She stated that neuroscience research has taught us much about the workings of the brain and can provide an understanding of what goes wrong with the brain in mental illness.[16] Then President Bush signed Executive Order 13217 on June 18, 2001, promoting community-based alternatives for individuals with disabilities and directing federal agencies to work with states to ensure full compliance with the *Olmstead vs. L.C.* decision and the Americans with Disabilities Act.

In the famous 1999 U.S. Supreme Court case of *Olmstead vs. L.C. and E.W.*, Lois Curtis and Elaine Wilson won the right to community living after many years of confinement in the State of Georgia's largest psychiatric hospital. The ruling upheld the integration mandate of the Americans with Disabilities Act to provide services in the most integrated setting appropriate to the needs of qualified individuals with disabilities. Tommy Olmstead was commissioner of the Georgia Department of Human Resources.[17]

The two women were diagnosed with life-long developmental disabilities and mental disorders (the latter most likely secondary to the developmental disabilities). Developmental disabilities are to be distinguished from "mental illness"—preferably called "emotional distress"—not a physical disability.

When Bush expressed his intentions to eliminate barriers that prevent people with disabilities from enjoying full access to opportunities available to non-disabled people, he categorized mental illness with physical disabilities. He didn't know any better: The surgeon general set the precedent. Both, no doubt, are influenced by prominent neurobiological theorists and the powerful pharmaceutical lobby. People who make policy and lay "believers" in the neurobiological model do not work in the trenches of mental health clinics. They put stock in their informers who represent mainstream psychiatry—strict proponents of the medical model. And they likely are too far removed from the clinical arena to appreciate the harm inflicted on children by the medical model of mental health care they espouse.

Thus *Achieving the Promise* and the *Federal Action Agenda of 2005* ultimately classify emotional distress as "mental illness," a physical disability. It is generally accepted that mental retardation and other developmental disabilities such as cerebral palsy, severe autism, and Down syndrome are physical conditions, usually of organic origin and readily diagnosed. Psychosocial proponents say this is not so with emotional distress. Lumping the two together is like comparing apples to oranges. But in the process leading up to *Achieving the Promise*, neurobiological theory prevailed over caveats regarding the uncertainty of mental disorders in very young children. "Mental illness," for all intents and purposes, became a physical illness of the brain. Let me reiterate: **This is only theory, not proven. There is no test for mental illness, and there is no proof that it is a disease**.

All of this is not to say that people disabled by the mental health system or those temporarily disabled by emotional distress should not enjoy the same rights as people with physical disabilities. The mistake is that the New Freedom Initiative fails to acknowledge a distinction between physical illness that is usually medically diagnosable and treatable and emotional conditions that cannot be medically diagnosed and have not been proven to have a medical origin.

Conference on Children's Mental Health of 2000

Let's move on to the Conference on Children's Mental Health that assembled on September 18 and 19, 2000. I compared their 2001 *Report of the Surgeon General's Conference on Children's Mental Health: A National Action Agenda* to the 2004 final report of the New Freedom Commission, *Achieving the Promise*. The first 11 pages of the 2001 document outline eight goals, along with action steps for achieving each goal. Goal 2 calls for the development and implementation of children's mental health prevention and treatment services. I chose 8 of 17 action steps for achieving Goal 2 that would have supported psychosocial theory:

- Recognize the importance of knowledge about child development.
- Consider familial, cultural, and ecological contexts in promoting mental health and preventing emotional problems.
- Recognize treatment modalities other than pharmacological ones, including behavioral and multimodal interventions.
- Promote research to assess psychotropic drugs' potential for damaging the genes as well as the brain.
- Promote research to determine the short- and long-term consequences of both acute and chronic exposure to pharmacological intervention.
- Promote research on the prognoses of mental illnesses treated very early in life.
- Heed ethical considerations of pharmacological research on children.
- Promote enhanced treatment interventions that preserve families.[18]

Unfortunately, those excellent eight steps became lost in the overall emphasis on neurobiologically driven concepts. Take them one at a time.

- The action step calling for further study of child development should discourage "early identification of mental illness," the phrase that becomes ubiquitous in subsequent reports. "Early identification," which usually means labeling and medicating children who deviate from a preconceived "normal" trajectory of development, flies in the face of the tenets of child development. Normal parameters of development envelop highly variable characteristics, such as physical and emotional maturation, and readiness and ability to learn. Inappropriate labeling (screening instruments have high rates of false positives) of an infant or toddler limits that child's potential. It stigmatizes him and lowers expectations of him. And it is likely that at some point his brain will be invaded with chemicals at the hands of professionals assigned to "treat" him.
- Considerations of familial, cultural, and ecological contexts, along with the recognition of non-drug treatment alternatives, went by the wayside in the tidal wave of neurobiological focus on brain pathology.
- These action steps underscore the need for pharmacological research, but the neurobiological enthusiasts ignore the research that has already demonstrated the deleterious effects of psychotropic medications on children. Pharmaceutical companies research their own products, and the U.S. Food and Drug Administration bases its approval on only two favorable outcomes, out of any number of studies unfavorable to their drug. Drug company research has been notoriously bad science, as discussed in previous chapters.

- As for ethical considerations associated with research on young children, this book documents in several places how little regard some neurobiological scientists have shown for the safety of children when exposing them to brain scans and worse procedures.
- Preservation of families is not the outcome of the kinds of interventions promulgated by the 2001 *National Action Agenda*. Rather, state interventions that disempower parents and threaten healthy child development have become universal. Moreover, the dulling effect of neurobiological treatment (medication) inhibits the family's ability to resolve the underlying causes of its distress.

Psychopharmacology for Young Children Meeting of 2000

The other meeting that contributed to the 2001 *National Action Agenda* convened October 2 and 3, 2000, and was summarized in "Psychopharmacology for Young Children: Clinical Needs and Research Opportunities" by Benedetto Vitiello, M.D., director of Child and Adolescent Treatment and Preventive Interventions Research Branch for the National Institute of Mental Health. He published the report in *Pediatrics*, October 2001. Vitiello repeatedly acknowledges the "diagnostic uncertainty surrounding most manifestations of psychopathology in early childhood."[19] Yet he goes on to say that children in this age group are most commonly diagnosed with ADHD, and he believes the symptoms of "valid" ADHD stay with children and "portend even more serious psychopathology" (p. 984). He does not acknowledge that "the more serious psychopathology" could be the result of early exposure to psychotropic medication. Yet he does acknowledge that, even though stimulants are used for preschoolers, no definitive study supports the efficacy or safety of these medications in this age group. Moving on to the topic of antidepressants and mood stabilizers, the author makes even more startling statements. He states clinical trials of medications on preschoolers would not seem possible because of the current uncertainties about diagnostic validity of mood disorders in children under age 6, and moreover, **"very little research has been done to demonstrate replicability across raters and external validity of these diagnoses in preschoolers"** (p. 984, emphasis added). Vitiello apparently foresaw the weaknesses of screening tools that have become evident since he wrote this article.

Under safety considerations Vitiello advises, "When possible, nonpharmacologic interventions should be considered before young children are given medications of unproven efficacy and safety" (p. 985). He expresses grave reservations about medicating young children because of risks of harm during early brain development (p. 986). Vitiello identifies the ethical consideration of risk minimization when testing psychotropic drugs on young children. He advises that when drugs are tried with preschoolers, they should be carefully monitored for side effects (p. 986).[20]

This raises another aspect of treatment with children. Monitoring for side effects is very difficult because children are often incapable of describing the subjective body feelings caused by the drugs they are ingesting. For example, how does a child describe the tortuous sensations associated with akathisia? Akathisia is a common side effect of many psychotropic drugs—a kind of inner urgent restlessness that causes the person to need to move about. (Such a symptom in a child may be observed by adults and interpreted as hyperactivity.) Another attribute of many children is tolerance for discomfort; they are apt not to complain.

Although Vitiello's report seems contradictory in places, in the last analysis it reflects a conservative attitude toward pharmacological treatment on young children. But by the time his report is subsumed under the New Freedom Initiative, the caveats in the report are thrown to the wind for the sake of advancing the neurobiological model of treatment.

NEW FREEDOM COMMISSION'S SUBCOMMITTEE ON CHILDREN AND FAMILY

The New Freedom Commission assigned subcommittees to develop the six goals. The subcommittee on Children and Family was responsible for Goal 4. Its subtitle became "Promoting, Preserving, and Restoring Children's Mental Health." This echoes the alarmist perspective that emanated from the Surgeon General's Report of 2001–the compelling myth that toddlers, children, and youth are so afflicted with mental health problems as to constitute a public health crisis. Someone sounded the alarm that each year large numbers of young children are expelled from preschools and childcare facilities for severely disruptive behaviors and emotional disorders.[21] The subcommittee set about to "fix" the children. Their recommendations led to Goal 4 of *Achieving the Promise*.

The commissioners in turn believed these youngsters are mentally ill or will become so unless mental health professionals intervene. They put forth "Early Mental Health Screening, Assessment, and Referral to Services" as the objective of Goal 4. Opponents' translation is that strangers will enter schools and family homes and manipulate parents into believing their children are disordered. The commissioners reveal their neurobiological bias on the first page of Goal 4, claiming that "[n]ew understanding of the brain indicates that early identification and intervention can sharply improve outcomes and that longer periods of abnormal thoughts and behavior have cumulative effects and can limit capacity for recovery."[22] We have critiqued "early identification and intervention," and explored the evidence that its exercise actually places children at risk. Chapter 2 elucidated that "new understanding of the brain" has given rise to different interpretations, not all of which support neurobiological treatments. Moreover, who knows what "abnormal thoughts and behavior" mean when dealing with vividly imaginative children?

Jude was an appealing 9-year-old client of mine, an enormously gifted artist with a lively imagination. When he told his school counselor that little bears were talking to him, she called me in alarm, accusing him of becoming psychotic. I disagreed and told her I had a poster of a bear family in my office and I believed he was alluding to the appealing cub faces poking over the protective arm of their mother. Jude was an animal lover who sometimes sported a stuffed "pet" animal on his shoulder—also causing school staff as well as our clinic psychiatrist to think he was not quite right in the head. He was, in fact, a lonely boy who had been abandoned by his father, but who had developed clever adaptive behaviors to help him cope. These mechanisms were working for him but, sadly, the alarmists assigned him a serious label and placed him in a day treatment program that heavily medicates its students.

The Children and Family Subcommittee would have fared better with Daniel Fisher at its helm. The notion that children need fixing is tantamount to blaming the victims of a society that has failed its children. As Fisher seems to suggest, repairing the infrastructure of American society would go far toward relieving children's emotional distress. A plethora of explanations is possible for the epidemic of troubled (not mentally ill) children. These are explored in chapter 8. Suffice it to say for now that professionals from many disciplines are seeking solutions in more appropriate places than inside the child, and mental health professionals would do well to heed their scholarly contributions.

TWO SUBCOMMITTEES DEPART FROM THE MEDICAL MODEL

Daniel Fisher was chair of the Subcommittee on Consumer Issues, which promoted a Recovery-Oriented Mental Health System. Its report starts with the assertion that mental health research shows that people can and do recover from even the most severe forms of mental illness.[23] Above all else, this model fosters self-determination for people served by the mental health system. The subcommittee urges governments at all levels to put consumers of mental health services in leadership roles to develop a National Recovery Initiative. Contrary to Goal 4's medical model, the Recovery Model empowers people. When Fisher's subcommittee recommended evidence-based practices, it mentioned peer support programs and initiatives that respect the wisdom and special knowledge of people who have lived with a mental illness label. Fisher also was co-chair of the Subcommittee on Rights and Engagement. This group, consistent with the Recovery Model, emphasized the key role that human rights of fairness and respect play in recovery from mental illness.[24] In line with the Recovery Model, it promoted self-determination for consumers about their treatment and their right to engage in mediation over their treatment. The recommendations of these two subcommittees comprise Goal 2 of *Achieving the Promise*: Mental Health Care Is Consumer and Family Driven. Central is the Recovery Model of treatment (focusing on adults), the one initiative in *Achieving the Promise* that deviates from the medical model. Now let's look at a promising outcome of Goal 2 before proceeding with the subcommittees.

Veterans Health Administration's Initiative

A U.S. Medicine Institute for Health Studies Roundtable Discussion occurred October 18, 2004, in Washington, D.C. Its executive summary, titled *The*

Changing Face of Mental Health Services in the Veterans Health Administration, reports that "paternalistic" programs do not involve the veteran in his own treatment and are less effective than programs that are veteran and family centered and utilize peer support.[25] This claim is based on an experiment involving veterans from the Southwest Asia conflict: The Veterans Health Administration (VHA) hired these veterans to reach out to their peers, and this proved a successful recovery technique. These peers trained VHA staff how to reach out with mental health care. The report mentions the President's New Freedom Commission on Mental Health and its charge that early detection of mental illness should occur followed by access to treatments that support and promote recovery. Daniel Fisher was a participant in this roundtable discussion.

On October 29, 2004, Deputy Under Secretary For Health, Veterans Health Administration, Frances Murphy, M.D., M.P.H., delivered "Recovery and Rehabilitation of the Client with Psychosis: Evidence Based Practices." Murphy stated:

The six goals of the [President's New Freedom] Commission on Mental Health and recommendations were turned into an 82-item Action Agenda designed to help the Veterans Health Administration transform its mental health delivery system to ensure that the mental health needs of veterans are met using a recovery model of treatment and to achieve the vision of the President's Commission on Mental Health where every veteran at risk for or having a mental illness has the opportunity to participate fully in his or her community.[26]

On April 1, 2008, Adrian M. Atizado, assistant national legislative director of the Disabled American Veterans, delivered a statement before the Subcommittee on Health, Committee on Veterans' Affairs, U.S. House of Representatives. He was reporting on progress of the Veterans Administration's Action Agenda that had commenced in 2005, as part of a five-year strategic plan designed to eliminate deficiencies and gaps in the Action Agenda. He noted several shortcomings in the implementation of the Recovery Model, such as conflict with the "evidence-based medical model"; possible difficulty in meeting the requirement for family inclusion in treatment planning; inconsistent efforts of program managers to involve veterans and their families locally; and the need for additional funding. Atizado requested of the House subcommittee that they continue their oversight on progress of the VA Strategic Plan.[27] His testimony is indicative of the challenge of instituting reform in a mental health system. The Veterans Administration deserves credit for its efforts. Now we return to our discussion of the New Freedom Commission's subcommittees.

TWO-SUBCOMMITTEE MERGER DISREGARDS ALTERNATIVES TO THE MEDICAL MODEL

The subcommittee on Medication Issues merged with the Subcommittee on Evidence-Based Practices. This combined subcommittee spoke of no alternatives to medication. Its discussion was exclusively on policies regarding psychotropic medication: access, cost, and knowledge.[28] The subcommittee did acknowledge the need to study long-term effects of psychotropic drugs on children, but in the context of medication as the treatment of choice for children. The subcommittee mentioned neither research that supports non-drug treatments nor research that reveals the disabling effects of psychotropic medication.

The above paragraphs demonstrate the contradictions between Fisher's sub-committees versus the Evidence-Based and Children and Family subcommittees. The Evidence-Based people apparently bore the heaviest influence on Goal 4, whose paternalistic screening methods disempower families and hijack children into a coercive mental health system. The recommendations of Fisher's subcom-mittees would rehabilitate the adult children victims of Goal 4!

We move ahead now to examine some projects currently in place, and how they have direct ties to the pharmaceutical industry and government, including former President George W. Bush. We also discuss why the screening models touted as "best practices" in *Achieving the Promise* were purportedly dropped from the *Federal Action Agenda of 2005*.

TEENSCREEN

Goal 4 features the TeenScreen program—the program responsible for the suffer-ing of Chelsea Rhoades and similar to the Texas program that hijacked Aliah Gleason—as a "best practice" model for youth screening.[29] Probably because this recommendation was met with such intense opposition, and possibly because of the pending lawsuit represented by the Rutherford Foundation (on behalf of the Rhoades family), the name TeenScreen was dropped in the 2005 *Federal Action Agenda*. But it reappeared, albeit with a face lift, as we shall soon see.

History of TeenScreen

A precursor to TeenScreen is described in the *Journal of the College of Physicians and Surgeons of Columbia University* in 1998.[30] At that time children were seen at the Ruane Diagnostic Unit (RDU) at Babies & Children's Hospital for half-day assessments using a questionnaire known as the Diagnostic Interview Schedule for Children (DISC). A psychologist headed the staff of two part-time psychologists and three lay interviewers. The children were seen with their parents. The unit was created and supported by philanthropists William and Joy Ruane, who also spon-sor the New York State Psychiatric Institute's Joy and William Ruane Center for the Early Identification and Treatment of Children with Mood Disorders.

Vera Hassner Sharav, founding director of The Alliance for Human Research Protection, informs us that the stated goals of the Ruane Center were to develop new diagnostic tools; to make DISC available to the academic and clinical com-munity at low cost; to establish professorships in pediatric psychopharmacology; to promote research on the use of psychopharmacological agents in children and adolescents; and to develop efficient high school programs to screen teenagers for the early signs of manic depression and suicidal risk.[31] The Ruane family has been notable in promoting these goals through its largess.

Sharav explains that three organizations at Columbia University worked together to further these goals of screening and medicating more children.[32] The three are the Diagnostic Interview Schedule for Children (DISC) Development Group, the Center for the Advancement of Children's Mental Health, and the National Alliance for the Mentally Ill (NAMI). The DISC Development Group at Columbia University was headed by Dr. David Shaffer, who went on to develop TeenScreen. DISC is a NIMH tool to be administered by lay (clinically untrained) interviewers.[33] Shaffer and the DISC Development Group developed mini-versions of the DISC questionnaire to screen school children. One is TeenScreen, a 14-item questionnaire completed in 10 minutes. The other is BSAD (Brief Screen for Adolescent Depression), an eight-item questionnaire completed in five minutes. Screening for Mental Health Inc. uses BSAD on an annual Depression Screening Day.

The Center for the Advancement of Children's Mental Health was established in 2000, a partnership of Columbia University and the National Alliance for the Mentally Ill (NAMI), and funded by the Carmel Hill Fund (formerly the William J. Ruane Family Foundation). Its stated goal is the early recognition of mental disorders in children. Mental disorders are defined as "a group of individual **illnesses of the brain** that affect behavior, mood and even thinking process."[34] Peter Jensen, who held the endowed chair as the Ruane Professor of Child Psychiatry at Columbia University from 2000 to 2007, was founding director of the center. He was associate director of child and adolescent research at the National Institute of Mental Health from 1989 to 2000. Currently, he leads the REACH Institute, an outgrowth of his work at the Center for the Advancement of Children's Mental Health.[35] NAMI seems to have taken ownership of the latter.[36]

NAMI is a large organization of people either with mental illness labels or related to someone with a mental illness diagnosis. It staunchly embraces the use of psychotropic medication and has close ties with the pharmaceutical industry. NAMI documents obtained by *Mother Jones* magazine revealed that between 1996 and mid-1999, 18 drug firms gave NAMI a total of 11.72 million dollars. Among these were Janssen, Novartis, Pfizer, Abbot Laboratories, Wyeth-Ayerst, and Bristol-Myers Squibb. The top donor was Eli Lilly.[37] Reporter Nicole Gaouette disclosed on April 6, 2009, that Senator Grassley has expanded his investigations into nonprofit groups, and specifically into NAMI. By letter, he asked NAMI to disclose any financial backing from drug companies or from foundations created by the industry. In the letter he stated, "I have come to understand that money from the pharmaceutical industry shapes the practices of nonprofit organizations which purport to be independent in their viewpoints and actions."[38]

Laurie Flynn served as executive director of NAMI for 16 years and in 2001 was recruited by Columbia University to help develop what became TeenScreen. She is now executive director of TeenScreen.

The three groups that developed TeenScreen—DISC, the Center for the Advancement of Children's Mental Health, and NAMI—have had connections with the National Institute of Mental Health (NIMH) and the Substance Abuse and Mental Health Services Administration (SAMHSA). All these alliances illustrate the monolithic influence that academia, private interest, the pharmaceutical industry, and government exert on attitudes toward mental health. Now we explore the miasma of funding and conflicting interests that characterize these entities.

TeenScreen's Tangled Webs of Funding and Influence

The updated 2008 TeenScreen Web site's financial link states it is funded by private foundations, individuals, and organizations committed to the early identification of mental illness in youth and the prevention of teen suicide. It states, "Neither the former TeenScreen or [sic] the National Center [new name] have never [sic] received support or funding from pharmaceutical companies for screening." The TeenScreen Primary Care branch, it says, is funded by a 4-year, $12 million commitment from the Carmel Hill Fund (formerly the William J. Ruane Foundation).[39]

Investigative reporters challenge the veracity of these statements. Evelyn Pringle states in a *Scoop Independent News* article that, when promoting the program to Congress, TeenScreen executive director Laurie Flynn told members of Congress that TeenScreen was free, and at that time TeenScreen's Web site apparently claimed it received no support from either the government or drug companies. Pringle cites the *Update Newsletter*, published by the Tennessee Department of Health, that reported 170 Nashville students had completed a TeenScreen survey. The publication said the survey was funded by grants from AdmoCare and Eli Lilly, both pharmaceutical companies. It was reported that 96 of the 170 ended up talking with a therapist, making the funding well worthwhile for the companies since it is likely the therapist recommended "a medical solution" (i.e., drugs).[40]

As for government support, Sharav reports that the DISC Development Group and TeenScreen are funded by tax dollars through SAMHSA, the same federal government agency that developed the *Federal Action Agenda of 2005*.[41] All Americans, then, pay for TeenScreen through federal taxes (and in many localities through state taxes—not only for programs, but also to line the pockets of pharmaceutical companies whose drugs are paid for by Medicaid—enormous sums!). Sharav's investigations revealed that Screening for Mental Health, Inc. (the group that uses the BSAD questionnaire developed by Shaffer and the DISC Development Group) received $2,823,425 in "donations" from the drug industry in 2001, 2003, and 2004, and $5,974,317 from the U.S. Department of Health and Human Services.

Pharmaceutical companies also indirectly support the TeenScreen programs. Drug companies donate money in the form of "educational grants" to the states. On June 10, 2005, Senators Chuck Grassley and Max Baucus of the Senate Finance Committee issued a press release calling for investigation into the practice of drug makers giving money to state legislators. Sepp Hasslberger[42] credits

Sharav's organization, the Alliance for Human Research Protection, for this information. The two senators were concerned that the money was influencing policy makers and promoting the companies' products more than "educating." Hasslberger cites a quote by Grassley: "We need to know how this behind-the-scenes funneling of money is influencing decision makers . . . The decisions result in the government spending billions of dollars on drugs. The tactics look aggressive, and the response on behalf of the public needs to be just as vigorous." Pringle corroborates this information.[43] She also uncovers a tactic used by TeenScreen executive director Laurie Flynn when trying to get the program established in Florida. Pringle reports that while testifying before Congress, Flynn bragged about her associations with government officials in Florida, stating she was "collaborating" with Jim McDonough, director of the Office of Drug Control and the state Suicide Prevention Task Force, "to achieve the goal of Governor Jeb Bush to reduce suicides in the state."

It turned out that "collaborating" meant gifting McDonough $180,000 to get TeenScreen set up in Florida. And an e-mail to McDonough read quite differently from her congressional testimony, according to Pringle's research: "I'm looking for a horse to ride in here! . . . I need to get some kids screened . . ." In the end, however, Flynn complained the money was not put to good use, because McDonough failed to get TeenScreen in all the schools as promised.[44] At least in one locality, Pinellas County, the school board turned away TeenScreen because of citizens' protests.[45]

Sharav reports that Shaffer has longstanding associations with drug companies whose drugs are prescribed to children. She specifies he was a consultant for Hoffman la Roche and GlaxoSmithKline, and was expert trial witness for Wyeth on the matter of Paxil and adolescent suicide.[46] (His group was designated by the Food and Drug Administration to review the studies on SSRI antidepressants inducing self-harm and suicide in children—a blatant conflict of interest.)[47]

As noted earlier, Laurie Flynn became executive director of TeenScreen in 2001, after serving as NAMI's executive director for 16 years. Deputy executive director Leslie McGuire has had roots at Columbia University since 1998, when she coordinated sites where the screening technique was being developed.[48] Sharav reveals that Michael F. Hogan, chairman of the New Freedom Commission on Mental Health, also served on TeenScreen's National Advisory Council and that he promoted the Texas Medication Algorithm Project (to be described shortly) while he served simultaneously as state mental health director from Ohio and on an advisory board for Janssen Pharmaceutica. Conflicts of interest could not be more obvious. (Hogan was confirmed commissioner of the New York State Office of Mental Health on March 14, 2007.)

TeenScreen Gets a Facelift

TeenScreen's updated (as of 2008) Web site portrays a booming organization that has given itself a new image.[49] It changed its name from the Columbia

University TeenScreen Program to the National Center for Mental Health Checkups. Subsumed under this heading are TeenScreen Schools and Communities and TeenScreen Primary Care. The former is dubbed the National Center's "flagship" program. It is described as a "voluntary" screening program for youth ages 11–18, operating at more than 500 (up 50 from the previous Web site) local sites in 43 states. There is no mention of change in the instrument or method of use. It still boasts its prominence as the Columbia TeenScreen Program, cited as a model program in *Achieving the Promise*; it is still based at Columbia University; and its core staff remains intact. TeenScreen Primary Care is described as a "mental health checkup" specifically designed to assist medical professionals in primary settings to—again, that euphemism—"check up" on the mental health of adolescent patients. But it goes on to say the "checkup" instrument is a "brief" questionnaire that can be completed in the waiting room. A "simple way," the summary boasts, of evaluating if a teen is suffering from depression, anxiety, or another mental health condition or is at risk for suicide. The "checkup" summary claims scientific support of its screening's effectiveness, as well as safety (ignoring widespread opposition based on known incidences— arguably as high as 84 percent of cases[50]—of false positives that compromise safety). TeenScreen surges ahead, despite no change in the statement of the U.S. Preventive Services Task Force that, according to task force research, screening does not prevent suicide, nor is there evidence that screening tools accurately identify persons at risk of suicide.[51]

MOVING AHEAD TO THE *FEDERAL ACTION AGENDA OF 2005*

Dr. Karen Effrem[52] summarizes some departures in the SAMHSA *Federal Action Agenda of 2005* from the New Freedom Commission's *Achieving the Promise* as they pertained to mental health screening. She explains that representatives from organizations opposing screening met with Charles Currie, administrator of SAMHSA (and a New Freedom commissioner). The organizations represented were EdWatch (Effrem was their representative), Eagle Forum, the Alliance for Human Research Protection, the International Center for the Study of Psychiatry and Psychology, the Association of American Physicians and Surgeons, the American Psychoanalytic Association, and Mind Freedom. Currie heard the concerns and criticisms of these groups. After the meeting he issued the following statements that indicated some progress on several important issues.

He noted the critical importance of parental consent and emphasized that consent for mental health screening must be based on full knowledge with a parent's signature and, again, full knowledge consent and signature for any follow-up treatment. He extended the requirement for parental consent to other federal programs such as Safe Schools and Healthy Students. Effrem acknowledges these concessions as improvements over the New Freedom Commission's *Achieving the Promise*, but notes they should be strengthened by legislation so that they apply to future federal administrations.

Currie highlighted the elimination of TeenScreen in the *Federal Action Agenda of 2005*. However, EdWatch and the Alliance for Human Research Protection learned, subsequent to the meeting with Currie, that SAMHSA intended to give $9.7 million in grants to four states to implement TeenScreen! Moreover, Effrem reports that Congress appropriated $20 million in 2004 and another $26 million in 2005 for grants to implement *Achieving the Promise* goals, including screening. It's as if to realize the vision of Kathryn Serkes, public affairs counsel for the Association of American Physicians and Surgeons. She was quoted on *Newsmax* on November 23, 2004: "Once it's established and has funding, a program exhibits the nettlesome property of being self-sustaining—it gets a life of its own. More funding follows."

It would seem that the two "best practice" models, TeenScreen and the Texas Medication Algorithm Project (TMAP—to be described shortly)—both programs already widely in practice—are here to stay. But within the states receiving grants, various groups are vigorously campaigning in opposition. They succeeded in 2005 in Minnesota and Texas. Effrem points out that unless the federal government actually stops funding grants for TeenScreen and TMAP types of treatment, and documents with an official statement that it does not recommend these, Currie's assurances are mere talk. The State Early Childhood Comprehensive System, discussed later in this chapter, is an indication of the meaninglessness of his assurances.

SCREENING CHILD MEDICAID RECIPIENTS

Many states have initiated other brands of mental health screening for children, such as the one referenced earlier, opposed by Daniel Fisher in his letter to the *Boston Globe*. Nevertheless, the *Globe* reported[53] on December 27, 2007, that within days the nearly half a million Massachusetts children on Medicaid would face mandated screening at their regular checkups. A lawsuit alleging that the state was not adequately serving its poor, mentally ill children resulted in a federal judge's ruling, which led to the requirement. The article acknowledges some controversy between those who applaud the ruling and others who worry about overloaded service providers and more children being medicated. The requirement affects 460,000 children and youth covered by Massachusetts' Medicaid program from birth to age 21. In the epilogue, I report that many states are now investigating Medicaid payments to pharmaceutical companies for purchases of psychotropic drugs not approved for children.

THE TEXAS MEDICATION ALGORITHM PROJECT (TMAP)

Another change in the *Federal Action Agenda of 2005* from *Achieving the Promise* concerns Goal 5, which reads: "Excellent Mental Health Care Is Delivered and Research Is Accelerated." Here the New Freedom commissioners tout the Texas Medication Algorithm Project (TMAP), alluded to previously as a "best practice," just as they did TeenScreen for minors.[54] Like TeenScreen, TMAP was dropped from the SAMHSA *Federal Action Agenda of 2005*, and for the same reasons.[55] It met with intense opposition from the same quarters that objected to TeenScreen. And, like TeenScreen, its model is still used in many states. TMAP was instituted in 1996, when George W. Bush was governor, in collaboration with pharmaceutical companies. It mandates all mental health professionals in the public sector to follow its formula in diagnosing "mental illness" and then mandates which of the most expensive drugs are prescribed for the given diagnosis. The ensuing skyrocketing sales of psychotropic drugs tell who benefits from this program. Investigative news reporter Nancy Wilson of *KEYE-TV News* in Texas revealed in 2004 the figures specific to three drug companies: how much they invested in the project and how much they profited from Medicaid payments on their drugs since implementation of the program. Pfizer expended $232,000 and made $233 million. Janssen contributed $224,000 and made $272 million. Eli Lilly contributed $109,000 and profits were $328 million. Furthermore, KEYE-TV reported that between 2002 and 2004, 107,000 children in Texas were prescribed psychiatric drugs, at a cost of $167 million.[56] These obscene profits came from the pockets of taxpayers.

Johnson & Johnson is the parent company of Janssen. The Robert Wood Johnson Foundation, an arm of Johnson & Johnson, donated $2.4 million for the initial creation of TMAP.[57] TMAP for children became CMAP, or Children's Medication Algorithm Project. This is the program that hijacked Aliah Gleason. We return to CMAP shortly.

Corruption in TMAP

The TMAP model has spread to many other states. In Pennsylvania, whistleblowers Allen Jones, an investigator, and Stefan Kruzewski, M.D., unveiled financial corruption and overuse of medication, respectively. Kruzewski believes drug toxicity caused the deaths of four children and one adult. Jones revealed that officials with influence over the Pennsylvania version of TMAP received money and perks from drug companies. The findings of both men were quelled when they were fired for talking to the news media. Jones has also pointed out that some members of the New Freedom Commission on Mental Health served on advisory boards for drug companies, and that others had direct ties to TMAP.[58]

Jeanne Lenzer reported on *WorldNetDaily* on June 21, 2004,[59] that Eli Lilly made $4.28 billion on olanzapine (Zyprexa) worldwide in 2003. Olanzapine is one of the first line drugs on TMAP (whose algorithm dictates which drug to use for each diagnosis). She reported that George Bush Sr. was on Lilly's board of directors, and George W. Bush appointed Lilly's chief executive officer to a seat on the Homeland Security Council. Lenzer further revealed that in 2000, Lilly gave $1.6 million in political contributions, 82 percent of which went to the Bush campaign and the Republican Party. Other drug companies involved with TMAP have been big contributors to election funds of George W. Bush, according to

Lenzer. She reported that drug companies and manufacturers of health products contributed $764,274 to the Bush campaign up to April 2004, compared to $149,400 to John Kerry.

2008 Update

The *Daily Texan* reported on August 25, 2008[60] that CMAP, the children's version of TMAP, has been halted by the Texas Attorney General's Office. This appears to be further fallout from the recent allegations concerning conflicts of interest on the part of researchers who receive money and gifts from drug companies. In this case, Janssen Pharmaceutica allegedly gave mental health program decision makers grants, trips, perks, travel expenses, and other payments. It is alleged Janssen and other companies also paid program decision makers to promote their medications. Furthermore, Janssen's product, Risperdal, was a preferred treatment on CMAP when it did not have U.S. FDA approval for children. The epilogue contains additional information about this development.

The final section describes specific government programs and explains why families are threatened by intrusion into their privacy and disrespected by state definitions of what is "normal."

KAREN EFFREM, M.D., AND COALITION OPPOSE SCREENING

No discussion of Goal 4 of *Achieving the Promise* would be complete without elaborating on Effrem's work. A pediatrician and researcher from Minnesota, she is a tireless advocate of children's mental health and the rights of families to nurture children free from state interference. Besides authoring many articles and delivering lectures nationwide, Effrem has testified before Congress on such legislation as the Child Medication Safety Act, the Reauthorization of the Individuals with Disabilities Act and Its Impact on Diagnosis and Treatment of Children with Mental and Emotional Disorders, and many others.

Effrem reveals the unlikely coalition of people who oppose screening children for mental illness as proposed by Goal 4 of *Achieving the Promise*. Liberal dissidents join forces with the very conservative Eagle Forum, Heritage Foundation, and Gun Owners of America. Congressman Ron Paul, founder of the Liberty Political Action Committee, tried first to prohibit screening by amending the Labor, Health and Human Services and Education Appropriations Act for Fiscal Year 2005 so it would disallow federal funding of any school mental health screening. When this measure failed to meet congressional approval, he offered an amendment to the New Freedom Initiative legislation that would have required parental consent prior to screening. This too failed, and he has since sponsored stand-alone bills requiring parental/caregiver consent for screening. So far these have not met with congressional approval. Paul is a member of the American Association of Physicians and Surgeons, which also opposes screening.[61]

MANDATORY SCREENING OF CHILDREN?

Some Existing Programs Look That Way

New Freedom Initiative proponents have argued vigorously since July 2004, when Jeanne Lenzer first announced the release of *Achieving the Promise* in the *British Medical Journal*, that the commission never recommended *universal* or *mandatory* mental health screening. Here is a quote from the Web site of the American Psychiatric Association from July 2004:

. . . the *British Medical Journal*, in anticipation of the roll-out [of the findings of the President's New Freedom Commission on Mental Health—its *Achieving the Promise*], alleged in a disjointed story that the Bush administration will announce a plan to screen all Americans for mental disorders and promote antidepressant and antipsychotic drug use—allegations which we are told are well beyond the scope of anything the administration has planned and which seem to stem from a psychiatric survivors group. The *BMJ* story has gained some traction in derivative reports on the Internet, though mainstream media have not touched the story, partly thanks to APA's work, for which the administration is appreciative.[62]

Yet all indications since that "roll-out" are that universal mental screening is indeed a primary objective of the New Freedom Initiative. In *The Dangers of Universal Mental Health Screening*,[63] Effrem reproduces a diagram of the mental health component of a program called the Early Childhood Comprehensive System (ECCS), or State Early Childhood Comprehensive System (SECCS), since states receive federal grants to develop and implement their respective programs. Administrators are the Maternal and Child Health Bureau in collaboration with Project THRIVE (a public policy analysis and education initiative at the National Center for Children in Poverty), under the auspices of the U.S. Department of Health and Human Services. I obtained information from the Web sites of these agencies in February 2009.[64] The broad goal of SECCS is to integrate services for children that reach out to families and foster healthy children ready to learn at school entry. Five components comprise ECCS: medical services, social-emotional development/mental health, early care and education, parenting education, and family support services. Early Childhood Comprehensive Systems currently exist in 47 states, funded by grants for years 2005 through 2010. Commensurate with the perceived epidemic of mentally ill preschoolers that provoked the misguided concern, much emphasis is placed on the social-emotional and mental health component. Services target children age 0–5.

Let's take a look at Effrem's diagram. The diagram illustrates three "Levels of Infant Mental Health Care." First come Universal/Preventive Services. These are aimed at **improving child development, parenting knowledge and behavior, and infant mental health for all families within their service range.** The second level, called Focused Services, is aimed at specifically identified groups considered **at risk for developing** potentially serious social or emotional problems **that could lead** to infant mental health problems. Examples of the types of services include home visiting services for first-time mothers or **preventive interventions** for abused or neglected children. And third, Tertiary Intervention Services serve infants and caregivers experiencing current difficulties, such as recent trauma. At this level ameliorative and preventive services are likely to be provided at mental health centers.

Level 1 entails screening. The National Early Childhood Technical Assistance Center (NECTAC) provides the instruments that purport to assess babies and toddlers (age 0–5) for social/emotional development or mental health. NECTAC compiled its instruments from the infant mental health literature and screening and assessment texts.[65] The Web site provides charts describing a host of instruments. Administration time for most of the tests is 10 to 15 minutes. Two of the tests take longer, up to 30 minutes.

Implications are that brief assessments (questionnaires completed by parents, caregivers, and/or professionals) at birth can set a course of treatment or prevention that may impact an individual from birth throughout his lifetime. Even to me, a professional, descriptions of the infant characteristics to be assessed are mind-boggling. For example, one social-emotional questionnaire (ASQ SE), designed for babies as young as 3 months, determines if further assessment is indicated. It measures self-regulation, communication, autonomy, coping, and relationships. Given the extreme variations in development at such early stages, how much stock can be put in a brief assessment tool, or any other tool for that matter? Another purports to assess temperament, ability to self-soothe, and regulatory processes for children ages 0–3 (BABES). Again, wide variations in development and personality put such early assessment processes into question. Many of the tools rate behaviors on a five- or six-point frequency of occurrence scale, from "never" to "very frequently," choices open to different individual interpretations.

Now let's critique the level 1 objectives of SECCS, via the diagram in Effrem's book. The first, **Improving child development**, just sounds so much like "making better people," a concept associated with eugenics. **Improving parent knowledge and behavior** resounds with arrogance. Years of working with families humbled me and instilled respect for differences in the manner in which parents raise their children. I found myself asking, "Who am I to tell these folks that they are doing this wrong?" By whose standards do we tell parents which way is the right way? Who decides what constitutes "normal" social development? Paternalistic programs such as this one seem to assume that low-income parents are less qualified to be parents. On the contrary, some economically disadvantaged families demonstrate effective parenting methods passed down through generations. The exception, of course, is cases of child abuse, but SECCS are not limited to abusive parents. According to the diagram, **all families within service range, starting with the birth of a child**, are to be assessed. When deemed appropriate, education and guidance follow the screening, or referral for more intensive interventions. Offering a service to parents who seek assistance is entirely different from sending strangers into homes at the birth of a child to check if mother "is doing this right." Beyond smacking of arrogance, this is Orwellian.

The second level aims Focused Services at groups identified as "at risk" for developing potentially serious social and emotional problems that could lead to infant mental health problems. Examples are home visiting services and preventive interventions. We saw above how "at risk" infants are identified with Ages and Stages questionnaires (ASQ). What are **preventive** services, or **preventive interventions**? A fearsome alternative has been proposed. Prominent neurobiological-oriented psychiatrists are talking about medicating very young children deemed **at risk** to keep their brains from malfunctioning later on. Kiki Chang discussed prevention on *Frontline*'s "The Medicated Child."[66] He believes some children are "genetically loaded" toward bipolar (despite lack of scientific evidence) and that when such children undergo stress, the latent disorder becomes manifest. He said once this occurs (a phenomenon he calls "kindling"), episodes "take on a life of their own."

Chang's use of the term "kindling" begs a brief digression. In "The Bipolar Bamboozle," appearing in the September/October 2008 issue of *Skeptical Inquirer*, Stephen Ray Flora and Sarah Elizabeth Bobby elucidate how anticonvulsant medications came into use to treat mania. They explain that seizures experienced by people with epilepsy are caused by the sudden excessive firing of neurons. This initial firing is known as "kindling." Anticonvulsants curtail or reduce further seizures by "stabilizing" the neurons. The authors credit R. M. Post and S. R. B. Weiss[67] with the idea that, since both mania and seizures involve high excitability, anticonvulsants might similarly stabilize the emotional excitability of mania. Flora and Bobby argue that there is no evidence of uncontrolled firing of neurons during the manic state. Electroencephalograms (EEGs) document brain abnormalities that accompany seizures. No such physical evidence has documented any brain abnormalities or "kindling" phenomenon[68] in children deemed bipolar to justify the use of anticonvulsants. The use of anticonvulsants to treat bipolar is discussed in chapter 4.

On *Frontline*'s "The Medicated Child," Kiki Chang said the first defense in preventing the manifestation of bipolar is therapy to help families avoid the stressors that might bring on symptoms. But he followed that statement with, "The second part of it is medications, and I'm really excited about medications." He expressed his conviction that the benefits of medication outweigh the risks. Insurance companies often require medication over therapy because it's quicker and therefore seems less costly (though in the long run it is not). I believe Chang's first line of defense will be lost in the real world. David Willis, Medical Director of the Northwest Early Childhood Institute in Portland, Oregon, takes this chilling idea further. Citing research that claims 20 percent of children ages 9 to 17 are affected by mental disorders, he opines that these disorders first manifest as difficult behaviors at early ages. He then suggests that general pediatricians don't have to be behavioral health specialists to intervene. He encourages them to identify preschoolers with these behaviors and either treat them or refer them to specialists. He goes on to state that **psychopharmacology is on the horizon as** "**preventive therapy** for children **with genetic suscepti-bility** to mental health problems."[69] Willis seems to imply that very young children, maybe even babies, can be drugged with powerful and dangerous medications just because they have relatives with mental illness. As Galves and Walker so thoroughly explained in chapter 2, there is no scientific basis for the myth that mental disorders are genetic in origin, despite the common assumption that mental illness is inherited. It's not a stretch, then, to imagine a government-sponsored "parent educator" in the home of a new mom, screening algorithm in hand, to assess mental illness "potential" and dictate what preventive medicine to apply! Vaccinating babies "at risk" (genetically loaded) is an ominous specter.

The third level of Infant Mental Health Care provides services to infants and caregivers who are experiencing trauma and other current difficulties. This presents no real threat, provided services are offered respectfully and appropriately. Mandated services are usually resented by recipients and are therefore not very helpful. When parents **choose** intervention, its chances of success increase manifold.

WHAT CAN WE EXPECT FROM PRESIDENT OBAMA?

Nurse-Family Partnership

We are now poised to observe President Obama's stance on mental health issues and screening as proposed in *Achieving the Promise*. Indications are that he strongly favors mental health screening. According to Unite for Life,[70] he stated during his presidential campaign that he would expand the "highly successful" Nurse-Family Partnership (NFP) to all low-income, first-time mothers. The New Freedom Commission on Mental Health identifies NFP as a model program in Goal 4 of *Achieving the Promise*.[71] It places registered nurses in homes of expectant mothers and claims to use "proven methods" to improve the mental and physical health of the family through counseling and teaching "effective methods of nurturing children." Most people, including Obama, would be impressed by the claims of NFP success included with its description in Goal 4. But critics such as Karen Effrem refute the claims of success.[72] Effrem cites research that counters the claims of NFP. While there were statistically significant effects on maternal behavior, there were no effects on child social-emotional development and behavior. And of six studies of other home visiting programs, five failed to show a significant impact on child abuse rates or measures of child abuse potential among first-time mothers enrolled in the program. In written testimony to the House of Representatives Subcommittee on Education Reform,[73] Effrem reasons that the validity and reliability of the research behind NFP's claims of success are doubtful because they start with a false premise: that is, its assumption that mental illness exists, is measurable, and is neurobiological in origin. She points to the absence of knowledge about the causes of mental illness (if indeed it exists), the lack of agreement on diagnostic criteria of childhood conditions, and especially the difficulty of identifying antecedents of those conditions. Obama and most of the general public remain unenlightened regarding these caveats of mental health treatment and research.

The Mothers Act

As senator, Mr. Obama co-sponsored the Melanie Blocker Stokes Mothers Act (hereafter referred to as the Mothers Act) during the 110th Congressional session. It never reached a vote in 2008, but has been reintroduced in both Houses of Congress in January 2009. The Mothers Act is intended to alleviate postpartum mental illness and requires all health professionals attending women in childbirth to offer a mental screening for risk of depression or psychosis during the first year of their infant's life. Like the NFP visitation program, such a plan would seem inviolate. Sponsors of the bills have the best intentions, and many citizens passionately support it. But again, seasoned critics of the medical model detect the inherent dangers because again, risk is to be assessed through the use of questionnaires. We saw how questionnaires failed many kids in TeenScreen due to a very high percentage of false positives. That is, perfectly normal youths were identified with mental illness just because their answers were inappropriate due to ambiguous questions. It would be tragic to label new mothers as mentally ill or "at risk" (even harder to detect) for depression or psychosis and recommend antidepressant or antipsychotic medications as preventives! That would really put them at risk. It would probably put the breast-feeding infant at risk as well. Yet this is most likely what the plan would call for. The elusive task of identifying at risk new mothers, and of preventing the emotional distress associated with childbirth, is a worthy goal indeed. I believe a qualitative approach of informal interviews by specialized mental health professionals would more accurately identify new mothers at risk than the quantitative approach attempted through the use of questionnaires. And a non-drug psychosocial preventive approach would be far preferable to a medication solution.

Early Childhood Education and Head Start

President Obama has been talking about reforming early childhood education. This is concerning, as I hope he does not mean to impose yet additional inappropriate academic pressure on toddlers. This brings us to the topic of Head Start, a federal program of the Administration for Children and Families. Like the Nurse-Family Partnership, it targets children from low-income families. These programs are reactive to conditions of poverty and aim to change people victimized by poverty (echoing eugenics). Their effectiveness is doubtful, as we will see below. I would encourage Obama to seek funding to develop proactive projects that eradicate the causes of cyclical poverty, and to focus less on changing the victims of poverty. Since the inception of Head Start 40 years ago we have heard of the widening gap between the most and least affluent, but not of dra-matic changes in upward mobility among Head Start participants. On August 27, 2008, National Public Radio's *Morning Edition* reporter Libby Lewis pre-sented statistics for the past year. She reported that the number of children living in poverty rose by half a million. Although the rise was blamed primarily on the economy, the numbers highlight the need to address the root causes of unequal opportunity between rich and poor instead of targeting "people change."

The *San Francisco Chronicle* issued a research-based report on universal pre-schools operating in some states.[74] In Oklahoma and Georgia, the fourth-grade National Assessment of Educational Progress (NAEP) was used to measure aca-demic progress. In Georgia, the score in 1992 when preschool commenced was 212—three points below the national average. In 2007, the score was 219—still one point below the national average. In Oklahoma, the fourth-grade NAEP in 1998, when the preschool was adopted, was 219—six points above the national average. In 2007, it dropped to 217—three points below the national average. Tenneesee's preschool is considered the gold standard. After three years, there was no statistically significant difference in educational performance between preschool attendees and non-attendees by second grade. Research on Head Start is also bleak. All results consistently show initial academic gains, but fadeout of gains soon after beginning elementary school. Karen Effrem compiled a list of 10 studies that yielded data unfavorable to preschool programs.[75] The following are some of her findings. The C.D. Howe Institute issued an e-brief in February 2006 whose authors concluded that children in Québec were worse off since the introduction of a universal childcare program.[76] Some studies showed higher academic skills among children who attended preschool, but only temporarily. Control children caught up, and continued to do well, while preschool attendees' academic skills faded. And preschool attendees demonstrated increased aggres-sive and oppositional behavior over time. All the remaining studies were of American children. The same results persisted throughout the studies. A Head Start study found negative impacts on social-emotional development among Head Start participants.[77] Effrem cites Stanley Greenspan, professor of pedi-atrics and psychiatry and a speaker for the Clinton White House Conference on Early Childhood at George Washington University School of Medicine. He asserted that most out-of-home care does not provide a number of essential building blocks that children need for healthy development. His advice is to bring about social arrangements such that parents can do home care for their children. Effrem goes on to quote from *The Harvard Guide to Psychiatry*: "Since the 1960s a vast body of research has stressed the importance to the developing child of the physical presence and emotional accessibility of both parents . . . the loss of a parent through death, divorce, . . . or a time demanding job contributes to many forms of emotional disorders . . ."[78] The experts in chapter 8 tell us this hasn't changed over the decades. Yet what do we see? More preschool at earlier and earlier ages, and the continued weakening of parental influence.

Ominous Legislation for Babies

House Bill 1429 was signed into law in December 2007. Its action was "Mental Screening & Federal Curriculum for Preschoolers." As we saw above, it is being implemented. This legislation extends services from ages 3 to 5 down to ages 0 to 3. Worse, it legislates for continual mental health assessment on Head Start children as well as curricula of topics that should be taught by parents at home. And if it could be worse, the bill was stripped of parental consent requirements for health care services (including mental health) just prior to passing.

Programs like SECCS, which explicitly set out "to improve child development," and Head Start's new earlier intervention, which implicitly does the same by teaching parents appropriate child-rearing behavior, establish norms of "correctness." We have in America many traditions, cultures, and subcultures, each with its own ideas of "normal." These enrich our nation. No professional—government, mental health, or otherwise—has the right to coerce families into a preconceived notion of "normal."

A meaningful agenda to address our troubled children would originate with professionals and lay people who share a common view of children vis-à-vis American society. They would agree that fostering happier and healthier children depends on a national holistic approach, not one that places the problem in the children or in their parents. And they would respect parents' needs and rights to be with their very young children, free from state intrusion into their privacy. The next chapter provides some history that supports the indignation and deep concern evoked by the threat of mental screening and its provocative implications.

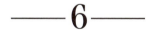

—6—

Lessons from Our Past

Indeed, future generations may look back on the early twenty-first century as an era when the chemical colonization of childhood really began in earnest.

—Daniel Burston

We'll look at parallels between our government's plan to universally screen for mental illness and past government initiatives that I believe most Americans would not be proud of. First we hear more from Karen Effrem and Congressman Ron Paul.

SCREENING AS A THREAT TO THE FREEDOM AND INTEGRITY OF THE FAMILY

Does the state own our children? According to Effrem, the issue boils down to that question.[1] She's concerned that mental health screening could lead to labeling children whose attitudes, religious beliefs, and political views conflict with "the secular orthodoxy that dominates our schools." Just as behavior that is individualistic has been pathologized, so might outstanding creative thoughts or unique perspectives. Moreover, the issue of parental consent remains tenuous. Reworded assurances of parental consent in SAMHSA's *Action Agenda* evoke skepticism. Worry lingers that "universal" screening as stated in *Achieving the Promise* really means "mandatory." After all, TeenScreen and TMAP are still very much alive, and both of these bureaucratic bodies have usurped from parents and private doctors the power to decide if a child is mentally ill. Ron Paul predicts that "[o]nce created, federal programs are nearly impossible to eliminate . . . Once the limited federal program is accepted, it will be expanded nationwide. Once in place throughout the country, the screening program will become mandatory."[2] Paul reminds us of Soviet communists who committed opponents of the state to mental institutions. He envisions American government psychiatrists similarly stigmatizing children whose religious, social, or political values are deemed incorrect. Paul adds, "American parents must do everything they can to remain responsible for their children's well-being. If we allow government to become intimately involved with our children's minds and bodies, we will have lost the final vestiges of parental authority. Strong families are the last line of defense against an overreaching bureaucratic state."

BRAVE NEW WORLD?

Now we travel back through time. Historian and political analyst Dennis Cuddy[3] constructs a version of the history behind former President Bush's New Freedom Commission on Mental Health. He recalls "The New Freedom" theme of President Woodrow Wilson's administration in 1912 inspired by President Wilson's chief advisor, Col. Edward M. House. Author of *Philip Dru: Administrator*, published in 1912, House wrote a fictional biography of a soldier turned social worker who built a utopian democracy aimed at leveling the social classes. Cuddy writes that House espoused "socialism as dreamed of by Karl Marx." Education was deemed the vehicle through which socialistic goals would be attained and, according to Cuddy, John Dewey emerged as "the father of progressive education" who promoted socialism. Cuddy attributes to Dewey the statement that the society or group is most important, and that independent individualists have a form of "insanity." Cuddy perceives John Dewey's progressive educational philosophy and mental health advocacy as pivotal in the instigation of the 1948 International Congress on Mental Health that convened in London and culminated in the publication of "Mental Health and World Citizenship." The document stated that "world citizenship can be widely extended among all peoples through the application of the principles of mental health." Cuddy also credits John Dewey and the growing strength of his progressive education in the 1950s and 1960s for the establishment of the Joint Commission on Mental Health of Children in 1965. According to Cuddy, a 1969 report by this commission recommended that schools assume responsibility for the emotional and moral development of children due to the decline of church and home. Cuddy states that the commission recommended aggressive outreach by child advocates, psychologists, and social and medical technicians; sending workers into children's homes, recreation facilities, and schools.

Cuddy continues his historical account of government's intrusion into the affairs of family. He reports that, at the urging of the Department of Health, Education and Welfare, North Carolina Governor James Hunt developed a model for child health care around the nation. Hunt's "Child Health Plan for Raising a New Generation" was released in 1979, the same year the North Carolina State Health Plan was adopted. The plan recommended that every child be assigned to a "health care home" that would require certain responsibilities of child and family. Cuddy said that in two places of the plan, religion was linked with mental illness and mental retardation.

Recent Trends Toward State Intrusion on Families

Also in 1979, Arkansas Governor Bill Clinton, supported by Hillary Clinton, began the Arkansas' Governor's School for the Gifted and Talented, modeled after the first Governor's School in North Carolina, established in 1963. Cuddy attended the North Carolina School (funded in part by the Carnegie Corporation, which funded eugenics programs at Cold Spring Harbor earlier in the century). He said students were given various psychological tests, and he believes students were guinea pigs to be used in the molding of humans for the creation of a Brave New World of the future.

Skipping ahead to Bill Clinton's presidency in the 1990s, Cuddy continues the saga. Hillary Clinton, in her capacity as head of a health care task force, awarded the now former Governor Hunt the directorship of Robert Wood Johnson Foundation's (R.W. Johnson is the same Johnson family of Johnson & Johnson Pharmaceuticals—makers of Risperdal) Mental Health Services for Youth program. In 1997, Hunt became chairman of the National Education Goals Panel (NEGP) and promoted the Early Childhood Public Engagement Campaign, also largely funded by the Carnegie Corporation. This panel, Cuddy reports, had a desire to create a nationalized system of child care from age 0, based on brain research. Cuddy alleges that another governor described an ideal system as one in which every community had a structure to be responsible for age levels up to age 6, adding that local governments' funding for needed projects should be contingent upon their adopting such a structure.

Cuddy suggests that coercive tactics such as this may be applied to establish the New Freedom Initiative: for example, attaching mental health screenings to vaccines that are required of all children in order to attend public school; or insurance companies requiring "voluntary" mental health screenings of older people in order to avoid higher premiums.

Cuddy associates this evolution of encroachment on families with socialist doctrine espoused in Arthur Calhoun's *A Social History of the American Family*, published in 1919 and used widely as a social service textbook. Cuddy quotes from this book:

> As soon as the new family, consisting of only the parents and the children, stood forth, society saw how many were unfit for parenthood and began to realize the need of community care . . . Kindergarten grows downward to the cradle and there arises talk of neighborhood nurseries . . . (pp. 174, 175) . . . in the new social order, extreme emphasis is sure to be placed upon eugenic procreation . . . we may expect . . . a system of public educational agencies that will begin with the nursery and follow the individual through life . . . (pp. 330, 331)

Some may believe this is far-fetched, but it is chilling to wonder where our nation is headed when we look at where we have been.

LATE 20TH CENTURY: OUR NATIONAL INSTITUTE OF MENTAL HEALTH-ASSAULTED CHILDREN

Now let's look at some recent initiatives that are not at all farfetched. Real and documented, they are exposed by Peter Breggin and Ginger Ross Breggin.[4] A federal violence initiative was announced in 1992 and the prestigious journal *Archives of General Psychiatry* devoted its June 1992 issue to violence research. One study in the journal described research on monkeys that found aggression correlated with low levels of serotonin. The researchers identified "aggressive" monkeys by the number of wounds and scars on their bodies (the monkeys were free ranging). The Breggins challenge the veracity of the study at the outset by pointing out that in all species the victims of violence, not the perpetrators, become most wounded (p. 88).

The violence issue of the journal also featured a study led by Mark Kruesi of the National Institute of Mental Health (NIMH) (pp. 89–90). Kruesi expressed his objective on National Public Radio: to identify and help individuals at high risk for violence with drugs and therapy early on. The implication is that children deemed to have low serotonin could be "vaccinated" with psychotropic medication to prevent potential violence later in life (similar to inoculating infants with antipsychotic medication to prevent potential bipolar, as suggested by prominent neurobiolocal theorists). Kruesi's team performed invasive spinal taps on 29 children ages 6 to 19 housed in NIMH hospital wards. Revealing their bias beforehand, the researchers stated it was likely that biology determines the violence potential in people ahead of environmental factors. Indeed, they found the same correlation as with the monkeys. Breggin challenges the validity of the study. Serotonin levels were identified by examining spinal fluid. But in spinal fluid it is actually the breakdown products, not the serotonin itself, that is used to "measure" serotonin levels. Breggin argues, "It is a leap of faith that correlates gross changes in spinal fluid with finely tuned activity in the brain." He also notes that no mention is made of double-blind procedures that would have prevented researchers from knowing spinal tap results when rating the behavior of the subjects; knowing these results likely would influence their judgment about behavior. However flawed the study, Kruesi's team concluded that low serotonin levels correlate with aggressive behavior (p. 89).

The Breggins describe studies on children and adolescents in NIMH wards by Judith Rapoport (who, we learned in chapter 2, continues brain-imaging experiments on children). She, too, performed spinal taps and other biological procedures on children from 1989 to at least 1995 for a costly project, "Neurology of Disruptive Behavior Disorders." Rapoport and her colleagues displayed callous disregard for the welfare of the research subjects, who were highly vulnerable inpatients in NIMH hospital wards. Breggin describes the invasive procedure of spinal taps. Lumbar punctures, terrifying in themselves, are used to extract spinal fluid. A child must lie extremely still for several minutes while the needle is inserted and then remain immobile while the needle draws out the fluid. Then he must lie immobile for 12 hours. The Breggins cite a 1987 neurology textbook that describes excruciating headaches that can extend down the spine and last from four to eight days, in 10 to 15 percent of cases. The textbook authors caution that spinal taps should never be performed routinely, but only when the information gained justifies the risk of the procedure (p. 91). Surely this is not a procedure to which most parents would consent.

In their final chapter, "Three Years Later," the Breggins report that abusive experiments on children were continuing at NIMH and elsewhere. But the good news is that Frederick Goodwin, dubbed by the Breggins the "mastermind" of the medical portion of the youth violence prevention initiative, ended his lifelong career with the federal government and no one has stepped in to maintain his advocacy for widespread screening and testing of children (p. 191). The Breggins write: "In the March 1995 *Scientific American*, W. Wayt Gibbs reported that efforts led by 'firebrand psychiatrist Peter Breggin' caused the government to abort its violence initiative."

MENTAL HEALTH SCREENING AND EUGENICS

Vera Sharav is a library scientist who specializes in law, and is founder of the Alliance for Human Research Protection (AHRP). She presented "Screening for Mental Illness: The Merger of Eugenics and the Drug Industry" at the 2004 annual conference of the International Center for the Study of Psychiatry and Psychology, which I attended. Her thesis was later published.[5] It takes no stretch of the imagination to recognize the analogies between psychiatry as proposed in Goal 4 of *Achieving the Promise* and the eugenics movement of past decades. First, both are based on the erroneous premise that deficiencies ("feeble-mindedness" in the case of eugenics and "disorder" in the case of mental health) are of biological origin. Eugenics held that genes were the cause of "feeble-mindedness" (which covered a host of "inferior" traits); psychiatry blames genes plus "brain disease" for the more euphemistic term "mental illness" or "disorder." Both minimize the effects of environment or personal history. Eugenics was seen as a solution to a broad range of human "afflictions," from mental or physical disability, to criminal behavior, to homelessness, disease, and low economic status. This is similar to the American Psychiatric Association's *Diagnostic and Statistical Manual of Mental Disorders* that categorizes a plethora of feelings and behaviors and labels them "disorders." Eugenics was first defined in 1883 by a cousin of Charles Darwin, Francis Galton: "the science of improvement of the human race . . . through better breeding." Respected scholars supported it, including British socialists George Bernard Shaw and Bertrand Russell. In the first decades of the 20th century, Charles Davenport, the most influential biological scientist of his day, presided over three eugenics institutions at Cold Spring Harbor, New York, then and now an esteemed research center.

Davenport, his colleague Laughlin, and leader in the American Eugenics Society Paul Popenoe collaborated with German eugenicists in the 1920s and '30s. Top financiers funded the eugenics movement, including the widow of railroad tycoon E.H. Harriman, the Carnegie Institute and Rockefeller Institute for Medical Research, the Ford and Kellogg foundations, J. P. Morgan, Procter and Gamble, and others. The Carnegie Institute and the Rockefeller Foundation financed German eugenicists, including Otmar Freiherr von Verschuer, who was Josef Mengele's mentor and collaborator during the infamous experiments on concentration camp prisoners during the Holocaust. The Nazis promulgated laws to promote "racial cleansing" and Laughlin translated them in *The Eugenical News*, for which he was awarded an honorary degree from the University of Heidelberg, while the American medical community praised Verschuer's work. The Nazi laws were published in the *Journal of the American Medical Association* and were accepted as if they were just a new medical treatment.

Here in America, the solutions recommended by prominent scientists were sterilization and even euthanasia. The eugenics movement started to wane when the depression struck, affecting people all along the socioeconomic spectrum and proving that misfortune befalls rich and poor alike. Yet between 1936 and 1960, two respected American neurologists, Foster Kennedy at Cornell and William G. Lennox of Harvard, persisted in promoting eugenics to sterilize the "feebleminded" and euthanize the "hopelessly unfit." They published in the *American Journal of Psychiatry*. One doctor, Leo Kanner, opposed them in 1942, and that journal belittled his contribution in an editorial.

As late as 1974, eugenics was still much alive in North Carolina. Between 1947 and 1974, the Eugenics Board ordered the sterilizations of more than 7,600 people, 2,000 of whom were under age 18. Most were against the wishes of the victims. In 1947 two prominent eugenicists, James Hanes (of hosiery fortune) and Clarence Gamble (Harvard-educated heir to Procter and Gamble fortune), funded massive IQ testing of 10,000 students in the Winston-Salem school system. Claims were made that a large number of students were "feeble-minded." Alarm spread throughout the state, and the Eugenics Board approved thousands of sterilizations. At the end of this period 99 percent of procedures performed were on women, over 60 percent of whom were black.

Sharav pinpoints the parallels between eugenicists' intent to excise bad genes by sterilization and government's intent today to improve "deficient" children through brain-altering medication. Her final paragraph is especially chilling. She states that German author Stefan Kuhl wrote in *The Nazi Connection* that Americans were intrigued by the idea of "a panacea that will cure human ills." Americans accepted eugenics and its methods; they were led to believe that laws supporting "racial purifying" and closing the nation's borders to "inferior hordes of degenerate peoples" were based on science. These "treatments" were the dominant model within the medical community, and scholars at leading universities endorsed them. All this illustrates that Americans are not immune to grossly misleading and dangerous trends. Eugenics and today's application of biological cures to a range of perceived mental disorders, based on bad science and supported by both the larger medical community and the government, bear ominous likenesses to each other.

CONCLUSION

I experienced conflicting emotions as I researched the material for this chapter. Early on I was led to read portions of House's *Philip Dru: Administrator*. I found it a compelling read as the biography unfolded of a young man with the most honorable ideals. The character started out as a West Point cadet who by fate could not serve in the army and instead became a social worker in the tenements of New York City's East side. He was driven to uplift the downtrodden by transforming the American economic, political, and social structure into one that equalized opportunities for all classes to pursue happiness and prosperity. Surely these ideals are worthy of aspiration. However, one glaring downside of the socialist movement prevails to this day. Its diversion into state control over families seems alive and well in the New Freedom Initiative. In a masquerade of benevolence, the state delegates caring human service workers the task of overseeing the development of citizens through their life cycle, starting with home visits to newborns. Those workers, however, don't know it's a masquerade; they really believe they are sent to do good work. And the really scary part is that the people in charge don't know it's a masquerade either.

It is a slippery slope upon which our current government rules. Reaching into the private lives of American families puts us at risk of repeating the mistakes of the past. In the early 20th century the eugenics movement, blended with the socialist ideal of state control over families, led to the incorporation of mental health into the schools in the 1940s. In turn, campaigns in the 1990s favored government takeover of child raising and, like all the above, today's New Freedom Initiative seeks to identify deficient children whom government will groom into superior beings.

—— 7 ——

Non-Drug Alternative Solutions

When fear, hate, greed, and the purely material conception of life passes out . . . and only wholesome thoughts will have a place in human minds, mental ills will take flight along with most of our bodily ills, and the miracle of the world's redemption will have been largely wrought.
—Colonel Edward M. House

MY HEALING

On our final school day of eighth grade, just before graduation from Guyton Elementary School, Kay Strangways and I wept for a good hour in the girls' lavatory before walking home. We'd attended this neighborhood school since kindergarten and were both in love with Mr. Deiss, our eighth grade teacher, who was indeed a gem of a man. I still remember with some sadness the sight of him walking away from the school that last day, briefcase in hand, down the sidewalk toward his home. Kay and I watched until he was out of sight. Then we fled to the lavatory.

Perhaps this was a prelude to the unhappiness that was to come the following fall when I entered the big world of the much larger Jackson Junior High School. While Guyton was a comfortable walking distance from home, Jackson was miles away. I had to take a city bus to get there. Most of the students at Jackson had started there in the seventh grade, but my elementary school went through eighth, so I was only at Jackson one year. It was hard to break into established social networks of kids I didn't know, although I eventually developed a few lasting friendships. Nevertheless, those few friends were no balm for the dark clouds gathering around me. Movies were the entertainment of that day, and there were theaters in our neighborhood. They were my escape that year. During the movie, I would be carried to another place where my daily travails fell away.

But when the movie ended, a feeling of dread descended over me with the falling curtain.

Perhaps my depression reached to my immune system. Toward the end of ninth grade, I came down with pneumonia. I think I was never so ill before or since. Our doctor, who practiced up the street, came to the house and gave me a penicillin shot the first day. It must have been a virus, as I was bedridden for a month. My mother nursed me with loving care. I remember sipping nutritious beverages through a bent straw because I wasn't able to negotiate a glass to my lips. She'd return from shopping trips to Jefferson Avenue, a block from our house, with ice cream sundaes that I was able to eat. She moved me into my brother's bed across the hall (he being away at college), from which I could view the street below. Now my mother was not great at listening. I would even have to say that rarely was I able to talk to her about anything that troubled me, at least if it had an emotional component. But she had a wonderful bedside manner. She would bring up her darning or knitting and sit by my bed just to keep me company; it didn't matter that we were mostly quiet.

Life improved after my pneumonia abated. For one thing, I had lost quite a few unwanted pounds; it was the beginning of that blessed "slimming down" my mother always promised. As I reminisce over that time, I think my mother nurtured away my depression. My physical illness provided her the opportunity to demonstrate her love through her devoted attention. Emotional distress, on the other hand, was something she seemed unable to deal with. I could not speak to her of my deeply felt unhappiness. I still don't know if she ever perceived how sad I often felt. But when my distress transformed to sickness, she knew just what to do.

This story came to mind as I contrasted how my childhood depression was alleviated back then versus how it might have been treated today. I don't recommend serious illness to get children the care they need, but I feel fortunate that my depression was resolved naturally, through loving care.

I cannot imagine addressing my childhood unhappiness with pills. Perturbing my brain with foreign chemicals would, at best, only have mesmerized me. Worse, pills might have exacerbated my emotional distress, or I might have commenced a path of lifelong dependence on chemical solutions to pain. In either case, the faulty family interactions would continue indefinitely. Ideally, my depression would have been acknowledged and addressed, but in the 1950s, it was uncommon for families to seek outside help. People handled their problems privately and coped, often quite successfully. Communication between my parents and me never really improved, but the opportunity my illness provided to feel loved and cared for lifted my spirits at a critical time.

If this had happened in the 1990s, it is likely my mother would have been unavailable to tend me as she did. I think growing numbers of children are troubled because they feel alone when in pain. I believe most parents lament the fact that their lives are so hectic they do not have enough time with their children. This is the real epidemic: Many families are caught up in frenzied activities that diminish a feeling of cohesion between members. The good news is that help for distressed children and families is more accessible today than in the 1950s, and that many viable treatment alternatives to psychiatric medications are available.

NON-DRUG SOLUTIONS TO CHILDHOOD DISTRESS

Howard Glasser's Nurtured Heart Approach[1]

Destructive interactional patterns often bring caregivers and their youngsters to counseling. I observed that power struggles, even between very young children and parents, were rife. Sometimes it seemed the children were in charge, while their parents just reacted—a no-win situation resulting in negative feelings all around. I was grateful for the introduction to Howard Glasser's Nurtured Heart Approach (NHA) in 2003 at a one-day workshop. His positive, gentle approach so impressed me that I ordered a carton of his books, *Transforming the Difficult Child: The Nurtured Heart Approach* and created a parent group for our clinic. Developing successful groups at public clinics is always a challenge. I received many referrals from our department of social services, probation, and family court of parents mandated for parent education. Others came voluntarily. My group was a participatory forum where we all learned from each other and all contributions were respected. Glasser's entertaining style commanded the attention of even the most resentful participants (no one likes being told they **have to** attend a group in order to retrieve their children from foster care). Metaphorical stories and an easy step-by-step process provide tools to facilitate positive communication with children. Ultimately, when NHA is applied consistently (which is of utmost importance), a child internalizes the desire to behave appropriately because he has learned that not breaking rules is far more rewarding than getting attention through misbehaving.

In 2004 I traveled to Tucson to participate in a five-day training with Glasser along with 25 other professionals from all over the country. Invigorated by the new knowledge that came with my certification as NHA trainer, I continued my group up to the last year of my employment in 2007. I received positive feedback from social service caseworkers and colleagues: Some of their referred people who attended other parent training programs preferred this one because it was upbeat and interesting. I think the respectful posture toward participants was empowering and esteem building. One father told me at the conclusion of the group that soon after the first session he gained so much insight into his self-defeating style of interacting with family members that he was transformed.

Glasser published *The Inner Wealth Initiative: The Nurtured Heart Approach for Educators*[2] in 2007. Tolson Elementary School in Tucson was mentioned earlier in this book as a success story for its students without the use of psychotropic drugs. In the seven years since NHA was introduced and the faculty trained, only one child was suspended, and no child was referred for an ADHD assessment or for medication. The number of students referred for special education services dropped from 15 percent to under 2 percent. Teacher attrition, previously at 50 percent annually, dropped to zero for the past three years as of

2007. Tolson's principal, Maria Figueroa, received regional recognition for the dramatic rise in test scores, even though she emphasizes they do not teach to the test. (She spoke to our group in Tucson.) Counselor Dawn Duncan-Lewis, of Skagit Discovery Center in Sedro-Woolley, Washington, reports similar impressive improvements in *The Inner Wealth Initiative* (pp. 2–4). She explained that this special school, "the last stop before institutionalization," gets the most challenging students from several school districts. Duncan-Lewis brought the NHA to the school, and faculty was trained over the summer. She reports that, within a few weeks of the new school year, the previously congested and chaotic halls were clear of students. Duncan-Lewis quantified the improvements by comparing incident reports after the first year to those of the previous year. For the seven most challenging students, the total incident reports numbered 518 for school year 2003–2004. For school year 2004–2005, the number was 94, an 82 percent improvement. Duncan-Lewis believes students are getting their needs met in the classrooms, by being appropriate instead of acting out in negative fashion. The benefit of NHA in schools is that it enhances the lives and learning of so many children simultaneously.

I recommend *Transforming the Difficult Child: The Nurtured Heart Approach* for parents and *The Inner Wealth Initiative: The Nurtured Heart Approach for Educators* for schools.

David B. Stein: Caregivers' Skills Program and the REST Program[3]

David Stein's Caregivers' Skills Program (CSP), in *Ritalin Is Not the Answer*, is designed for young children up to about age 12. Stein recommends that caregivers identify target behaviors and shape children's desired behaviors through social reinforcement (encouragement by positive attention rather than tangible rewards). His goals for children are to develop self-efficacy and internal control. This is accomplished through a strict system of time-out without warning or prompting. He is very clear why he believes punishment does more harm than good. At length and in detail, he describes how to apply three forms of discipline (to be distinguished from punishment). Once behavior is under control at home, Stein instructs how to improve school performance. But he notes that often problems at school resolve in pace with resolution of problems at home.

Stein's book, *Stop Medicating, Start Parenting: Real Solutions for your "Problem" Teenager*, explains the Real Economy System for Teens (REST). I attended Stein's presentation of this program at a conference of the International Center for the Study of Psychiatry and Psychology. It teaches parents to instill self-reliance, dependability, self-discipline, and responsibility in their teenagers. Parents accomplish this by establishing weekly expectations and providing an economy system contingent upon meeting those expectations. Stein helps parents help their teen to master the basics of home rules, and then to meet more complex expectations. He emphasizes the avoidance of force and confrontation. Parents are led through increasingly individualized steps to match their youngster's special needs or disposition. Stein is adept at pinpointing the most common sources of discord and telling caregivers how to resolve them. As with all programs, consistency on the part of parents is the key to success. Both of Stein's books have met with acclaim, and are fine resources for parents.

Other Books

In *The Myth of the A.D.D. Child*,[4] Thomas Armstrong offers fifty ways to improve behavior and attention span without drugs, labels, or coercion. I found his book very interesting reading. In *Curing ADD/ADHD Children*,[5] Peter Oas offers a psychodynamic, or therapeutic, approach through which parents are led to understand their own parts in their children's development and to deepen their relationships with their children. This approach is a departure from the behavior management techniques of other programs.

I'll describe two parenting approaches with very different views of the family. The first emphasizes the authority of parents and places them central to the family. The second is a child-centered approach that makes the children the focus.

John Rosemond has written a number of books about parenting. I own *A Six-Point Plan for Raising Happy, Healthy Children*.[6] Rosemond advocates traditional parenting as an alternative to the current trend toward child-centered parenting. I recommend the traditional approach, as research demonstrates the success of the model of authoritative parenting combined with a great deal of warmth, affection, and love. Its rationale is that parents require time alone with each other to nurture their own needs for intimacy and pursuits that feed their self-esteem, as opposed to pouring their energy into their children most hours of the day. Rosemond believes parents whose own needs are met are well equipped to meet the needs of their children. I believe too that children learn self-soothing and independence when they have time alone to explore their own private space. I notice often adults who think babies want to be held all the time. And when the baby starts to squirm and fuss, someone else will grab the baby, who still squirms and fusses. When my turn comes, I'll put the baby down in his carrier, and usually he stops fussing and enjoys just looking and listening to all that's going on around him. The baby seems relieved to have freedom and space to do his own thing. And everyone else in the room sighs with relief and resumes their enjoyment.

John Bowlby's *A Secure Base: Parent-Child Attachment and Healthy Human Development*[7] takes a 90-degree departure from Rosemond. Attachment parenting is an example of child-centered parenting, and was embraced by Cornell professor of human development Urie Bronfenbrenner, whose model is featured in chapter 8. The rationale often given by its proponents is that primitive cultures used attachment parenting; their babies were wrapped closely to their mothers constantly, were breast-fed long term, and bedded with parents. New parents often start out with the best intentions, and defend their desire to have the infant close at all times by citing "attachment parenting" and the experts who recommend it. But they run the risk of developing second thoughts about this arrangement.

They may find themselves feeling like hostages when, for example, they tire of co-sleeping and find the children adamantly opposed to sleeping alone. Or when the child becomes too heavy to wear constantly, she might feel abandoned when mother goes out of sight. Then parents may have to deal with a very upset and distressed child because she has not learned to self-soothe. But for parents who are prepared to stick with attachment parenting, I say, "Go for it." The children will feel loved and secure as long as it's done consistently, as is true for all parenting models that emphasize the love bond between parent and child.

Two Physicians' Alternative Approaches

Sami Timimi, Child Psychiatrist[8]

Sami Timimi, a child psychiatrist in the United Kingdom, wrote *Pathological Child Psychiatry and the Medicalization of Childhood* in 2003. Timimi slows down the assessment period and evaluates in three stages: the office visit with the whole family, the school visit, and the home visit. He elicits the child's positive qualities and asks parents and children for ideas about what might help. A strength-based therapist, he identifies the things parents are doing well, and encourages them to keep doing those things. He asks about times when the child is behaving appropriately and what is different about those times so they can duplicate situations that work for the child.

Timimi believes diet is important. He might prescribe supplements, most commonly a multivitamin and mineral preparation, and an essential fatty acid-based preparation. He, like others in succeeding pages, might recommend additive-free food (no preservatives, MSG, or dyes, for example), or a lactose-free or gluten-free diet. Timimi asks about lifestyle, such as exercise patterns, television-viewing, computer games, and social activities. He encourages activity-based groups. More than his professional expertise, Timimi lends great importance to local knowledge and old school advice that may have been handed down for generations, such as firm discipline, nurturing, spirituality, fresh air, and other old-fashioned, ageless, commonsense knowledge. Timimi describes himself as transparent. He operates on a level playing field, eliminates a hierarchical posture, admits if he is stumped, gets angry sometimes, and explains why.

Larry Diller, Behavioral Pediatrician

When I met Diller at the Point Park symposium, I expressed puzzlement regarding his eloquence in explaining reasons for not prescribing drugs to children, while at the same time prescribing stimulants. He good-naturedly admitted his ambivalence, and writes about it in *The Last Normal Child*.[9] He decries the use of antipsychotics and other newer powerful drugs. I never want children on drugs, but for parents who are intent on trying stimulants for their child, it is critical that these parents seek out a doctor like Diller. Like Timimi, his evaluations of children are complete and lengthy. In *Should I Medicate My Child?* he states,

"I believe the evaluation and treatment of children is neither complete nor ethical unless it looks beyond the symptoms, to the fullest possible understanding of a child's brain and behavior within the context of that child's world."[10] Diller evaluates in multiple visits that include the entire family: children and both parents (if available). He communicates directly with school personnel to get other perspectives and to offer suggestions that might enhance the child's success at school. Diller encourages parents to avoid thinking of their child as "disordered" and to focus on his strengths and ability to take responsibility for his actions. Then he asks them to provide a secure and loving presence, but also one that sets and maintains rules and limits. Diller remains available to support families over the long term to help maintain improvements.

Finding physicians like Diller and Timimi is a challenge. If the search for one is futile, families should seek therapists who have the freedom to practice according to their own unique and ethical standards. For those whose insurance covers a therapist in private practice, I suggest looking in the private sector. Therapists in clinics are generally constrained by agency protocols that promote a medical model (brief assessment, diagnosis, psychiatric referral, and, likely, medicine).

Parent Modeling and Training for Self-Control

DuBose Ravenel offers his "A Child of Competence and Character" curriculum,[11] a framework solidly grounded in research, both his own and that of others. His tenets combine his best selections from careful studies. D. Baumrind[12] concluded that the goal of parenting is to produce a child who is competent and of good character. His studies showed that parents who combine high nurturance with high demands—or powerful love with powerful discipline—achieve this goal most successfully. R. F. Baumeister et al.[13] conclude that high self-esteem is a good thing for a child to have *when it is a product of ethical behavior and worthy achievement.* On the other hand, self-esteem by itself can lead to detrimental characteristics such as narcissism. J. M. Strayhorn[14] asserts that self-control is a skill that children can be taught and that can aid in managing "vast amounts of psychopathology." D. A. Christakis, et al. and L. J. Stevens[15] demonstrated that self-control can be modeled and taught by parents. Whether a child displays the behaviors of ADHD or oppositional defiance, he can be trained and encouraged to develop self-control. Other enhancements for success without the use of drugs include: limited exposure to electronic media; healthy nutrition; and, in some cases, educational interventions such as *avoiding* early preschool formal instruction. Ravenel cites his own work and R. A. Marcon[16] with the latter advice about preschool. More about the cons of preschool are discussed in chapter 8.

Phonics

DuBose Ravenel, in a presentation at the 2007 annual convention of the International Center for the Study of Psychiatry and Psychology, offered an alternative for children who have difficulty learning to read. He lauded the old-fashioned method of teaching reading through pure phonics-based instruction. James Campbell, a pediatrician from Fulton, New York, is one of Ravenel's sources. Campbell has had success in helping children with severe reading difficulties and associated ADHD behavior by arranging for tutoring that applies the basic skills of phonics. In some cases this approach completely resolved ADHD behaviors when children finally experienced success, often after years of frustration.

Ravenel expounds further on older methods in a review of "The Right to Read" by Jan Strydon and Susan du Plessis, which he discovered on the Internet while seeking a better understanding of learning disabilities. Ravenel characterizes these authors' work as logical, intuitively understandable, and commonsensical. These two, like Ravenel himself, were puzzled by the pervasive and persistent presence of learning disabilities, despite an explosion of early intervention and remedial teaching in the schools. Strydon and du Plessis demonstrate that conventional methods have not reduced the incidence of learning disabilities. They offer, in Ravenel's words, "a disarmingly understandable and sound framework for conceptualizing and approaching the problem." Their ideas are based on: 1) learning is a "stratified process"—meaning that it is built upon sequential acquisition of skills and knowledge; 2) learning cannot occur without repetition—as in the old days, "drilling" is central to learning; and 3) application of skills. Strydon and du Plessis maintain that, since 1970, remedial programs have lacked the foundation building of skills necessary to master reading. Ravenel lauds the results of their approach. He recommends it to parents of children who struggle with reading the way it is currently taught, which he believes is unnecessarily complicated.

NATURAL ALTERNATIVES TO DRUGS

Dietary Adjustments

A great deal of documentation supports the significance of diet on behavior. Let me respond emphatically to the protest that special diets are expensive. I understand that for some families they may be too expensive. But minor alterations can be made to regular diets that, in fact, save money because some of the worst choices of foods are more expensive than healthy ones. For some families, changing priorities is imperative. Certain luxuries can be eliminated, like eating out, buying brand name clothing, buying expensive computer games, and the list goes on and on. The peace and happiness that well-behaved, content children contribute to the family is well worth the exchange, not to mention the physical health benefits of eating fresh organic foods.

My otherwise perfect young granddaughters can, at times, be prone to oppositional behavior and meltdowns. Their parents discovered certain foods triggered these behaviors. Their mother, Anna, researched and experimented with dietary solutions and discovered that a lactose- and gluten-free diet helps. Since we share lots of meals, I now cook to their requirements. It isn't as hard as it sounds at all. Gluten-free flours, made from rice (from unprocessed rice with intact hulls—brown is a good choice), quinoa, tapioca, pecan or almond meal, garbanzos, and others make very good substitutes for baking and thickening. Xanthan gum, just a pinch, can serve to hold batters together in place of gluten.

I have recommendations for all families. Milk with growth hormones and foods with dyes and other additives should be avoided. All people, especially children, should avoid high fructose corn syrup, as it is suspected to contribute to the surge of type II diabetes among Americans, including children. It is found in everything from juices to ketchup to yogurt. So read labels carefully before buying. Our family uses only evaporated cane sugar or honey, never processed sugar. It is more expensive, but children should not eat that much sugar in any event. Raw sugar (unprocessed) is less expensive than evaporated cane and is much preferred over processed. We eat well and enjoy a delicious variety of dishes.

Whenever possible, buy organic foods, both vegetables and meats. Conventional produce may have toxins, and meats are infused with antibiotics and growth hormones, both potentially dangerous, especially for children. Where I live, the prices of organic vegetables are approaching the prices of conventional. If you can't afford grass-fed meat or organically fed poultry, try eating less meat and chicken and increasing your intake of vegetables and grains. We shop at an Amish market where both can be bought at reasonable prices. We also joined a farm group (called a CSA, acronym for Community Supported Agriculture). For a cost per season, families get local organic produce weekly, year round.

For families starting out, or for those who choose less extreme changes, I suggest eliminating those especially offending ingredients such as high fructose corn syrup and dyes. Cut out junk food like packaged pastries and fast food. Children should avoid soft drinks such as colas and other carbonated sodas. Substitute natural fruit juices (but read the label—many contain that high fructose corn syrup!). Do this first, and see the difference it makes for your children's behavior or learning problem. If a problem persists, try eliminating lactose, glutens or corn, one at a time so you'll know which ingredient is causing the problem. Or consult a nutritionist at a local hospital or health center.

Research Supports the Dietary Solution

How to Raise a Healthy Child . . . in Spite of Your Doctor by Robert S. Mendelsohn was written in 1984, but its revelations still apply. Mendelsohn wrote, "More recently, there has been a mass of evidence that demonstrates a Feingold diet does work with many [ADHD] children." Benjamin Feingold, known as "the pioneer of dietary control of hyperactive behavior," observed that nervous system symptoms related to food hypersensitivity had been described repeatedly for at least half a century. As chief of the Allergy Clinics of Kaiser Foundation in California, his studies documented that food colorings, flavorings, preservatives, and stabilizers were especially offensive in causing hyperactive behavior in children. His studies have been duplicated; for example, William Crook, pediatrician and allergist at Children's Clinic in Jackson, Tennessee, found that food allergies accompanied ADHD three-quarters of the time. The most frequent offenders were milk and refined cane sugar. Also he found that corn, wheat, eggs, soy, citrus, and others exacerbated hyperactive behavior.[17]

"Hyper Kids? Check Their Diet" appeared in *Time* on September 24, 2007.[18] It said that research confirmed a long-suspected link between hyperactivity and food additives. It cited a study published in the British journal *Lancet* that showed a variety of common food dyes and the preservative sodium benzoate— found in many soft drinks, fruit juices, and salad dressings—cause some kids to become measurably more hyperactive and distractible. Jim Stevenson, professor of psychology at the University of Southampton, led the study involving about 300 typical (non-ADHD) children in two age groups: 3-year-olds and 8- and 9-year-olds. Children from each group were assigned to three groups. Each group drank fruit juice for a one-week period. One group's juice had the amount of dye and sodium benzoate typically found in a British child's diet. A second group had lesser concentrations of the additives in their juice, and the third group drank juice with no additives. Each child was evaluated for restlessness, lack of concentration, fidgeting, interrupting, and other typical ADHD behaviors. Children in both age groups were significantly more hyperactive when drinking juice with the typical amount of additives. Three-year-olds had a greater hyperactive response than the older kids to the juice with lower concentrations of additives. These children did vary in their degree of hyperactivity. Stevenson's research prompted Britain's Food Standards Agency to immediately warn parents to limit their children's intake of additives if they notice an effect on behavior.

"Outcome-based Comparison of Ritalin versus Food-Supplement Treated Children with ADHD" appeared in *Altern Medical Review* in August 2003.[19] Researchers compared a group of children treated with Ritalin to another group that received a mix of vitamins, minerals, phytonutrients, amino acids, essential fatty acids, phospholipids, and probiotics. They based their study on "eight known risk factors for ADHD: food and additive allergies, heavy metal toxicity and other environmental toxins, low-protein/high carbohydrate diets, mineral imbalances, essential fatty acid and phospholipid deficiencies, amino acid deficiencies, thyroid disorders, and B-vitamin deficiencies." The children's improvements in the supplement group exactly matched those in the Ritalin group. I would point out, though, that for many children the effects of Ritalin are short term, while supplements are likely to provide a long-term solution. Chapter 8 reveals more about the deficiencies noted by the researchers in the study.

Fatty Acids as Supplements for ADHD and Learning

Fatty acids, most common in fish oils, are essential for brain development. The Oxford-Durham study was published in the journal *Pediatrics* in May 2005. Its authors, A. J. Richardson and P. Montgomery, experimented with fatty acids omega-3 and omega-6 on children ages 5 to 12 with developmental coordination disorder (affecting motor skills). Of the 117 children, 32 were diagnosed with

ADHD. Divided in half, one group was given supplements consisting of 80 percent fish oil and 20 percent evening primrose, together providing omega-3 and some omega-6 fatty acids. The other group was given a placebo (olive oil). Evenly divided, 16 children in each group had the ADHD diagnosis. While the fatty acids had no effect on the motor skill disorder, their effect on ADHD was significant. In the group receiving the fatty acids, 7 of the 16, after three months, no longer displayed symptoms of ADHD. Only 1 of the 16 in the placebo group no longer met the criteria for ADHD. After the first three months, children in the placebo group were also administered the same dose of fatty acids. At the end of this period, the ADHD children in this group achieved similar improvement as the group receiving the supplements all along. And in that group, the improvements were maintained or accelerated. The improvements were observed in reading, spelling, and behavior.

Exercise

Michael Wendt, superintendent of the Wilson Central School District in Niagara County, New York, studied the effect of aerobic exercise on children diagnosed with ADHD.[20] Wendt explained that aerobic exercise increases healthy chemicals like endorphins, dopamine, epinephrine, and serotonin, and increases blood flow to the brain, which is very important for brain development. In his study the overall behavior of children improved after only two weeks, and continued to improve throughout the six-week program. Most notable was the drop in conflict and oppositional behaviors.

Newfield Central Schools in rural upstate New York adopted a six-week pilot program for fourth- and fifth-graders based on Wendt's study.[21] Physical education teachers Christine Williams and David Green introduced "KEEP 57," short for "kid's early exercise program, five to seven days a week." They sought a natural solution to rising behavioral problems in the school, as opposed to medication. Students chosen for the project had high rates of disciplinary referrals and/or rated high for ADHD traits. Ten of the 40-minute exercise sessions five days a week included aerobic workouts to keep heart rates between 135 and 175 beats per minute. I spoke with Newfield Elementary School principal Vicki Volpicelli in August 2008 for a follow-up interview. She reported that the children who stuck with KEEP 57 showed improvements. But she believes results were somewhat disappointing because the teachers didn't get commitment from parents. They wanted to run the program in the morning before the start of school, but parents were not willing or able to make their children available that early, so kids had to perform the exercises at 3 o'clock in the afternoon. Also, parents did not provide extra encouragement to children who refused to fully participate during the program. However, the school continues to incorporate movement and exercise into the curriculum. Classroom teachers collaborate with physical education teachers to have movement breaks during academic periods, such as performing jumping jacks. And during recess, aerobic exercises are organized for part of the period. Volpicelli reported that fewer children at Newfield now take psychotropic drugs than five years ago. She said Newfield school staff never recommend drugs, but non-drug alternative suggestions are offered parents of challenging children.

In March 2009 I heard a report on NPR's *Morning Edition* regarding movement being incorporated into classroom agendas. Research supports this trend.

Neurokinesiologist (movement specialist) Jean Blaydes Madigan[22] states that movement enhances focus and attention, spatial awareness, and motor skills that are foundations for reading. It can bring a lethargic or hyperactive child back into balance. Instead of sitting for hours loading up on academics, students should have movement breaks. Madigan cites Eric Jensen's *Teaching with the Brain in Mind* and *Learning with the Body in Mind*[23] as sources of research summaries that support her statements. One was a study by Caterino and Polak in 1999 that suggests physical exercise, like jumping and aerobic game playing, has a definite impact on children's frontal lobed primary brain areas, those responsible for mental concentration, planning, and decision-making. Madigan explains that exercise increases the flow of blood that feeds the needed nutrients of oxygen and glucose to the brain. Lack of oxygen, she says, results in disorientation, confusion, fatigue, poor concentration, and memory problems.

Madigan suggests a possible link between violent behavior and early motor development. Infants deprived of stimulation through touch and handling may fail to develop the movement-pleasure link in the brain because of lack of connection between the cerebellum (movement center) and the pleasure/pain centers. So an inactive child may be unable to experience pleasure in the way a typical child does. The outcome may be the development of an intense state of behavior, such as violence. She says the good news is that the child can develop the ability to experience pleasure by becoming active and engaging in exercises like tag games, flag football, and sports, under adult supervision.

The Guardian of May 20, 2004,[24] reported on a study that showed exercise helped children with dyslexia, ADD, and ADHD. Researchers at Exeter University in the United Kingdom provided students at a primary school with twice-daily exercises designed to stimulate the cerebellum part of the brain, which is understood to be responsible for balance and coordination. Researchers have come to believe it may also be responsible for the way in which reading and writing become automatic processes. The exercises included balancing techniques, such as balancing on a wobbly board, or juggling objects from one hand to the other. The study lasted two years, at the end of which pupils with learning difficulties had improved faster than did their "normal" peers during that time, as well as the year after. They remained behind the peers academically, but their improvement was characterized as remarkable. Teachers noticed dramatic improvements in the children after only six weeks of participation. For example, one child mentioned enjoyed a marked increase in self-esteem; he started expressing himself more, in both spoken and written words.

In August 2007, the *New York Times*[25] reported that a study at the Salk Institute for Biological Studies showed that mice with running wheels in their cages had superior spatial memory and cognitive processing speed than those that did not exercise. Neuroscientist Fred H. Gage and colleagues made another remarkable discovery when the brains of these mice were examined following euthanasia. Through a technique using dye, they detected the creation of new neurons (neurogenesis). In other words, their brains were regenerating themselves. The mice that exercised showed many more new neurons, two to three times more.

Next the scientists at Salk investigated humans to see if the same phenomenon occurs. They studied the brain tissue of deceased cancer patients who donated their remains to science. They, too, showed evidence of neurogenesis. It is very difficult to study the brains of living people. But the article goes on to report that neuroscientists at Columbia University in spring 2007 studied humans with the aid of functional MRIs (magnetic resonance imaging). Humans, ages 21 to 45, who worked out for one hour four times a week demonstrated much higher volumes of blood flow to a part of the brain responsible for neurogenesis. In particular, the hippocampus received almost twice the blood volume as before the exercise regimen. The hippocampus is largely responsible for how mammals create and process memories, and plays a role in cognition. The study yielded another discovery: The subjects who exercised took in greater amounts of oxygen during exercise. The subjects with the greatest increases in oxygen consumption showed the best improvement in memory, measured by a word-recall test.

The article reports that still another study, at the University of Illinois, demonstrated that elderly people who did aerobic (walking) exercise for at least one hour three times a week showed significant growth in several areas of their brains (reversing brain shrinkage that occurs with age). The scientists believe the study suggests that exercise can stimulate the brain not only to produce new cells but also to add new blood vessels and strengthen neural connections, allowing new neurons to integrate themselves into the neural network.

What does this have to do with children? The scientists cite colleagues at the University of Illinois who demonstrated that children similarly benefit from aerobic exercise. It promotes their ability to process information more efficiently and perform better on standardized tests. Exercise is good for the brain at any age.

When students have the opportunity for unstructured time out of doors, or in large spaces indoors in inclement weather, they seem to engage in running and other forms of aerobic exercise naturally. Pediatrician Romina Barros documented the value of recess[26] in a study published in the journal *Pediatrics* in 2009. She found that children who had even 15 minutes of recess a day behaved better in class. She noted some studies document a dramatic decrease in recess time since No Child Left Behind was implemented in 2001. Ironically, low test scores of American students prompted legislation that led schools to cut back free time in order to avoid penalties associated with low test scores. They cut back on the very component of the school day that helps students perform better academically. Countries that demonstrate high scores, such as Japan and Finland, provide

10- to 15-minute free play after every 40 to 50 minutes of academic time. Experts say children learn as much on breaks as they do in traditional classrooms, experimenting with creativity and imagination and interacting socially. Barros quotes pediatric psychiatrist Jane Ripperger-Suhler: "Conflict resolution is solved on the playground, not in the classroom."

ANIMAL THERAPY

Pets

I was visiting family in Owings Mills, Maryland, with my two dogs, Leo and Sparky. We were walking along a small outdoor mall when we encountered a lady who showed great interest in the two miniature poodles. I explained that they were registered therapy dogs. Introductions were exchanged, and Marie told me about her 12-year-old twin grandsons, Lonnie and Benjamin, who are autistic. She said the boys' parents depend on the family dog, a black lab named Chester, to calm the boys when they get out of control. When a meltdown is about to occur, the parents call for Chester. Chester approaches the room where the boy is, sits, sighs, and surveys the situation. Then he goes to work. If it's Lonnie, he approaches the boy very calmly and sits on him. On the other hand, if it's Benjamin, Chester snuggles up with him and licks his face. This remarkable dog knows what works for each boy. He is not a formally trained service or therapy dog; he's just a natural.

Resources on therapy dogs can be found on the Internet. I located some useful books at http://www.workingdogs.com/book031.htm. It is also possible to choose a family dog for temperament, complete a basic obedience training course, and then find an organization online, such as Therapy Dogs International or Delta, and receive special training for assisting children.

Service dogs are not to be confused with therapy dogs. Service dogs are specially trained to assist children or adults with disabilities. In the news recently was a dog trained to sense peanuts in any form. She went everywhere with her elementary school-aged mistress, who had a very severe allergy to peanuts. Dogs have an uncanny ability to sense all kinds of danger, such as a child who is about to have a seizure. A list of organizations through which a service dog can be obtained in each of the United States can be accessed at http://www.inch.com/~dogs/service.html. A number of service dog resources for children diagnosed with autism are also available online.

Unconditional attachment and loyalty make the animal/human bond very therapeutic. I recommend pets for relief of enduring stress or distress in children and adults. If a dog is not possible, a cat or rabbit can also be therapeutic, or even a small animal: a hamster, a gerbil, or a carefully chosen bird.

Dogs as Co-therapists

In chapter 3 I mentioned my therapy dog, Solo, who assisted me at the mental health clinic until he passed away in 2004. Staff and clients alike shared my grief at his loss. Solo accompanied me to Tucson for the Nurtured Heart Approach training with Howard Glasser. The training included a demonstration by a family who practiced the Nurtured Heart Approach. One of the daughters was electively mute. She had not spoken outside of the home, and rarely there, for a couple of years. She was not about to speak in front of all of us. However, she was quite taken with Solo. I offered her his leash, and as she walked him around the conference room, she was heard talking softly to him.

Leo commenced his training at our clinic as a 10-week-old puppy, soon after Solo's demise. One of his first clients was 5-year-old Jerold who very recently discovered his twin brother had died in his sleep. Being so young, he was unable to verbalize or process his suffering. I mentioned to Jerold that I had also recently lost my best friend, Solo. Jerold's translation was that Leo lost a brother, like he did. Very soon he was lying on the floor, head to head with Leo. He talked intimately with Leo, about both their losses, their wishes to bring their brothers back to life, and how it felt to be suddenly alone. Leo was attentive and responded lovingly. Even though he was only a puppy, he was learning how to do his work.

Children also benefited from a cat that a colleague brought to work. Another colleague brought mice and small animals in cages, and even these drew some children out of their shells.

MEDITATION

Some schools are using transcendental meditation (TM) for kids diagnosed with ADHD. Reporter for Carolina 14 News, Casey Taylor, updated a previous video newscast titled "Meditation Can Reduce Bouts of ADHD" on November 25, 2006. Neuropsychologist William Stixrud and educator Sarina Grosswald were interviewed. Stixrud explained that TM allows one to experience very profound levels of relaxation while wide awake. Children sit with their eyes closed for 10 minutes, twice a day, while focusing on a mantra. Several children were shown testifying about how this easy and effective technique also makes them feel good. Studies on kids with ADHD behaviors by Grosswald and Stixrud demonstrated a 45 to 50 percent reduction in stress, anxiety, and depression among the study participants.

The researchers noted that organization, memory, strategizing skills, mental flexibility, and attention improved, while impulsivity decreased. Grosswald said the results exceeded her expectations. She explained that during TM there is increased blood flow to the brain (the same beneficial effect as exercise). Taylor reported that other studies have shown that TM can lower blood pressure and even increase IQ in children without ADHD. The researchers said the benefits for ADHD children run much deeper and they would like to see TM in all schools. Parents can access information about TM at www.tm.org to locate trainers for themselves, their children, or their school. A short video at that site corroborates the reports of Grosswald and Stixrud with a study in a Detroit school by University of Michigan researchers.

WRAPAROUND PROGRAMS

Peter Breggin applauds the concept of "wrapping around the child."[27] He described the Alaska Youth Initiative, where the most difficult and often most violent youngsters were treated. To qualify, everything else had to have failed. This kind of program takes over the care of the youngster as an alternative to long-term institutionalization. The basic tenets are keeping the youth in the community and providing everything his family and the community need in order to do this. Wraparound is less costly than long-term institutional care.

Many communities in the United States have wraparound services. Counties with good financial resources are able to meet the needs of both child and family. In Tompkins County, New York, a Family Resolutions Project was established in 1997. This partnership between the department of social services and Cornell University teaches strength-based techniques to county caseworkers—a departure from the traditional approach that most families find intimidating and punitive. Children targeted might be persons in need of supervision (PINS), or they might be in foster care. Family group gatherings meet early in treatment, usually in the home of the child. Every significant person in the child's life is invited: relatives, teachers, friends, anyone with a stake in the child's welfare. A professional facilitates the conference. Everyone shares a meal, gets acquainted, and then identifies the strengths and needs of the child and her family. Everyone participates in setting goals. Then all professionals leave so the significant others can make a plan to achieve the goals. This is very empowering to families. Helpers, who might be people who attended the conference or trained parent advocates, aid in the achievement of the goals. They collaborate with family members to provide recreational activities, transportation, and other services. They are go-betweens for the family and professionals. A crucial tenet of wraparound treatment is that the caregivers are in it for the long haul. Sometimes this means years, waiting for a probation period to end, or even an incarceration. The family is never abandoned.

Unfortunately, many counties lack the financial resources to meet this model. In the economically depressed county where I worked, the program called "wraparound" did not match the concept. But even its bare-bones program did help some children and families due to the efforts of some dedicated people.

Breggin points out that medication is not eschewed in wraparound. Virtually all the children eligible for the program in our clinic had been on medication cocktails for years. One could hope that an empowered family would eventually tell their doctor it was time to gradually discontinue the medications.

I end with a Breggin remark about wraparound: "The approach requires personal self-restraint on the part of the adult rather than restraint of the child. The aim is to break the cycle of unfulfilled needs and mutual coercion, by reaching out with love against the onrush of anger and violence."[28]

COMMUNITY ORGANIZING

Community organizing helps children indirectly by empowering their communities from the ground up. Community organizers come in many guises, but always they strive to empower people who face oppression or poverty. An example was Adrienne Anderson,[29] a professor at the University of Colorado, who helped citizens in a Colorado community whose children were dying mysteriously. When neither big business nor the government would reveal the source of the deadly malady, she organized the citizens to perform their own investigation. They discovered deadly pollution of the water supply that authorities had known about all the time. They got the water supply shut down so that babies no longer suffered fetal defects. The complete story is told in the next chapter.

As a young Columbia University graduate in the 1980s, President Obama chose community organizing on Chicago's south side over a traditional job. Most residents had lost their jobs when steel mills shut down. We are witnessing in 2009 the same phenomenon as that community experienced in the '80s: The consequences of unemployment reverberate deep into the community and into the lives of families. *The Nation*[30] featured a story about Obama's work with the Developing Communities Project in Chicago. Obama organized citizens to accomplish the protection of community interests regarding landfills. Against the odds of corrupt officials, he led a group of citizens to obtain asbestos removal from their apartments. He helped build playgrounds and develop afterschool programs. He inspired school reform, and helped create employment training services.

Community organizing accomplishes positive goals of the New Freedom Initiative: self-determination, infrastructure building, and grassroots reform, goals that David Fisher advocated for in chapter 5. It has the potential to interrupt cycles of poverty. Community organizing is not a panacea, though. Obama decided he could be more effective in higher levels of office. However, unlike mental screening, community organizing reaches to the roots of poverty and disenfranchisement that jeopardize children's development.

EARLY NON-DRUG INTERVENTIONS

Quakers and Moral Treatment

Robert Whitaker[31] traces very early movement in the revolutionary idea that severe emotional distress is best treated with kindness, good nutrition, constructive activity, and a clean, pleasant environment. Traditional inhumane methods of treating the insane up to 1750 were first challenged by Quakers in England, who believed the insane were entitled to the amenities mentioned above. Quakers brought this approach to America in the 1800s with impressive results. Their institutions were kept small, their caretakers were carefully selected to be respectful, and the patients were stimulated with pleasantries in their physical surroundings and intellectual pursuits. They spared no expense in providing the best care. Many people were released fully cured and went on to lead normal lives. Ironically, a heroine in the fight for humane treatment, Dorothea Dix, in-advertently brought an end to this Moral Treatment. So brilliant was her activism that the institutions expanded and became very large. But necessary to the success of the Moral Treatment was keeping the institutions small so that treatment providers could maintain the quality of care and keep expense manageable. The quality diminished rapidly when institutions greatly expanded in size. Medical people again usurped care of the insane after the Civil War. Once the war veterans were taken care of, these doctors took over the care of psychiatric patients and the medical model flourished again. To justify their roles as scientific healers, they needed to believe in a biological or neurological cause of mental illness. So they revived the notion that mental illness was caused by brain lesions and the like.

World Health Organization Studies[32]

The studies discussed below concern adults diagnosed with schizophrenia, but they support non-drug treatment alternatives, and the drugs implicated are the powerful antipsychotics long prescribed to adults, and now liberally prescribed to very young children.

The World Health Organization (WHO) compared outcomes for people diagnosed with schizophrenia. The United States and four other developed countries were compared to the poor countries of Nigeria, India, and Colombia. It was discovered that patients in the poor countries had dramatically better outcomes than those in developed countries. A 1969 study showed that after five years, about 64 percent of patients in the poor countries were cured and functioning well. But in the developed countries, about the same percentage of patients were doing poorly. So dubious were these results that another study was undertaken using more scrupulous methods and controlling for more variables. The results were published in 1992. Outcomes were the same; people in poor countries had far higher rates of recovery. Having ruled out all other factors, the only explanation for the difference was that the poor countries did not have ready access to neuroleptic (antipsychotic) medication. Sixteen percent were maintained on these drugs in those countries, versus 61 percent in the developed countries. The only feasible explanation is that these drugs kept people sicker. This has been a bitter pill for the psychiatric profession and the pharmaceutical companies. Schizophrenia had always been considered incurable, "a brain disease." Now we know that it is curable, especially with minimal drug use. Yet Robert Whitaker's statistics show that 92 percent of all people in America diagnosed with schizophrenia in 1998 were taking antipsychotic medication.

The Soteria Project[33]

Loren Mosher's convictions about treating schizophrenia were in harmony with Moral Treatment and the results of the World Health Organization studies. As director of schizophrenia research at the National Institute of Mental Health, he opened Soteria (Greek for deliverance) House, a small residential treatment center in California. It operated between 1971 and 1983. A second residence, Emanon, operated for a shorter time. These projects employed kindness, friendship, as little medication as possible, and "being with" instead of "doing to" against the symptoms of schizophrenia. Their results were compared to outcomes in a traditional community mental health treatment facility (that prescribed antipsychotic drugs).

Non-professionals cared for the six individuals who were struggling with extreme emotional distress at Soteria House. Caregivers were screened for compassion, optimism, tolerance, and interest in reaching out to residents as friendly peers. Antipsychotic drugs were administered only minimally, at low doses and for a short time to manage extreme psychosis. Mosher assigned independent researchers from outside the project to compare outcomes. After six weeks, Soteria residents were improving at the same rate as those in traditional care. But they were staying well longer. At both one-year and two-year follow-ups, relapse rates were lower for the Soteria group. And they were functioning better socially, attending school and working. The psychiatric establishment did not like these results. Mosher was accused of being "antiscientific." Gradually his funding was decreased until it was virtually withdrawn altogether. A temporary reprieve came in the way of a different funding stream. But when the results of the ongoing experiment continued to show Soteria treatment superior to that of traditional care, further funding became contingent upon his being replaced by another investigator. Finally, even though authorities admitted that non-professional care like that administered at Soteria could do as well as a more conventional community mental health program, the project was shut down. Mosher was pushed out of the National Institute of Mental Health. He responded with an eloquent letter of resignation to the American Psychiatric Association.

Robert Whitaker speaks of envying the caregivers of Soteria residents: "They had the unique opportunity to 'be with' unmedicated people who were battling with 'madness.' They clearly learned a great deal from this experience . . ." Of the gift bequeathed by Loren Mosher, who died much too soon, he said, "The disappearance of a place like Soteria from our society is not just a loss for those who might find a refuge there, but also for those who work in the field of 'mental health.'"[34]

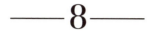

—8—

Other Voices Explain Rising Rates of Childhood Distress

The harder we work to demonstrate the power of heredity, the harder it is to escape the potency of experience . . . the way to intervene in human lives and improve them, to ameliorate mental illness, addictions and criminal behavior, is to enrich impoverished environments . . .

—W. Herbert

My eldest granddaughter, Rosa, had dinner with me the other night. During our conversation, she said, "Even though I wasn't there, I long for the 1950s. Tell me what it was like growing up then." Rosa was born in 1978. I was glad to tell her how, although I grew up in a big city, I had community. We bought our clothes at local shops along Jefferson Avenue, within blocks of home. I walked to school and home for lunch every day. After school my friends and I had free play in the neighborhood. We knew all the neighbors and they didn't mind us running through their yards, playing hide and seek. We organized our own baseball games and made up lots of imaginary games as well. We had a "monkey club" that met in my friend's silver maple tree.

Rosa agreed that was a contrast from today's scenario for kids. But she said that wasn't it. Because she had a great childhood too, growing up in the beautiful Shenandoah Valley and having a mom who worked from home. She said, "Children now know too much for their age. What happened to happy-go-lucky innocence?" Then I added to my chronicle that, indeed, as a child I had none of the technology to burden me with information. We were protected from the ills of society and premature worry about sex and other worldly matters.

James Garbarino, professor of child development at Cornell University and author of *Raising Children in a Socially Toxic Environment*, narrates a similar theme.[1] He said children today pine for what we older adults experienced growing up, like the examples I mentioned above. His phrase "toxic environment" captures that loss of innocence as well. I recommend his book to parents. Garbarino is one of those voices that explains why our children are distressed and that offers suggestions for protecting them from noxious influences.

QUESTIONS

How do computers and television impact the neurotransmitter functions in young children that might contribute to attention problems? Does academic pressure, especially at preschool levels, set the brain up for later imbalances? What is the effect of exercise, versus the lifestyle of a couch potato, on the functionality of the brain? And what part do environmental factors—physical, emotional, or cognitive—play in the current "epidemic" of childhood disabilities and disorders? Educational psychologist Jane Healy laments how little attention has been paid these questions, despite their pressing nature. We return to Healy later in this chapter.

First we'll hear other voices of reason and common sense from fields of medicine, psychology, environmental science, education, and child development. I believe they put to rest the simplistic neurobiological explanation of the "epidemic" of disturbed children and its corollary of treatment with psychotropic drugs. These scientists and scholars do not negate the role of neurobiology, but identify multiple factors outside the child that may cause alterations in the very plastic brains of young children.

ONE PHYSICIAN'S SUMMARY

I recently heard a replay of physician Stephen Bezruchka's 2006 address on NPR, "Is America Driving You Crazy?"[2] Bezruchka specializes in population health, societal hierarchy, and their application to health. This provides him a unique perspective on what he calls the "plague of mental illness" across America. Like Robert Whitaker, he observes that since 1987, when Prozac became a household name and many "wonder drugs" followed, rates of mental illness have escalated dramatically. He too asks if the medicine is making us sicker. He has other theories as well. Bezruchka talks about right brain development in the first year of life that facilitates early bonding through visual connection with primary caregivers. He believes American babies are often deprived the opportunity to bond with parents in those crucial early months because for many families economic necessity forces both parents to work. But in many countries babies are not deprived under the same circumstances. Bezruchka compares America to a system in Sweden where mothers are *required* to take a year's leave with full pay after childbirth, and can opt for a second year at 80 percent pay. Fathers are given twelve weeks' leave with full pay. After that, the government provides day care facilitated by master's level professional childcare workers.

Bezruchka believes the economic hierarchy in this country also contributes to high levels of emotional distress: for example, widespread poverty and the uneven delivery of health care, compared to other developed countries. He anticipates an unstable future with factors of war, global warming, advanced technology, and globalization; we face all of these with fewer family and community ties.

The remainder of this chapter takes an in-depth view of the issues raised by Bezruchka and other experts. Other voices offer logical explanations for the rising rates of troubled children in America. Their voices deliver the final chinks in the armor of "brain disease" theory and underscore the fallacy of medication as solution. They identify the social and environmental causes of childhood distress. Solutions to these causes of distress remain complicated and highly challenging. Parents, families, and ordinary citizens must demand they be given the highest priority. With a reallocation of tax monies and realignment of political agendas, the solutions are attainable.

AN ECOLOGICAL PERSPECTIVE

Child development professor Jeanne Stolzer summarizes Cornell professor of human development Urie Bronfenbrenner's bioecological model of three systems that impact on human development, and applies it to ADHD.[3] The microsystem consists of family and close associates. Stolzer identifies methods of parenting from primitive times, still practiced in some societies, that promote parent/child bonding. Attachment parenting, as it is known, consists of long-term breast-feeding, child-led weaning, co-sleeping, and being in close and continuous proximity to parents or other family caregivers.

Stolzer highlights the benefits of long-term breast-feeding, which often means up until age 4. Studies have shown that during lactation, when breast milk is being produced, hormones secreted by the pituitary gland reduce anxiety, as they enhance maternal nurturing and a desire to be physically close to the infant. Stolzer refers to the special relationship enjoyed by mother and infant during this extended period of breast-feeding as a "dance." She suggests that when this "dance" is disrupted, as it has been in American modern society, a mother's perception is altered, possibly "opening the door for the unprecedented acceptance of ADHD in America." She cites studies such as Maslow's of 1946[4] that concluded breast-fed children displayed significantly fewer behavioral problems than artificially fed cohorts. She cites the 1949 work of Holloway[5] that demonstrated breast-fed children were more pro-social and more apt to engage in self-regulation. Other researchers, she says, have determined that human milk is a dynamic substance that changes day by day according to the needs of its infant consumer. Linkages between breast-feeding and ADHD have not been established, but the United States has the lowest breast-feeding rates in the world, and the surgeon general decreed in 2000 that it must increase in order to ensure optimal developmental processes for both infants and mothers. When one ponders the eons of evolution that led to close parent/infant ties, the departure from practices that nurture those ties is cause for concern, considering the differences it has wrought in the typical American family.

In Bronfenbrenner's mesosystem, linkages occur between two or more settings and the developing child. These can include day care settings, schools, and the workplace. Contrasting the traditions of parenting in days past with practices in America today makes parents seem almost dispensable, states Stolzer. This is evidenced by the assumption that children and parents can be separated from each other during most of children's formative years, and still be well connected with each other. She cites Fogel: In 2001, 75 percent of American infants under the age of 12 months were in full-time non-parental care.[6] This situation worsens with the lack of federal regulations regarding training or education for day care workers. They are poorly paid, receive little if any benefits, and report high stress levels.

Stolzer refers to ethologists (animal behaviorists) who have demonstrated repeatedly that any other mammalian species so separated from its primary caregivers suffers catastrophic consequences in the attachment process. She asks why it is assumed that working and mothering cannot occur simultaneously. Some workplaces have responded by providing childcare centers in close proximity to parents. It's a start, but Stolzer highlights the recommendations of Baumslag and Michels: expanded national policies that would promote attachment parenting.[7] Examples are a federally mandated maternal health policy that includes guaranteed job reinstatement, flexible work schedules, flextime, part-time work, working from home, and guaranteed parental leave options.

Stolzer turns to our schools, another important component of the mesosystem, and one that is failing kids. Like so many child development experts, she disparages the trend of cutting back on physical education and decreasing recess time. She cites Pellegrini,[8] who documents that children who engage in large motor outdoor activity several times in the course of a day exhibit significantly fewer behavioral problems. Yet staying in from recess is a regular, approved method of punishment in many schools.

The exosystem consists of linkages and processes taking place between two or more settings, at least one of which does not contain the developing person, but in which events occur that influence the person's setting. Stolzer's examples include the pharmaceutical industry's vested economic interest in promoting ADHD. Its rampant presence in the media has virtually convinced parents that ADHD is a "brain disease," and that it has nothing to do with parenting, schooling, national policies, or cultural ideologies. She finds even more disturbing the economic alliance that exists between the pharmaceutical industry and the medical community. Besides noting the financial incentives to physicians for prescribing psychotropic drugs, she cites the drug industry's financial support of CHADD, the organization of Children and Adults with ADHD, which openly promotes the chemical infiltration of children's brains. Last, Stolzer puts the U.S. government on her list of exosystem offenders in its role of promoting the mental screening of all schoolchildren through the so-called New Freedom Initiative. That topic comprises chapter 5.

Exosystem Stirs Conjecture about Evolution

Finally, the overarching patterns found in a culture comprise the macrosystem. Bronfenbrenner hypothesized that these include the ideologies, activities, world-views, and belief systems that determine the blueprint of a particular culture. Stolzer points out how differently the beliefs about children have been perceived over time. Once considered normal traits of children, rambunctiousness and high energy are now attributed to "disordered brains." She asks how, in the space of a few decades, the brains of American children could become neurologically impaired. Neurologist Fred Baughman assures us that children's brains have not become diseased within the span of one generation.[9]

Glasser, author of the Nurtured Heart Approach[10] model described in chapter 7, reframes so-called hyperactivity using terms like super-energized, enthusiastic, exuberant, and spontaneous—traits that can be great assets when channeled positively. If childhood traits are incompatible with a society that **has** changed in a generation, we should examine the society's influence on the developing brain.

Stolzer identifies changes in the 21st century that indeed create an environment incompatible with these potentially advantageous traits. Children now are encouraged to engage in sedentary activities: watching television, playing computer games, attending preschools that inhibit spontaneity, and spending less time in free play out of doors. Stolzer credits John Bowlby[11] for his observation that boys have been especially targeted because, from the evolutionary perspective, they were socialized to be extremely active, combative, physical, and protective as a function of preserving the species. Peter Jensen and his colleagues[12] also suggested that ADHD behaviors were adaptive in what he termed "a pathological" environment. Now these ancient male traits have been categorized as pathological. Stolzer adds that we have responded by constructing a mythical brain disorder and applying psychotropic drugs to change the male brain so boys' behavior will comply with new cultural scripts.

CHEMICAL TOXINS IN THE ENVIRONMENT

Environmentalists Varda Burstyn and David Fenton[13] identify socio-cultural forces that are causing the following troubling trends among growing numbers of American children: failure to thrive, increases in youth violence, emotional volatility, depression, neuro-developmental disorders, substance abuse, and plummeting educational achievement. The authors describe the devastating impact of synthetic chemicals—ubiquitous in our environment—on children's development. They focus on a few of many pollutants known to compromise children's neurological development and mental health: a group of toxins called persistent organic pollutants (POPS), lead, and mercury. They mention the huge health implications for children of the sex hormone-disrupting effects of

POPS—usually known for neurological harm. Girls are victims of precocious puberty, while boys are victims of delayed sexual development. Both put children at risk of emotional problems. Although the threats of global warming, extreme weather, water shortages, and other significant environmental challenges are not central to their treatise, the authors acknowledge that all serious environmental health problems compromise the emotional well-being of children and put them at risk of inappropriate psychotropic drugging. For example, toxic mold—a contaminant of homes and schools—can jeopardize academic performance and cause depression due to the effect of mold on the immune and nervous systems. Another example is petroleum-based food additives, shown to provoke extreme reactions in many children, from ADHD-like symptoms to storms of temper often attributed to "bipolar" disorder. It is misguided treatment that attempts to mask these reactions with medication instead of removing the mold in buildings or eliminating the offending additives in food.

Nearly everywhere studies have been done, high levels of persistent chemical and agricultural contaminants have been found in our waterways, soil, and air. *The Globe and Mail*[14] released the results of a special study on flame retardants: These chemicals were found not only in soil and water, but also in food, household carpets, and dust bunnies under beds. Given such omnipresence, it is no wonder that toxins are carried in our bodies. A 2004 study in England by the European Public Health Alliance found a "toxic cocktail" in the blood of every one of 155 volunteers.[15] These included sex-disrupting polychlorinated biphenyls (PCBs), flame retardants, and pesticides—the same chemicals rampant in American waters, air, and soil. The persistence of these chemicals is demonstrated by the fact that breakdown products of DDT, a pesticide banned more than 30 years ago in the United Kingdom and Europe, were found in 99 percent of the volunteers. Moreover, PCBs, industrial chemicals banned in the United States for decades, still persist in our environment. Their health risks include impaired fetal brain development and cancer. The report *In Harm's Way*,[16] by the Boston Physicians for Social Responsibility, alerts the public to the special threats posed to children by environmental toxicants. The alerts included: an epidemic of developmental, learning, and behavioral disabilities has become evident among children; animal and human studies demonstrate that many chemicals commonly encountered in industry and the home are developmental neurotoxicants that can contribute to developmental, learning, and behavioral disabilities. Neurotoxins are not merely a **potential** threat to children. With increased knowledge of the vast quantities of neurotoxic chemicals released into the environment each year, the "safe thresholds" for known neurotoxins in the body have continuously been revised down. The Boston physicians assert that a regulatory process is necessary, especially to protect children.

Children Are Especially Vulnerable to Toxins

Until recently, most studies on environmental toxins were performed on adults, mostly males, and mostly mindful of the risk of cancer. Burstyn and Fenton attest that we now know men and women react differently to toxins and that many more diseases besides cancer result from exposure. But they emphasize that we **know** fetuses, infants, and children respond uniquely to environmental hazards. They are much more vulnerable than adults in ways that are qualitatively different, and those hazards pose lifelong consequences. They offer this 2004 quote from the Children's Environmental Health Network (CEHN):[17] "The elegance and delicacy of the development of a human being from conception through adolescence affords particular windows of vulnerability to environmental hazards. Exposure at those moments of vulnerability can lead to permanent and irreversible damage."

Burstyn and Fenton elaborate on this statement, drawing on the knowledge base of numerous authorities. They tell us fetuses cannot defend against environmental toxins because their underdeveloped nervous, respiratory, reproductive, and immune systems are in the process of dynamic change. Fetuses can be grievously and irreversibly damaged by toxins via the placenta, especially by those that harm the nervous system, such as lead, PCBs, mercury, ethanol, flame retardants, and nicotine from tobacco smoke. Babies and toddlers spend much time close to the ground, where toxins accumulate; some of these mimic the body's hormones and have been shown to disrupt reproductive and hormone systems in wildlife. Children have higher metabolisms and proportional food and liquid intake than do adults. So too, then, is their potential exposure to ingested pollutants such as lead, pesticides, and nitrates greater than that of adults. But their developing metabolic systems are much less capable of detoxifying and excreting toxins than those of adults. The cells of infants and children are multiplying, and their organ systems are developing at a very rapid rate. Children need more calcium than adults, but their bodies will absorb lead in preference to calcium if lead is present. Exposure to toxins at an earlier age can trigger diseases with long latency periods, such as cancer, Parkinson's disease, allergies, autoimmune disorders, and chemical sensitivities. All of these factors are potential causes of childhood emotional distress, behavioral disturbances, and mental disabilities.

Heavy Metals

Lead

Burstyn and Fenton draw from the work of Howard Hu[18] at Harvard University, who has written extensively about lead. Lead exposure to children and adults can cause wide-ranging health problems: from coma, convulsions, renal failure, and death to subtle effects on metabolism and intelligence. Hu notes that developing fetuses and children are especially vulnerable. Citing "a plethora" of well-designed studies, he reports that low-level exposure to lead in children less than 5 years of age results in lost intelligent quotient (IQ) points. As a result, the Centers for Disease Control and Prevention lowered the allowable amount of lead in a child's blood, and recommended blood lead screening of all children between the ages of 6 months and 5 years.

Herbert Needleman[19] of the University of Pittsburgh is the authors' source for research that led to the ban on lead in fuel in 1979. His work is noteworthy in that he was among the first to demonstrate that lower IQs, poor reading skills, and attention problems could be attributed to lead exposure; these deficits had traditionally been considered genetic or psychogenic in origin. He also demonstrated that lead exposure was linked to disruptive classroom behavior, failure to graduate high school, violent tendencies, addictive predispositions, and other behavioral and emotional problems that often resulted in self-destructive and criminal behaviors. Needleman estimated that 11 to 38 percent of America's delinquency is attributable to high lead exposure.[20]

Burstyn and Fenton refer to the research of Roger Masters,[21] president of the Foundation for Neuroscience and Society. He found a disturbing correlation between high lead rates and the use of silicofluoride to fluoridate water systems. In states where he measured high lead levels in blood, he also found silicofluoride in the water. And he claims to have found "a kind of doubling" of violent crime rates where this chemical is used. He believes silicofluoride breaks down the barrier between blood and the gut, so that more toxins enter the bloodstream.

Masters highlights the importance of nutrition in cases of lead exposure. A child low in calcium will pick up more lead, so we see how poverty can impact risk, especially with rising food prices.

I digress now to an interview with Adrienne Anderson,[22] professor of environmental and ethnic studies at the University of Colorado that aired on *Alternative Radio*. Her subject, "Planetary Casualties: The Hidden Costs of War," was a personal account of what happened when she learned that poisoned water was being delivered to a Colorado community called Friendly Hills. The source was a Lockheed Martin plant. While organizing that community between 1984 and 1986, she discovered a cluster of children (16 by her count) who mysteriously died there. State officials and the Environmental Protection Agency (EPA) claimed to have no knowledge of the cause of the deaths, so she and the citizens urged the federal government to open an investigation. Federal efforts yielded no explanation, so Anderson and the citizens commenced their own investigation. They learned that for 30 years Lockheed Martin (known as Martin Marrieta at the time) had been contaminating that region's water supply as well as a source of water just below their plant, southwest of Denver. They learned that the Denver Water Board, the State of Colorado, and the EPA, to whom they had appealed, were aware of this contamination all along. Lockheed Martin had protested any investigation because of a civil action that had been brought by citizens whose babies died, and whose children contracted cancers. The public water supply was shut down in 1985, followed by plummeting rates of babies born with fetal defects. But concerns about cancers remained. The federal government gave the state thousands of dollars to conduct a health assessment of area residents, which is required under Superfund Law. The research showed that the contaminated water not only affected Friendly Hills, but also all of those feeder communities to the Columbine High School area in Littleton, Colorado.

Anderson called for more health assessments in January 1999, a few months before the Columbine High School shootings. After the shootings, the kinds of contaminants emitted—lead, cadmium, and manganese—became paramount. Roger Masters, cited earlier, joined the investigation with Anderson because of his research linking crime with exposure to these toxic metals. Despite their hard work, they failed to elicit interest or support from governments, as Lockheed Martin continued to protest further health assessments, and the two scientists were ridiculed in the *Denver Post*. Anderson asks, "if rocket fuel propellants such as the chemicals at Aerojet in California, the Lockheed Martin plant in Colorado, and other facilities around the country are capable of causing cancers in any organ system in tiny doses, then what kind of impacts can they have on behavioral health?" And why is this not an area of concern regarding the Littleton community? Anderson states unequivocally that Dylan Klebold, one of the Columbine shooters, was exposed to contaminated water as a baby and as a toddler. Furthermore, his companion in the shooting, Eric Harris, grew up at Superfund sites near Sandia labs, in New Mexico, and every place he had ever lived was an area designated as a Superfund site, because his father was in the Air Force.

Mercury

The authors continue with testimony from Howard Hu,[23] an expert in mercury as well as lead and other heavy metals. Hu sounds a global alarm: that mercury has been increasing in importance as a widespread contaminant. He warns that atmospheric dispersion of mercury has increased markedly, and the medical industry is a major contributor to this form of pollution. He notes that fish, especially tuna, mackerel, and swordfish, can concentrate methylmercury (the toxic form of mercury) at high levels. Hu underscores the special danger to fetal and infant nervous systems from mercury exposure. He cites a 1955 disaster in Minamata Bay, Japan, when women victims of this disaster gave birth to infants with mental retardation, retention of primitive reflexes, cerebellar symptoms, and other abnormalities. He adds that research at the Faroe Islands has demonstrated that, even at much lower levels, mercury exposure to pregnant women through fish and whale meat ingestion is linked to decrements in motor function, language, memory, and neural transmission in their offspring. Organic mercury, as is found in fish and whale meat, readily crosses the placenta to the fetus and also appears in breast milk.

A nationwide survey of women by the Centers for Disease Control and Prevention revealed that 1 in 12 women of childbearing age already carry unsafe levels of mercury and that as many as 600,000 American babies could be at risk. Researchers at Mount Sinai Center for Children's Health and the Environment reported in 2005 that IQ losses linked to mercury range from one-fifth of an IQ point to 24 points. They calculated that mercury damage in the womb costs the United States $8.7 billion a year in lost earnings potential of those babies affected.[24]

Mercury and Autism

For many years, a debate has brewed over whether mercury exposure is the cause of autism. Several years ago, I attended a workshop facilitated by a group of specialists in autism who stated unequivocally that mercury as a cause of autism had been ruled out. But Burstyn and Fenton report that just a month before they wrote their chapter, a study was released by researchers at the University of Texas[25] that examined 254 counties and 1,200 school districts in Texas, comparing 2001 mercury emission levels with rates of autism and special education services. The scientists reported a high correlation between the disorder and high mercury emission rates from coal burning plants. Coal burning power plants are the largest source of mercury in the United States today—producing 48 tons of the poison annually. The Texas researchers report that Texas plants emit more than those in any other state. And they found a 17 percent increase in autism for every 1,000 pounds of mercury released into the environment. Autism, once thought to occur in 1 of every 10,000 children, is now estimated at 1 in every 250 children, according to the researchers.

The *Environmental News Network, Associated Press* released "Mercury Study Identifies Problem Spots" on March 9, 2005.[26] It was the product of a four-year study in the northeastern United States and eastern Canada, funded by the U.S. Department of Agriculture's Northeastern States Research Cooperative. The study shed new light on the long-held assumption that toxic mercury was found primarily in water. The last year of the study showed that toxic mercury is found on land as well, in "mercury hot spots" (four in Maine, one each in New York and Massachusetts, and three in Canada); that it is found in non-fish-eating birds; and that just how widespread and bio-available it actually is remains unknown. But it is now recognized to be a situation much worse than previously known.

Conclusions

Children who suffer the effects of environmental pollution often become labeled as "disordered" with ADHD or bipolar, and then "treated" with psychotropic drugs, putting them at risk of further neurological and metabolic challenges. And the parents may be subjected to accusations of child neglect or abuse. Instead, these children actually need detoxification treatment and nutritional remediation, say Burstyn and Fenton. They assert that researchers and professionals in fields of environmental epidemiology, biostatistics, occupational health, toxicology, medicine, education, and mental health need to pool their expertise to ensure accurate diagnoses and effective treatment of children with mental and emotional disabilities.

Burstyn and Fenton recommend amelioration on three other fronts: families, communities, and government.

Families

Books that can help parents include Herbert Needleman and Philip Landrigan's *Raising Children Toxic Free: How to Keep Your Child Free from Lead,*

Asbestos, Pesticides and Other Environmental Hazards[27] and Doris Rapp's *Our Toxic World*.[28] Both provide a great deal of information to help families avoid toxic contamination to the highest degree possible. But families alone cannot solve the enormous challenge of pollution.

Community

Burstyn and Fenton agree that schools are in an excellent position to advocate for children's environmental health. They can serve as liaisons between parents and local public authorities and policy makers.[29] California schools are a good example. For eight years, as of 2008, the California Safe Schools program has focused on banning pesticides, and many other schools are following their example.[30] Our authors recommend that schools institute a policy of serving organic foods in cafeterias to further protect children from pesticides. Furthermore, if they used only nontoxic cleaning and construction materials, they would create a great market for these "green" products.

The authors stress the imperative that training programs for health practitioners integrate information about environmental threats to health into their curricula and provide continuing education on that special topic. They point out that the damage being done to the physical and emotional health of children by environmental toxins amounts to a public health crisis that will only worsen rapidly. Therefore, public health officials must play a major role in communities to curb the crisis.

Government: Local, State, and National

Burstyn and Fenton liken the increasing amount of environmental toxins to a tsunami in its enormity. They maintain that the crisis is the result of industrial modes of production that placed profit above all other considerations. It requires a national government to legislate massive reform, a challenging task for the best intentioned administration. The authors disparage the George W. Bush administration for setting back the environmental agenda in monumental proportions. Until a new administration takes office that gives the welfare of children the high priority it deserves, they suggest that each state could create an interdepartmental body. It would have funding, personnel, and power to animate citizens and community groups as well as its own departments and agencies "into a system that makes the term *guardian* real in practice as well as rhetoric." They visualize municipal and county governments rallying into the movement, and eventually, "when the national capital regains its environmental senses, providing generous federal support." Now that President Obama is in office, perhaps appropriate action will emanate from the federal government. We can hope.

COMPUTERS AND TELEVISION

Educational psychologist Jane Healy, who specializes in developmental neuropsychology, authored two books on the impact of media on child development:

Endangered Minds[31] and *Failure to Connect: How Computers Affect Our Children's Minds and What We Can Do About It*,[32] published in 1990 and 1998, respectively. In the first book, Healy reveals that the brains of today's students have been shaped by our fast-paced lifestyle, coupled with "heavy media diets of visual immediacy." The result is a mismatch between kids' brains and traditional modes of academic learning. Today's children have shorter attention spans and are less able to reason analytically, express ideas verbally, and attend to complex problems. Healy suggests that the neuronal connections in the brain develop according to experience. If the brain's synapses develop by a heavy diet of video and rushed adult-organized afterschool activities, then that brain's neuronal connections will be quite different from the brain shaped by meaningful verbal exchange and creative play. Healy is talking about "neural plasticity," or malleability. While this science is young, what we do know is that repeated experiences cause synaptic differences, such as the ability of deaf children's brains to develop differently from those of hearing children because of differences in the types of input to which they respond. Healy also tells us that there appear to be sensitive periods in the course of development when the brain is more amenable to stimulation. Lack of appropriate stimulation during those windows of opportunity may leave permanent decrements. Much of what is known comes from animal research, but it has been demonstrated regarding language development in humans. Little is known about its applicability to higher-level learning, for which the brain may retain its plasticity into adolescence. Healy tells us these higher-level learning skills appear to be endangered in today's environment.

The good news, however, is that it is possible that today's children's brains are being shaped for new and different modes of learning: more immediate and hands-on learning instead of passive listening to lectures and reading. Healy has some innovative ideas of how teaching might adapt to the different kinds of stimuli that children require in a new age of technology and fast lifestyle. She has concrete suggestions for schools and parents regarding the kinds of new modes of communication that can enhance problem solving, following sequential directions, and planning behavior. Healy says these skills must be in place before children can learn to read in any meaningful manner. Until children learn to use language, they cannot think effectively. She charges that the television programs children are apt to watch use language at about a fourth grade level. Healy suggests that language deficits brought about by today's lifestyle could explain the increase in ADHD-like behaviors: Without the inner speech, children cannot mediate their thinking, and therefore cannot mediate behavior. They lack the ability to plan ahead or perceive cause and effect in their behavior, which requires complex language relationships. Healy believes, too, that the software flooding the market for kids is training them to be attention deficit disordered and impulsive. Furthermore, most of it limits motor activity to the fingers alone. (The Wii Fit Program is an exception—a system that makes the viewer do large muscle activities and aerobics.)

Healy concedes that not all children lack language skills. It depends upon the kind of language input they have had at home. She said some children from all socio-economic levels have careful language input from parents, and these are the youngsters who get into good colleges.

Andrew Leonard's review of *Failure to Connect* appeared on *Salon.com* on August 28, 1998. The following statements reflect his interpretations of Healy's ideas. Those in quotes are extracted from her book. Healy writes that some of the most popular educational software may be damaging to creativity, attention, and motivation. In 1998, what she calls the "edutainment" market for home use in the United States was growing by 20 to 30 percent a year. And in 1997, school expenditures on technology reached $4.34 billion. "At the same time, music and art programs—which, unlike computers, *have* been demonstrated to increase 'intelligence'—are constantly being defunded."

Healy acknowledges a place for computers in schools, but argues there is no need until age 10 or 11. Her considerable research on neuroanatomical development demonstrates that older children can learn computer literacy very quickly, equally as well as children with preschool computer experience: There is no need to "jump start" (alluding to one of the most popular software programs) the immature brain. She reiterates from her earlier book: The brain goes through critical windows in both childhood and adolescence "when learning environments exert special kinds of effects and when certain types of activities and stimulation are most appropriate and necessary for the brain to reach its potential. If we waste or subvert these developmental windows, the losses may be irrecoverable."

Healy elaborates: Too many kids' programs merely consist of clicking on a cute object to get a reward "like experimental rats," rather than gaining any real understanding of cause and effect. She deplores classrooms where students spend more time playing "reward" games than solving the original problem. She informs us that computers are not preferable to TV because children are prone to vision problems and repetitive motion injuries. Furthermore, the nature of computer screen animation is conducive to mind-dulling, transfixed attention. And parents should not substitute computers for TV in order to limit TV watching. Doing so is just replacing TV with another technical device that tunes parents out! Healy is adamant that parents' time with their kids is still worth more than any equipment, no matter how "glitzy."

PLAY

Rat Studies

Secondary school teacher Matthew Harvey[33] suggests lack of natural play may cause ADHD. His *New York Times* article cited an interesting study by physiological psychologist Jaak Panksepp, professor emeritus and director of the Memorial Foundation for Lost Children (which helps parents and children with neuropsychiatric disabilities). In the mid-1990s, Panksepp made the surprising discovery that rats laugh. He and his team noticed that rat pups emitted high-frequency chirps when involved in rough-and-tumble play with each other. Panksepp had suspected that rats, like many mammals, share some emotional traits with humans, and this seemed to lend veracity to his hunch. Then in 2003, Panksepp and his team discovered that the rats they allowed to play went on to become less impulsive and more socially successful than their cousins who were deprived of play. In 2007 the researchers found that the brain differences between rats that played abundantly and rats deprived of play matched the brain differences between non-ADHD and ADHD human children, respectively, in imaging studies performed by Castellanos and colleagues (discussed in chapter 2). Panksepp's work supports the importance of play and its possible link to ADHD traits.

But also, just as I pointed out in chapter 2 regarding the research of Castellanos and Rapoport, the rat studies also support psychosocial theory in that **experience and behavior** appear to have influenced brain development.

Children and Play

Clinical psychologist Sharna Olfman's contribution to her anthology, *Childhood Lost*, is "Where Do the Children Play?"[34] In years past children engaged in imaginative play, whereas they now spend about 40 hours each week engaged with media. A generation ago, children were encouraged to go outside to play after school. Relatives were available to keep a watchful eye, and neighborhoods were conducive to free and imaginative play. Today, economic and cultural constraints force many parents to work long hours, and children are confined more within day care or organized afterschool programs. Furthermore, national policy mandates standardized testing that pits school against school for funding; this has resulted in more and more emphasis on early academic work instead of play. Olfman tells why the deprivation of imaginative free play hurts children in the following paragraphs.

Essential for Wholesome Development

Erik Erikson's theory of psychosocial stages has long been a mainstay of developmental and social scientists. It charts the developmental stages through which humans pass, from infancy through the waning years of life. Each life stage presents a challenge; meeting the challenge prepares one for the next stage. Failing to meet the challenge makes the successful attainment of further challenges difficult, if not impossible, jeopardizing further healthy development. For young children, Erikson's stage of *initiative* challenges children everywhere to engage in vivid fantasy play between the ages of 3 and 5. Erikson's admonition: If children are foreclosed on this stage and rushed into the next stage of *industry*, they may indeed learn to read, write, and do math precociously, but (quoting Olfman) "we may be creating a cohort of children who lack spontaneity, creativity, and a love of learning."

Olfman excoriates the current American public educational system, where early academic exposure is paramount, at the expense of essential play. Public school curricula, especially since No Child Left Behind, flies in the face of the tenets of child development known to professionals for decades. Little wonder America does not rate high in academic success compared to other countries.

Olfman cites a highly respected international survey conducted in 2004 by the Organization of Economic Cooperation and Development (OECD).[35] Finland rated first in literacy and placed in the top five in math and science tests given to a sample of 15-year-olds attending both public and private schools. American students placed in the middle. Quite naturally, other countries wanted to emulate Finland's success. How does Finland do it? Children start to learn to read at age 7, in first grade, on the premise that play is the most important building block in the early years and sets the stage for lifelong love of learning. Preschool for 6-year-olds is optional. Seven-year-olds quickly catch up to their peers in other countries in reading and then excel. In grades one through nine, students are set loose to play for 15 minutes following every 45-minute lesson; they can engage in play or musical activities. Subjects deemed expendable in the United States— art, music, physical education, woodwork, and crafts—are all required subjects throughout the grades. Teachers in Finland are highly respected and are given latitude to adjust the national curricula according to their judgments.

Olfman cites C. Clouder,[36] who observes that even as America continues to slash play from preschool and kindergarten curricula, many European countries, including the United Kingdom, are following Finland's example: increasing the age at which academics are introduced, using play curricula in the early years, and eliminating standardized testing in the early grades. Olfman quotes from the British House of Commons Education Select Committee's report of December 2000:[37] "Inappropriate formalized assessment of children at an early age currently results in too many children being labeled as failures, when the failure, in fact, lies with the system."

Anyone familiar with young children knows the variability of their rates of readiness for academic pursuits.

Garbarino[38] on Play

Cornell professor Garbarino notes, "And if we are to be successful parents in a socially toxic environment, we must understand that children develop largely through play." Extolling further on the importance of play, Garbarino says this about lessons and other organized activities in the name of creating "learning experiences": "Play becomes work, and this contributes to the social toxicity of the environment for children." Fantasy, says Garbarino, is the child's vehicle for processing experiences, testing hypotheses about the world, and having fun. Garbarino quotes Paley:[39] "In that world [child's], children play. Through their play, they come to live better. They figure things out. They learn. They become more fully human."

Nature Deficit

When I was an elementary school teacher's aide back in the '70s, I volunteered to host an "ecology club." To my surprise, I attracted a gang of the most challenging and truculent fourth- and fifth-grade boys. Were they enthusiastic!—and well behaved! I took them to a pond in the woods, where we collected insect larvae and other critters with nets. We took them back to the classroom, identified them, and released them back to the pond. We returned to the pond over the next weeks to see how the tadpoles and dragonfly larvae were developing. We made a big diagram of the pond with its life and its surrounds and hung it in the hallway of the school. These boys turned out to be very special. Nature brought out the best in them. I still feel a glow when I think back to that time.

Richard Louv,[40] author of *Last Child in the Woods: Saving Our Children From Nature-Deficit Disorder*, quoted Roszak,[41] who remarked on the American Psychiatric Association's list of more than 300 mental diseases in its *Diagnostic and Statistical Manual*: "Psychotherapists have exhaustively analyzed every form of dysfunctional family and social relations, but 'dysfunctional environmental relations' does not exist even as a concept . . . The *Diagnostic and Statistical Manual* defines 'separation anxiety disorder' as 'excessive anxiety concerning separation from home and from those to whom the individual is attached.' But no separation is more pervasive in this Age of Anxiety than our disconnection from the natural world."

Louv introduces us to "ecopsychology," which refers to our symbiotic relationship with the natural world, or nature therapy: what the earth does for us—for our health—and what we do for the earth.[42] Louv's thesis is that today's American children have lost the opportunity for free play in woods, fields, streams, and other places where they can observe and absorb nature. And this loss is enormous. He cites reasons for this deficit: suburban communities where there are rules against climbing trees, building tree houses, or tramping through the patches of trees that were intentionally left for wildlife. But the wildlife is not available to the children. Then there is the issue of time. Many children attend afterschool latchkey programs. Others arrive home laden with knapsacks heavier than they are, full of homework to occupy whatever free time they may have. Neighborhoods aren't what they used to be. Neighbors don't know each other, and don't condone kids running through their yards playing hide and seek. Fortunately, this isn't universally true. The fortunate child still lives with access to the world of nature and knows the bliss of lying in the grass gazing at the clouds or exploring a stream. But unfortunately, too many do not have this luxury. Louv defines "nature deficit disorder" as the human cost of alienation from nature. Among these costs are diminished use of the senses, attention difficulties, and higher rates of physical and emotional illnesses. Louv says the disorder can even affect cities: It can change human behavior as seen by a relationship between the absence, or inaccessibility, of parks and open space with high crime rates, depression, and other urban maladies. Some city planners are heeding the studies of these phenomena and designing communities accordingly.

The Virtues of Make-Believe

Olfman praises the early work of Lev Vygotsky, a Russian psychologist who analyzed the attributes of make-believe, especially sociodramatic play (when two or more children construct and act out play scenes together). His work in the 1920s became recognized in the 1970s in the United States and had a profound effect on developmental scientists and educators. Citing Berk,[43] Olfman explains why sociodramatic play has significant applications to development. Unlike solitary play, social play requires children to cooperate in the making of rules and deciding what objects stand for: beds, the stove, or room boundaries, for example. They must agree on characters—who's the mother, the baby, the dad, the grandparent—and then on how these characters relate and act toward each other. To stay in the game, the children have to subordinate their impulses and delay gratification to the will of the group. Then during play, children learn through direct experience the importance of rules, impulse control, and cooperation. In acting out their roles, they learn the art of social discourse. Sometimes their characters are imaginary, like fairies, monsters, good and evil animals, kings, queens, magicians, and all sorts of beings that only the imaginations of children can conjure up. They might give them names, and perpetuate the scenario repeatedly over weeks, months, or even years. In so doing, they experiment, explore, and develop their emotional lives.

Solitary dramatic play is equally valuable to healthy emotional and intellectual growth. I remember observing my 9-year-old neighbor Nora, an only child. Draped in a makeshift gauzy fabric, she was transformed into an Arabian princess. Her "tent" was a sheet thrown over a bush. As she gracefully lifted the "door" of her "tent," and disappeared inside, I momentarily revisited the wonder and joy of imaginary play.

Nora was a perfect example of the child not merely mimicking an Arabian princess, but actually living, feeling, and moving like one. Olfman refers to educational philosopher Jeffrey Kane,[44] who contrasts "disembodied facts" that are *learned* with knowledge that is *discovered*. The kind of play that Nora engaged in provided her infinitely deeper knowledge than any she would encounter in a school lesson or on the Internet. Kane elaborates eloquently. He compares the child, let's call him Joey, observing a butterfly in its natural environment to the child studying a case of butterflies in a museum. In watching the living, "breathing" insect, Joey might imagine himself as that butterfly. He might touch it gently, feeling the softness of its wings and the slight air movement created by their fluttering. He might be drawn to this being emotionally and develop a concern for its welfare. The experience of the butterfly becomes part of Joey's repertoire of knowledge that he can apply to new artistic or scientific discoveries. There are infinite ways that direct experience surpasses formal instruction. Yet for many of our children, time alone in nature is a rare opportunity during their tightly regimented day. Kane and Louv are on the same wavelength.

PARENTAL AVAILABILITY

Olfman concludes her chapter with sad commentary regarding the American family's ability to foster the kinds of imaginary play and learning described above. She understands the plight of the swelling numbers of the "working poor," who toil long hours for little pay while the government fails to provide quality day care for their children. More affluent parents also often get caught up in overspending, running up debts, and having to leave children in the care of others in order to meet financial responsibilities. And so the children are abandoned to screens, structured activities, or the streets, while exhausted parents retreat to their own screens.

So concludes our partial accounting of environmental and societal influences on American children. These comprise alternative explanations for the swelling numbers of distressed children. Throughout this book, I have contrasted two theories with opposing views regarding the causes of this "epidemic": the psychosocial and the neurobiological. Yet in the writing, I repeatedly stumbled across signs that, increasingly, the two theories converge in significant ways. I pointed these out in chapter 2 and other places. Could it be that the two are moving from opposition to juxtaposition?

IS CONSENSUS POSSIBLE?

As elucidated in chapter 2, National Institute of Mental Health researchers concluded that the brains of children with ADHD were normal, at least 50 percent of the time, merely lagging in development by about three years behind non-ADHD peers. These researchers also acknowledged that experience and behavior influence brain development. Jensen and colleagues acknowledge the role of evolution in shaping behavior. I visualize a convergence of neurobiological with psychosocial theorists in many respects, but not in the choice of solutions—and that is a huge departure, considering what is at stake.

Consensus among mental health professionals on the wrong-headedness of putting foreign chemicals into people's brains, especially those of children, will happen only when the pharmaceutical industry takes a backseat in the pursuit of remedies. Financial gain must be eliminated as a motivating factor in the treatment of emotional distress. Children will have a fair shake at healthy, wholesome development when, instead of perturbing their brains with toxic chemicals, we put our resources into addressing the roots of childhood distress as outlined in this chapter.

Epilogue

It is easier for a camel to go through
the eye of a needle,
than for a rich man
to enter into the kingdom of heaven.

—Matthew 19:24

Like a bad penny, the lucrative relationship between psychiatrists and pharmaceutical companies emerges persistently throughout this book, a relationship so pervasive that Peter Breggin dubbed it the "psychopharmaceutical complex." Chapter 4 explained how this merger evolved. It has long been a thorn in the side of psychosocial advocates: a thorn, it seemed, we were destined to endure indefinitely. However, the summer of 2008 marked a turn of events that continue to unfold with revelations of skullduggery in that mighty fortress. First we return to Joseph Biederman.

BIEDERMAN'S ALLEGED FAILURE TO DISCLOSE PAYMENTS BY DRUG COMPANY: FALLOUT CONTINUES

The *New York Times*, June 8, 2008: "Researchers Fail to Reveal Full Drug Pay"

The front page of the *New York Times* bore this explosive headline. Mental health reporters Gardiner Harris and Benedict Carey, speaking of Joseph Biederman, opened with "[a] world-renowned child psychiatrist whose work has helped fuel an explosion in the use of powerful antipsychotic medicines in children earned at least $1.6 million in consulting fees from drug makers from 2000 to 2007 but for years did not report much of this income to university officials, according to information given Congressional investigators." Senator Charles Grassley, Republican from Iowa and ranking member of the Senate Finance Committee, led the investigation and declared that failure to report the income may have violated federal (some of Biederman's research is funded by government grants) and university research rules meant to police potential conflicts of interest. The investigators also revealed that Biederman's colleague Timothy Wilens belatedly reported $1.6 million in the same time period, and that colleague Thomas Spencer reported earning at least $1 million after being pressed by the investigators. The article said Biederman reported no income from Johnson & Johnson for 2001 in a disclosure filed with Harvard University. When asked to check again, he said he received $3,500. But Johnson & Johnson revealed to the Grassley investigators it paid him $58,169 in 2001. Investigators believe some figures may still be understated since the companies' disclosures contradict them.

A National Institutes of Health (NIH) spokesman said if NIH policy has been violated and Biederman research was found to be compromised, those responsible would be held accountable. He added it would be completely unacceptable and not tolerated. A Harvard spokeswoman said the doctors had been referred to a university conflict committee for review. The NIH requires researchers to report university earnings of $10,000 or more per year in order to ensure research integrity. But there is no system of accountability. It's been an honor system. Grassley wants a national registry for oversight of outside earnings now.

This news attracted much attention because of the immense influence of the Harvard group. The *Times* article described Biederman as much admired since he treats highly distressed children, and it said his work helped fuel the 40-fold increase in bipolar diagnoses in a 10-year period.

Director of the Child and Adolescent Bipolar Foundation Susan Resko defended Biederman, saying he is a true visionary who has saved many lives. Critic Vera Sharav, president and founder of the Alliance for Human Research Protection, said, "They have given the Harvard imprimatur [license or approval] to this commercial experimentation on children."

The *Times* article quotes experts' descriptions of the Biederman research as "a string of drug trials from 2001 to 2006, but the studies were so small and loosely designed that they were largely inconclusive." They criticized further that "improvement" in subjects meant a decline of 30 percent or more on a mania rating scale, well below the 50 percent improvement of symptoms most researchers use as the standard.

Also quoted was E. Fuller Torrey, executive director of the Stanley Medical Research Institute, which finances psychiatric studies. He stated the price paid for revelations such as these is credibility. He added, "In the area of child psychiatry, in particular, we know much less than we should, and we desperately need research that is not influenced by industry money."

The *New York Times*, June 12, 2008: "Psychiatric Group Faces Scrutiny Over Drug Industry Ties"

This story by the same authors reported that Congress now is attacking the American Psychiatric Association (APA) for allowing the cozy relationship between psychiatrists and the drug industry. Grassley reportedly wrote a letter to the APA saying he now understands that money from industry can shape the practices of nonprofit organizations that purport to be independent in their viewpoints and actions. It was learned that in 2006 drug companies provided 30 percent of the APA's financing. Furthermore, Grassley expressed concern about the APA's president-elect, Alan F. Schatzberg of Stanford University, and his $4.8 million stock holdings in a drug development company. A Stanford spokesperson denied the doctor had violated any research rules, and the APA will go ahead with his induction as APA president. The article reported that psychiatrists earn less than other specialists, but when consulting income from drug companies is added to their salaries, they surpass the others. The worry is that this money may influence which medicines they prescribe. Minnesota keeps records that enable a check on this information. An analysis of that state's data by the *New York Times* last year found that on average, psychiatrists who received at least $5,000 from makers of the "atypical" antipsychotics appear to have written three times as many prescriptions to children for those drugs than psychiatrists who received less money or none.

Update on Alan Schatzberg

The *Wall Street Journal*'s Health Blog journalist, Jacob Goldstein,[1] elaborated on Senator Grassley's investigation of Alan Schatzberg, mentioned in the paragraph above as president-elect of the American Psychiatric Association. Schatzberg is also chair of Stanford University's department of psychiatry, and is alleged to have conflicts of interest regarding his stake in Corcept Therapeutics, developer of a drug, mifepristone to treat psychotic depression. He is co-owner of the patent on the drug, and principal overseer of the research on the drug. The research on mifepristone is funded by a National Institutes of Health (NIH) grant. Schatzberg reported having a stake of over $100,000 in Corcept, but Grassley alleges his stake is about $6 million, substantially more than $100,000. Then on August 1, 2008,[2] it was reported that Grassley was intensifying his probe into NIH and the convoluted Stanford research. Stanford officials were minimizing Schatzberg's role in the research of mifepristone, yet Grassley presses the question of how Schatzberg could not be closely involved in the research since he is the primary investigator. Grassley demanded an answer to the question "How could Dr. Schatzberg monitor the research funded with his NIH grants if he was not involved closely in the study?" The Senate Finance Committee states its primary investigations concern research grants and how the NIH and universities manage conflicts of interest when academic researchers receive both NIH funding and have ties to drugmakers. This news was followed up within hours by the announcement that Stanford had pulled the NIH grant from Schatzberg and replaced him with another investigator.[3]

July 13, 2008: Diller's Opinion—*San Francisco Chronicle*[4]

Diller asks if leading pediatricians are industry shills. He cites Biederman as his prime example, but he alludes to pediatricians in general for their tactics. Diller identifies Biederman as a doctor so influential that when he merely mentions a drug, even one not yet tested, tens of thousands of children end up taking it. Of the scandal over the withholding of drug company payments he states, "If true, this scandal is yet one more stake in the heart of American academic medicine's credibility with frontline doctors like me—and more importantly, with the parents of the patients I deal with every day." He says the $1.6 million Biederman didn't declare is only a fraction of drug money his department gets from a dozen pharmaceutical companies, to pay for the studies and also the salaries of the researchers. He goes on, "Virtually all doctors who receive drug company money say they are not influenced, but every independent study examining the effects of such money says they are." Diller notes the Harvard psychiatric department's strange silence or even defense of Biederman. He commends them as "good men with solid reputations both in drug and nondrug aspects of treatment." But he acknowledges how dependent they are on drug company money; in fact, he says the psychiatry department could not exist without it. He noted the Physician Payments Sunshine Act, introduced by Senators Grassley and Kohl that will require more vigorous reporting and enforcement regarding payments to doctors, but Diller calls for other "laws to have the federal government, along with major academic research centers, coordinate and direct the use of drug company money in medical research."

On a related matter, on May 10, 2007, *New York Times* journalists Harris, Carey, and Roberts[5] quoted Steven Hyman, provost of Harvard University and former director of the National Institute of Mental Health. The article focused on Anya Bailey (the child who developed a painful dystonia from Risperdal) and the increasing awareness of conflicting interests on the part of psychiatrists. Hyman, talking about drug payments to doctors, acknowledged that such payments could result in doctors using drugs in ways that endanger patients' physical health. He added, "There's an irony that psychiatrists ask patients to have insights into themselves, but we don't connect the wires in our own lives about how money is affecting our profession and putting our patients at risk." He said this before the scandal erupted at his own university. This article described payments to doctors in Minnesota, one of the only states that require transparency in drug payments, and therefore one that fosters research into the consequences of such payments. The journalists reported that from 2000 to 2005, payments to doctors increased more than sixfold, to $1.6 million. At the same time, prescriptions for children on Medicaid for antipsychotic drugs increased more than ninefold. The same investigation yielded the data alluded to previously: Minnesota psychiatrists who received at least $5,000 from atypical drug makers appear to have written three times as many atypical prescriptions for children than psychiatrists who didn't receive drug money.

November 30, 2008: *New York Times* Editorial

Its heading is "Expert of Shill?" and it reveals more inciting information about Biederman. This editorial reports that internal documents that emerged as a result of a lawsuit "have sketched out what looks like an unsavory collaboration between Dr. Biederman and Johnson & Johnson to generate and disseminate data that would support the use of an antipsychotic drug, Risperdal [a Johnson & Johnson drug]." The editorial alleges that Biederman repeatedly asked Johnson & Johnson to fund a center at Massachusetts General Hospital to focus on juvenile bipolar disorder and that the company responded with almost $1 million. It alleges further that a stated mission of the center, besides improving the psychiatric care of children, was to "move forward the commercial goals of J. & J."

December 30, 2008: The *Wall Street Journal*[6]

"Drug Researcher Agrees to Curb Role" is the title. The article reports that Biederman, "a top researcher on the use of psychiatric drugs in children," agreed to stop participating in drug company-funded clinical trials at Massachusetts General Hospital. He would also not participate in any outside activities such as presentations or consultations that are funded by or sponsored by drug companies, according to the article. It reports further that the hospital expresses concern that an institute was created by Biederman and Johnson & Johnson to promote the use of Risperdal on children rather than to pursue scientific or scientific objectives. Consequently, Massachusetts General is conducting its own investigation. Senator Grassley has accused many schools of failing to supervise researchers adequately, and he sees the hospital's investigation as a positive move.

INVESTIGATION OF MELISSA DELBELLO PRECEDED THAT OF BIEDERMAN

Bad Science Rewarded Handsomely, but Disclosure Fell Short

I disclosed DelBello's unscientific study regarding the use of Seroquel with Depakote on children in chapter 4. It was published, nevertheless, and was even acclaimed as "rigorous." Consequently, thousands of children have been exposed to the toxic cocktail. This information came to light in 2007.[7] DelBello's lucrative association with the maker of Seroquel (AstraZeneca) caught up with her in 2008.

The Cincinnati-based Internet news source *The Enquirer*[8] reported on April 21, 2008, that Senator Grassley unveiled DelBello's failure to report the hundreds of thousands of dollars in corporate research money she received from AstraZeneca in the last decade. DelBello's boss, the vice president of research at the University of Cincinnati, told reporters that DelBello now has to review all of her drug company interactions with her department chairman. Grassley discovered DelBello received more than $238,000 from AstraZeneca from 2005 to 2007, but reported only about $100,000 to university authorities. She also received $100,000 from AstraZeneca in 2003, the year she led the infamous study on pediatric Seroquel use mentioned in chapter 4 and above. She did report that income. The article said the University of Cincinnati now prohibits gifts from drug companies and bans drug representatives from campus unless they have an appointment.

APRIL 4, 2008: REBECCA RILEY'S DOCTOR SUED[9]

The *Boston Globe* reported that while Rebecca's parents await trial on charges of murder, Andrew Meyer—the lawyer representing Rebecca's estate—filed suit against the girl's psychiatrist, Dr. Kayoko Kifuji, in Suffolk Superior Court. Meyer cites evidence that the nurse of the school attended by Rebecca warned Kifuji that she suspected Rebecca was overdosed on powerful psychiatric drugs; Rebecca was so weak, she was described to appear like "a floppy doll." Meyer charges that Kifuji, after examining Rebecca, still did not reduce her medication. He believes Rebecca was misdiagnosed and medicated inappropriately.

AUGUST 2008: TEXAS CHILDREN'S MEDICATION ALGORITHM PROJECT (CMAP) HALTED[10]

The Daily Texan writer Stephany Garza reported in August 2008 that the children's version of the algorithm mental screening instrument has been halted due to allegations of pharmaceutical companies influencing its researchers. The State of Texas filed a lawsuit in 2004 against Janssen Pharmaceutica, alleging Janssen paid for grants, trips, perks, travel expenses, and made other payments to decision makers associated with the Texas Medication Algorithm Project (TMAP). The lawsuit states that some proponents of TMAP also worked on CMAP. The state further alleges that Janssen paid decision makers to promote their product, Risperdal, and that Risperdal was listed as a drug of choice to treat children and adolescents when it was not approved by the FDA for use among that age group.

Investigators learned that the Robert Wood Johnson Foundation, an arm of Johnson & Johnson (parent company of Janssen), donated $2.4 million toward initiating TMAP. Other drug companies poured in hundreds of thousands of dollars. The lawsuit states that TMAP and CMAP became powerful marketing tools for the drug companies. Therefore, the companies developed a marketing plan to extend the algorithm project to other states. This was successful, and in Pennsylvania corruption was discovered and reported by Allen Jones, a state official.

BRISTOL-MYERS SQUIBB PAYS $389 MILLION FOR ILLEGAL PRICING AND MARKETING

In mid-July 2008, news releases from several states[11] announced that 43 states, the District of Columbia, and the federal government would receive $389 million plus interest from Bristol-Myers Squibb (BMS) in a settlement. The company was accused of improper practices, including reporting inflated prices for prescription drugs; paying physicians, health care providers, and pharmacies to sell its products; illegally promoting its antipsychotic Abilify for use not approved by the FDA—in children and for dementia-related psychosis; and for misreporting sales prices for the antidepressant Serzone. The settlement restores money to Medicaid, which paid for most of the products. Medicaid will pay only for drugs that are approved for the given condition, not for "off-label" use. "Off label" refers to drugs prescribed for conditions other than those for which the FDA has given approval, or prescribed to an age group for which the drug is not approved. Those antipsychotics now approved for pediatric use have been widely prescribed for ADHD, and for children under age 6, not FDA-approved uses.

EARLIER CONCERNS OVER MEDICAID SPENDING ON ANTIPSYCHOTICS

The settlement was preceded by concerns in many states over the burgeoning rate of antipsychotic prescriptions written for children on Medicaid. On February 4, 2008, Ed Silverman[12] reported on *Pharmalot.com* that New York state senator Tom Morahan, chair of the state senate's Committee on Mental Health and Developmental Disabilities, learned that Medicaid paid $82.8 million in 2006 for multiple pills for thousands of children, even though many of the medications were not approved by the FDA for pediatric use. New York health department officials do not even know what conditions the pills are prescribed for, since pharmacies do not require diagnoses. Claims have always been paid on faith that the doctor deemed the medications were "medically necessary." The article mentions other states that are investigating off-label promotion of drugs by pharmaceutical companies.

Ed Silverman[13] next unveils sales of more than $73 million for antipsychotic medication for children under 18 between 2000 and 2007, paid for by New Jersey Medicaid. A state official acknowledged the drugs may have been prescribed for conditions other than schizophrenia and bipolar, the approved uses. Pat Diegnan, a New Jersey assemblyman, wrote to the New Jersey Attorney General calling for an investigation to ascertain the safety and effectiveness of antipsychotic drugs. The article goes on to report that several states are filing lawsuits against drug makers—Lilly, AstraZeneca, and Johnson & Johnson—for alleged improper marketing and failure to disclose serious side effects. It was reported that only hours ago (at the time the article was being written), Lilly agreed to pay $15 million to settle a lawsuit filed by the state of Alaska, that claimed Lilly hid side effects of Zyprexa. Since Alaska spent $40 million over five years on Zyprexa, this isn't much of a settlement.

GOOD NEWS FOR JIM GOTTSTEIN: ELI LILLY DOESN'T FOOL JUDGE THIS TIME

An update on Zyprexa appeared in the *Indianapolis Star* July 3, 2008.[14] It mentioned that Eli Lilly is the largest private employer in Indianapolis. The same U.S. District Judge, Jack Weinstein, who presided over the case involving Attorney Gottstein this time issued a draft order saying the case against Lilly is strong enough to warrant a trial and is encouraging Lilly to settle for the $7.7 billion sought by the plaintiffs. The company is charged with illegally marketing Zyprexa for conditions the drug is not approved for and for overcharging insurance companies for the drug. The article added that Lilly still faces criminal and civil investigations by federal and state officials on charges of hiding the risks of Zyprexa and spreading misinformation about the effectiveness and safety of the drug. In this case, insurers and labor unions sued Lilly under the Racketeer Influenced and Corrupt Organizations Act (RICO). Judge Weinstein wrote in a draft order that there is sufficient evidence of fraud under RICO to go to a jury. Dates for jury trial as of July 2008 have not been set.

ASTRAZENECA

Delaware Online[15] reported on June 20, 2008, that the CEO of London-based AstraZeneca pharmaceutical company, who formerly led the company's U.S. unit in Fairfax, Delaware, faced questioning in London by attorneys representing thousands of plaintiffs across the United States. Paul Pennock of the New York law firm Weitz & Luxenberg, which is handling about 2,500 Seroquel cases in federal and state courts, stated that many people have been severely injured permanently because of the conduct of AstraZeneca and the effects of Seroquel. The drug was developed in Delaware by AstraZeneca's predecessor, Zeneca Group. The company admits it faces 8,440 personal injury lawsuits from more than 12,000 plaintiffs over Seroquel. Pennock believes the evidence at trial will show that AstraZeneca knew Seroquel could potentially cause high blood sugar levels, weight gain, and diabetes and that the company hid the dangers and avoided studying the issue.

　AstraZeneca said it had incurred legal costs of about $200 million, and that it expects its product liability insurance to cover its legal costs in all cases. It is just part of doing business. Obviously, we need measures that are more effective than punitive monetary damages to protect children from the avarice of the pharmaceutical industry.

Attorneys General in Three States Say AstraZeneca Illegally Promotes Seroquel[16]

Finally, on August 3, 2008, *Delaware Online* reported that AstraZeneca's phenomenal $4 billion in sales of Seroquel in 2007 is believed by attorneys general in Pennsylvania, Montana, and Arkansas to be due to illegal marketing of the drug. They believe company representatives promoted Seroquel for conditions it was not approved by the FDA to treat. These included use in children, mostly for bipolar; dementia in seniors; and use as a sleep aid. AstraZeneca in Fairfax, Delaware, is a major employer for people of that state.

I know that the AstraZeneca drug representative pushed Seroquel at our clinic for use in children. He paid at least weekly visits to our child psychiatrist, who chose Seroquel as his favorite antipsychotic for his child patients. But a loophole is that the psychiatrist probably invited him and sought his advice.

Even as the company seeks approval for additional uses of Seroquel, it is reported that it faces thousands of lawsuits brought by patients with serious side effects; 8,500 were filed for developing diabetes. Attorneys for the plaintiffs claim they can prove AstraZeneca hid the risks that Seroquel could cause high blood sugar levels, weight gain, and diabetes. Warnings about these risks did not appear on the drug's label until seven years after it was approved.

This article included information that challenges the effectiveness of the atypicals, including Seroquel. The 18-month study conducted in 2005 on more than 1,400 participants with schizophrenia found the atypicals no more effective than an older, cheaper neuroleptic. The Clinical Antipsychotic Trials of Intervention Effectiveness, or CATIE, compared four atypicals with "first generation" perphenazine (Trileptal). Nearly 75 percent of participants dropped out of the trials, either because they could not tolerate the drug, or because the drug was ineffective. Only 18 percent of patients on Seroquel stayed on the drug for the full course of the trial, the worst rate of the five drugs tested. Robert Rosenheck, psychiatry professor at Yale and co-sponsor of the CATIE trials, told reporters he has seen no reduction in the use of atypicals, despite their poor showing. He believes doctors have been swayed by drug company marketing and industry-sponsored research. Rosenheck is quoted: "You had 10 to 15 years of marketing in which the companies controlled the journal publications, controlled the speakers bureaus, controlled the dinners, controlled the patient advocacy groups, all of which communicated these drugs were a breakthrough. But there was little independent research."

Biederman is mentioned in the article in connection with his role as principal investigator in a study currently recruiting children ages 4 to 6, diagnosed as bipolar, on which to test Seroquel.

Damning Evidence Emerges on AstraZeneca's Silenced Study[17]

Even as charges continue to mount against AstraZeneca for alleged illegal tactics, the *Washington Post* revealed Study 15, which came to be called "cursed." It was a long-term trial of Seroquel that seemed to disprove the long-held assumption of the superiority of the atypical antipsychotics. Now critics' charges that AstraZeneca hid unfavorable results appear to have a factual basis. Study 15 was silenced in 1997, the same year the drug was approved by the FDA! Study 15 was never published or shared with doctors, while less rigorous studies with positive results were published and used in marketing campaigns. Study 15 was given to the FDA, but the administration strenuously maintains it cannot place such studies in the public domain. Study 15 came to light through lawsuits occurring across the nation alleging that Seroquel caused weight gain, hyperglycemia, and diabetes in thousands of patients. A Houston-based law firm, Blizzard, McCarthy & Nabers, one of several that have filed about 9,210 lawsuits over Seroquel, publicized the documents. A *Washington Post* analysis of the data from Study 15 showed that four out of five patients quit taking Seroquel in less than a year, raising doubts about its effectiveness. An AstraZeneca physician, Lisa Arvanitis, worried because 45 percent of the Seroquel patients experienced significant weight gain. But she made ambiguous statements and was praised by company strategist Richard Lawrence for "a great 'smoke and mirrors' job." He praised the company for putting a "positive spin" on "this cursed study."

THE PHYSICIAN PAYMENTS SUNSHINE ACT OF 2009[18]

U.S. Senators Grassley and Kohl introduced this act, which would require makers of pharmaceuticals, medical devices, and biologics to publicly report payments given to doctors that exceed $100 every year. These entities would report to the Department of Health and Human Services, and those payments would be posted online in a user-friendly way for public consumption. Failing to do so could result in fines as high as $1 million. A similar bill was introduced in 2007, but it was never considered by the 110th Congress. Kohl said he is confident it will pass this year, as he feels there is a "groundswell of support from every corner."

TWO STATES' PLANS TO REDUCE ANTIPSYCHOTIC PRESCRIPTIONS FOR CHILDREN

Florida took steps in 2008[19] to stem the number of antipsychotic prescriptions written for children under age 6. Doctors are required to get permission from the state before writing such a prescription. The dramatic reduction in prescriptions is described as "seismic change." Statistics show a nearly 75 percent drop overall, and a 40 percent drop among preschoolers. The state was approving nearly three out of four requests submitted. But when Medicaid took a closer look at the off-label prescribing of these drugs to preschoolers, about 200 doctors changed their minds about prescribing. (They obviously knew the drugs weren't FDA approved for this age group.)

The *Dallas Morning News*[20] reported on April 1, 2009, that Texas lawmakers are considering similar legislation to prohibit doctors from prescribing antipsychotic medications to children under the age of 11 without state permission. It applies to children covered by Medicaid. The article said thousands of Texas children under the age of 2 have been prescribed drugs like Seroquel and Risperdal. It reported that the drug industry, medical professionals, and mental health organizations staunchly oppose the bill.

So concludes my report of current affairs in the world of tainted ethics among doctors and the pharmaceutical industry—the psychopharmaceutical complex, that is.

IN CLOSING

I end with some beacons of hope that psychiatrists and medical doctors at large do care about their sacred oaths and do wish to curtail the cozy arrangements between their colleagues and the drug industry.

In August 2005, Steven Sharfstein, as president of the American Psychiatric Association, published a letter in *Psychiatric News* titled "Big Pharma and American Psychiatry: The Good, the Bad, and the Ugly."[21] He juxtaposed the ideal relationship between psychiatrists and the drug industry next to what actually existed then and now. He said that when the profit motive (of drug companies) and human good (role of psychiatry) are aligned it's a win-win situation. But the interests of big pharma and psychiatry often are not aligned, he lamented. He acknowledged the overmedicalization of mental disorders, saying psychiatrists have allowed the biopsychosocial model to become the bio-bio-bio model. He said continuing medical education (CME) sponsored by pharmaceutical companies has become more akin to marketing than to CME.

Sharfstein acknowledged the "ugly" practices that undermine the credibility of psychiatry. Doctors request fancy dinners, cruises, tickets to athletic events, and so on. And especially ugly, he said, are so-called "preceptorships," where drug representatives are allowed to sit in on patient sessions, allegedly to learn more about care for patients, and then advise the doctor about appropriate prescribing. He said psychiatrists should have the wisdom and distance to call drug company gifts what they really are: kickbacks and bribes.

Sharfstein's recommendations:

> We need to embrace a new professional ethic. The doctor-patient relationship should not be a market-driven phenomenon. Preceptorships should be considered unethical. Enticements, such as gifts and other perks, should be reined in . . . We must re-evaluate single-sponsored medical education events and phase them out in favor of a more general support for CME, along with careful policing of these events for bias. The amount and support received by individual clinicians and researchers from industry should be transparent . . . When we attend lectures at annual meetings and other educational events, and read journals and textbooks, we should know very clearly about the industry support given to presenters and authors . . . we should all be grateful for the modern pharmacopia and the promise of more improvements in the future . . . however, we must be very mindful that we cannot accept gratuities in the new medical marketplace.

What a pity that years following this excellent advice, little has changed. We can thank policy makers like Senator Grassley for taking charge and creating legislation to enforce Sharfstein's excellent recommendations.

Another positive sign came from medical students. A press release on October 22, 2007,[22] announced, "Thousands of medical students call on schools to eliminate pharmaceutical marketing influence." With the creation of National Pharm-Free Week, sponsored by the American Medical Student Association (AMSA), it was announced that thousands of future physicians and health care leaders would hold events across the country to promote liberation from pharmaceutical company influence. These included a Capitol Hill briefing, a new policy announcement at the University of Connecticut Medical Center regarding its new pharmaceutical policy, and a symposium to provide skills to become more critical and evidence-based prescribers. AMSA national president Michael Ehlert was quoted: "These marketing practices [those described in Sharfstein's letter above] . . . have led to over-medicating of the U.S. population. There is substantial evidence that marketing shapes physician prescribing habits. By eradicating pharmaceutical companies from all medical schools, hospitals, and academic medical centers, physicians will be able to go back to practicing evidence-based medicine."

In May 2007, AMSA released its PharmFree Scorecard, which ranks medical schools according to their pharmaceutical influence policies. Of all medical schools in the United States, five received a grade of "A," which translates into comprehensive school policy that restricts pharmaceutical representatives' presence at both the medical school campus and its academic medical centers. Forty schools received a grade of "F" for their lack of policy.

The press release ends by proclaiming that AMSA remains one of the few national organizations to completely reject all pharmaceutical advertisements and sponsorships. Its Web site is pharmfree.org.

Blessings and best wishes, AMSA.

Notes

CHAPTER 1

Epigraph: Breggin, Peter R. and Ginger Ross Breggin. *The War Against Children of Color* (Monroe, ME: Common Courage Press), p. 66.

1. All names are pseudonyms.

2. New York State has prohibited school staff from mentioning diagnoses. Instead, they recommend "medical assessments," which is euphemistic for being evaluated by a doctor for medication. They still talk liberally about medication without mentioning a diagnosis.

3. CHADD is an acronym for Children and Adults with Attention Deficit Disorder. It is a nationwide organization of lay people diagnosed with ADHD. It endorses neurobiological theory and stimulant medication.

4. Albee, George W. "A Radical View of the Causes, Prevention, and Treatment of Mental Disorders." Plenary presentation at the 2004 Conference of the International Center for the Study of Psychiatry and Psychology, Flushing, NY, October 8–10, 2004.

5. Psychotropic medication is synonymous with psychiatric medication; that is, chemicals that are prescribed for so-called "mental disorders," for the purpose of changing the chemistry in the brain.

6. The DSM is a publication of the American Psychiatric Association, used nationwide by all mental health professionals who are required to assign diagnoses to their patients or clients. All clinicians who collect third party reimbursement from insurance companies are required to assign diagnoses.

7. Kutchins, Herb and Stuart A. Kirk. *Making Us Crazy: The Psychiatric Bible and the Creation of Mental Disorders* (New York: The Free Press, 1997).

8. Abramson, John. *Overdosed America: The Broken Promise of American Medicine* (New York: HarperCollins, 2004).

9. Petersen, Melody. *Our Daily Meds: How the Pharmaceutical Companies Transformed Themselves Into Slick Marketing Machines and Hooked the Nation on Prescription Drugs* (New York: Sarah Crichton Books, 2008).

10. Vergano, Dan. "Study: Medical Manual's Authors Often Tied to Drugmakers." *USA Today,* April 20, 2006. Accessed June 15, 2009, at http:/usatoday.com/news/health/2006-04-19-manuals-drugmakers_x.htm.

11. Parker-Pope, Tara. "Psychiatry Handbook Linked to Drug Industry." The *New York Times*, May 6, 2008, Health section. Accessed December 31, 2008, at http://well.blogs.nytimes.com/2008/05/06/psychiatry-handbook-linked-to-drug-industry/?

12. Ulrich, Carolyn. "'Greening' of Mental Health?" *Eugene Weekly*, December 24, 2008, Happening People section. Accessed December 31, 2008, at http://www.eugeneweekly.com/2008/12/24/news.html.

13. Founded in 1988, MindFreedom advocates against forced medication, physical restraints, and electroconvulsive therapy (ECT). Its members worldwide identify themselves as survivors of human rights violations in a mental health system heavily influenced by outdated practices and pharmaceutical interests.

14. Ameen, Shahul. *Organic Mental Disorders.* Online book from Psyplexus. Accessed January 31, 2008, at http://www.psyplexus.com/neuropsychiatry/introduction.htm.

15. Burston, Daniel. "Diagnosis, Drugs, and Bipolar Disorder in Children." In *No Child Left Different*, Ed. Sharna Olfman (Westport, CT: Praeger Publishers, 2006), pp. 121–140, p. 135.

16. Foster children are especially vulnerable and are often alone in the world to the extent that no adult follows them with watchful and loving regard. Parents may have lost the right to advocate for their child. Not uncommonly, parents lose rights without just cause. Often caseworkers, not to be confused with master's level social workers, have no education in child development or previous experience with children. Yet they are empowered to make decisions that change lives. Qualifications of caseworkers vary from county to county and state to state, mostly depending upon the financial resources of the locality.

CHAPTER 2

Epigraph: Leo, Jonathan. "American Preschoolers on Ritalin." *Social Science and Modern Society.* January/February, 2002.

1. ADHD is the most commonly recognized acronym for attention deficit hyperactivity disorder.

2. Diller, Lawrence. *Should I Medicate My Child? Sane Solutions for Troubled Kids With—and Without—Psychiatric Drugs* (New York: Basic Books, 2002), p. 9.

3. Seidman, Larry. "An Overview of ADHD." *Helpletter*, Fall, 2005.

4. Peter Breggin, prolific author and co-author with Ginger Ross Breggin, is a long-time advocate for the ethical treatment of people afflicted with emotional distress. Since the 1970s he has issued warnings about the dangers of biological treatments, including psychotropic medications, psychosurgery, and institutionalization of mental patients. His warnings about these methods have been borne out time and time again.

5. Breggin, Peter. "Upcoming Government Conference on ADHD and Psychostimulants Asks the Wrong Questions," *ICSPP News* (International Center for the Study of Psychiatry and Psychology), Spring/Summer, 1998, p. 4.

6. U.S. Department of Justice, Drug Enforcement Administration, "METHYLPHENIDATE, Death from Ritalin." Accessed March 5, 2009, at http://ritalindeath.com/methylphenidate.htm.

7. International Narcotics Control Board, "Convention on Psychotropic Substances 1971," International Narcotics Control Board Web site. Accessed March 6, 2009, at http://www.incb.org/incb/convention_1971.html.

8. Breggin, Peter. "Report to the Consensus Development Conference on ADHD and Its Treatment," Peter Breggin Web site. Accessed February 16, 2008, at http://www.breggin.com/consensuscsppstmt.html.

9. Carey, William B. "What To Do About the ADHD Epidemic," *American Academy of Pediatrics Newsletter,* Autumn, 2003, 6–7. Accessed February 2, 2008, at http://www.ahrp.org/children/CareyADHD0603.php.

10. http://www.politicalwatchdog.com/psych_fraud/baughman.htm. Accessed March 5, 2009.

11. Diller, Lawrence. "When Your Life's Work Falls Outside the Demanded Result." In *The Last Normal Child: Essays on the Intersection of Kids, Culture, and Psychiatric Drugs.* (Westport, CT: Praeger Publishers, 2006), p. 94.

12. Bluestone, Judith. "Spurious Diagnosis, Specious Treatment," The Handle Institute. Accessed February 16, 2008, at http://www.handle.org/miscinfo/adhdconf.html.

13. Accessed February 16, 2008, at http://consensus.nih.gov/1998/1998Attention-DeficitHyperactivityDisorder110html.htm.

14. In the years since this correspondence occurred, no additional scientific studies have yielded evidence that would affect the veracity of these critics' arguments.

15. *Ethical Human Sciences and Services* 2002 (Number unavailable). Reproduced with the Permission of Springer Publishing Company, LLC, New York, NY 10036. Accessed June 5, 2009, at http://www.academyanalyticarts.org/galveswalker.htm.

16. Schwartz, J. M., P. W. Stoessel, L. R. Baxter, M. Karron, et al. "Systematic Changes in Cerebral Glucose Metabolic Rate After Successful Behavior Modification Treatment of Obsessive-Compulsive Disorder," *Archives of General Psychiatry* 53 (1996): 109–113.

17. Baumeister, A. and M. Hawkins. "Incoherence of Neuroimaging Studies of Attention Deficit/Hyperactivity Disorder, *Clinical Neuropharmacology* 24 (2001): 2–10.

18. Council of Regional Networks for Genetic Services. *Guidelines for Clinical Genetic Services for the Public's Health,* First Edition, April 1997.

19. Joseph, J. *The Gene Illusion: Genetic Research in Psychiatry and Psychology Under the Microscope* (Ross-on-Rye, UK: PCCS Books, 2003).

20. Lewis, T., F. Amini, and R. Lannon, *A General Theory of Love* (New York: Random House, 2000), pp. 149–153.

21. Holt, J. *How Children Fail* (New York: Perseus Books, 2000).

22. Leonard, G. *Education and Ecstasy* (Berkeley: North Atlantic Books, 1987).

23. Gatto, *The Underground History of American Education* (Oxford, NY: Oxford Village Press, 2001).

24. NAMI is a large organization of individuals who claim ownership of a mental health diagnosis or are related to someone who does. Like CHADD, it strongly advocates a neurobiological view and psychotropic medication treatment.

25. Petersen, Melody. *Our Daily Meds: How the Pharmaceutical Companies Transformed Themselves Into Slick Marketing Machines and Hooked the Nation on Prescription Drugs* (New York: Sarah Crichton Books, 2008), p. 96.

26. Breggin, Peter. *Toxic Psychiatry* (New York: St. Martin's Press, 1991), p. 308.

27. DeGrandpre, Richard. *Ritalin Nation* (New York: W.W. Norton, 2000), pp. 141–143.

28. Armstrong, Thomas. *The Myth of the A.D.D. Child* (New York: Plume, 1997), pp. 20–21.

29. Breggin, Peter R. and Ginger Ross Breggin. *The War Against Children of Color: Psychiatry Targets Inner City Youth* (Monroe, ME: Common Courage Press, 1998), p. 91.

30. Fred Baughman e-mailed this document on February 1, 2008.

31. "Medicating Kids." *Frontline,* PBS, April 10, 2001. Transcript of program accessed March 7, 2009, at http://www.pbs.org/wgbh/pages/frontline/shows/medicating/interviews/castellanos.html.

32. A Drug Recall Web site, "MRI Dye and Nephrogenic Systemic Fibrosis." Accessed February 4, 2008, at http://www.adrugrecall.com/mri-dye/mri-dye-nsf.html.

33. Castellanos, F. Xavier, Patti P. Lee, Wendy Sharp, Neal O. Jeffries, et al. "Developmental Trajectories of Brain Volume Abnormalities in Children and Adolescents With Attention-Deficit/Hyperactivity Disorder," *JAMA* (2002): 1740–1748.

34. Ravenel, S. DuBose. "A New Paradigm for ADD/ADHD and Behavioral Management Without Medication," *Ethical Human Sciences and Services*, Summer, 2002. The information comes from an updated version dated July 1, 2003, and accessed January 27, 2004, at http://www.icspp.org/research/anewparadigm.htm.

35. Leo, J. and D. Cohen. "Broken Brains or Flawed Studies? A Critical Review of ADHD Neuroimaging Research." *Journal of Mind and Behavior* 24 (2002): 29–55.

36. National Institutes of Health, "Brain Shrinkage in ADHD Not Caused by Medications," NIH News Release, October 8, 2002. Accessed October 2, 2008, at http://www.nih.gov/news/pr/oct2002/nimh-08.htm. (Emphasis added.)

37. NIMH, Science Update, "Brain Changes Mirror Symptoms in ADHD," National Institute of Mental Health. Accessed February 11, 2008, at http://www.nimh.nih.gov/science-news/2006/brain-changes-mirror-symptoms-in-adhd.shtml.

38. Shute, Nancy. "ADHD Brains Might Need More Growing Time," *U.S. News and World Report*, November 12, 2007. Accessed June 7, 2009, at http://health.usnews.com/articles/health/2007/adhd-brains-might-need-more-growing-time.html. (Emphasis added.)

39. NIMH, "Gene Predicts Better Outcome as Cortex Normalizes in Teens with ADHD," National Institute of Mental Health. Accessed June 4, 2009, at http://www.nimh.nih.gov/science-news/2007/gene-predicts-better-outcome-as-cortex-normalizes-in-teens-with-adhd.shtml. (Emphasis added.)

40. Jensen, Peter S., David Mrazek, Penelope K. Knapp, Laurence Steinberg, et al. "Evolution and Revolution in Child Psychiatry: ADHD as a Disorder of Adaptation." *Journal of the American Academy of Child & Adolescent Psychiatry* 36 (1997): 1672–1679. Accessed June 4, 2009, at http://www.ohsu.edu/psychiatry/pdfs/course%20Lectures%20&%20Lecture%20Materials%20-%20Child%20Psychiatry%20Handout%20B.pdf.

41. Jackson, Grace E. "A Curious Consensus." *Ethical Human Psychology and Psychiatry* 8 (2006): 55–60. Reproduced with the Permission of Springer Publishing Company, LLC, New York, NY 10036.

42. Ibid. p. 58.

43. Amen clinics, "ADHD/ADD How Brain SPECT Imaging Can Help." Accessed March 4, 2009, at http://www.amenclinics.com/clinics/information/ways-we-can-help/adhd-add/.

44. Flaherty, Lois, William Arroyo, Irene Chatoor, Roxanne Dryden Edwards, et al. *Brain Imaging and Child and Adolescent Psychiatry With Special Emphasis On SPECT.*

American Psychiatric Association, Council on Children, Adolescents and Their Families. January 2005. Accessed February 5, 2008, at http://www.psych.org/psych_pract/clin_ issues/populations/children/SPECT.pdf.

45. Bush, George. "Neuroimaging of Attention Deficit Hyperactivity Disorder: Can New Imaging Findings Be Integrated in Clinical Practice?" *Child and Adolescent Psychiatric Clinics of North America* 17 (2008): 385–404. Accessed March 4, 2009, at http://www.nmr.mgh.harvard.edu/BushLab/Site/Publications_files/Bush-2007-PCNA-Imaging+ADHD%20Dx.pdf.

46. add adhd advances Web site, Kane, Anthony, "The Use of Brain SPECT Imaging in ADHD." Accessed March 4, 2009, at http://addadhdadvances.com/SPECT.html.

CHAPTER 3

Epigraph: Hart, Tobin. "Spiritual Parenting." *Psychotherapy Networker*, May/June 2004, p. 53.
Progoff, Ira. Cited by Hart, from *The Symbolic and the Real: A New Psychological Approach to the Fuller Experience of Personal Existence* (New York: Julian, 1963), pp. 165–166.

1. Moreno, C., G. Lahe, C. Blanco, et al. "National Trends in the Outpatient Diagnosis and Treatment of Bipolar Disorder in Youth." *Archives of General Psychiatry* 64 (2007): 1032–1039.

2. Carey, Benedict and Katie Zezima. "Debate Over Children and Psychiatric Drugs." The *New York Times*, February 15, 2007. Accessed February 15, 2007, at http://www.nytimes.com/2007/02/15/us/15bipolar.html?_r=1&th&emc=th&oref=slogin.

3. Murphy, Shelley. "Doctor Is Sued in Death of Girl, 4—Her Psychiatrist Treated Her with Powerful Drugs." *Boston Globe*, April 4, 2008. Accessed June 5, 2009, at http://www.boston.com/news/local/articles/2008/04/04/doctor_is_sued_in_death_of_girl_4/.

4. Harris, Gardiner, Benedict Carey, and Janet Roberts. "Psychiatrists, Children and Drug Industry's Role." The *New York Times*, May 10, 2007.

5. This Associated Press article was printed in the *Ithaca Journal*, March 24, 2007.

6. Groopman, Jerome. "What's Normal?" The *New Yorker*, April 9, 2007, pp. 28–33.

7. *ABC News* reported on May 17, 2006, that the Massachusetts General Hospital's Department of Pediatric Psychopharmacology (Biederman's group) was recruiting 4- to 6-year-olds to establish "the effectiveness and tolerability" of Seroquel, still another powerful antipsychotic drug. The report mentioned that previous experiments by Biederman's group to test Risperdal and Zyprexa used children as young as 3. It noted that none of these drugs was FDA approved for children, and were known to cause diabetes, a deadly nervous disorder called neuroleptic malignant syndrome, low blood pressure, and to lead to higher deaths among the elderly. In fact, they carry "Black Box" warnings, the strongest warning the FDA can give. Vera Hassner Sharav of the Alliance for Human Research Protection, was quoted as saying these children may be at risk of permanent brain and nervous system damage by these drugs, and "We believe that physicians who subject children to the toxic effects of these drugs . . . are practicing outside medically accepted standards." This information was accessed February 15, 2009, at http://blogs.abcnews.com/theblotter/2006/05/tots_used_as_hu.html.

8. Diller, Lawrence. *Should I Medicate My Child? Sane Solutions for Troubled Kids With—and Without—Psychiatric Drugs* (New York: Basic Books, 2002), pp. 173–175.

9. Harris, Gardiner and Benedict Carey. "Researchers Fail to Reveal Full Drug Pay." The *New York Times,* June 8, 2008. Accessed June 5, 2009, at http://www.nytimes.com/2008/06/08/us/08conflict.html?ei=5124&en=62ad8cb804db003a&ex=1370750400&partner=permalink&exprod=permalink&pagewanted.

10. DSS case file, *Boston Globe*, February 8, 2007. Accessed March 12, 2009, at http://www.boston.com/news/local/massachusetts/articles/2007/02/08/dss_case_file/.

11. Tanner, Lindsey. "Study Finds More Bipolar Diagnoses in Kids: Experts Question Whether It's Real." *The Ithaca Journal*, September 4, 2007.

12. *Frontline*, PBS. "The Medicated Child," January 8, 2008. (Emphasis added).

13. Breggin, Peter. "Psychiatry Makes War on 'Bipolar Children.'" *Huffington Post,* May 23, 2008. Accessed at http://www.huffingtonpost.com/dr-peter-breggin/psychiatry-makes-war-on-b_b_103337.html.

14. None of the drugs recommended for bipolar disorder were, at that time, approved by the Food and Drug Administration (FDA) for pediatric use.

15. The URL used to access this information is no longer available. In place of Biederman's extensive home page is a general description of the department where he is still listed as head. As of April 2009 it can be accessed at http://www.massgeneral.org/children/research/researchers/biederman.aspx.

16. Diller, Lawrence. *Should I Medicate My Child? Sane Solutions for Troubled Kids With—and Without—Psychiatric Drugs* (New York: Basic Books, 2002), pp. 173–175.

17. Harris, Gardiner. "Use of Antipsychotics in Children Is Criticized." The *New York Times*, November 19, 2008. Accessed November 22, 2008, at http://www.nytimes.com/2008/11/19/health/policy/19fda.html.

18. Papolos, Dmitri and Janice Papolos. *The Bipolar Child: The Definitive and Reassuring Guide to Childhood's Most Misunderstood Disorder* (New York: Broadway Books, 2002. Hereafter cited in the text by page numbers).

19. Groopman, Jerome. "What's Normal?" *The New Yorker*, April 9, 2007, pp. 28–33.

20. Breggin, Peter. "Electroshock: Scientific, Ethical, and Political Issues." *International Journal of Risk and Safety in Medicine* 11 (1998).

21. Burston, Daniel. "Diagnosis, Drugs, and Bipolar Disorder in Children." In *No Child Left Different,* ed. Sharna Olfman (Westport, CT: Praeger Publishing, 2006), pp. 121–140.

22. Lewinsohn, P. M., J. R. Seeley, and D. M. Klein. "Bipolar Disorder in Adolescents: Epidemiology and Suicidal Behavior." In *Bipolar Disorder in Childhood and Early Adolescence,* ed. B. Geller and M.P. DelBello (New York: Guilford Press, 2003), pp. 7–24.

23. McLellan, J. Editorial in *Journal of the American Academy of Child and Adolescent Psychiatry* 44 (March, 2005): 236–239.

24. Ibid.

25. Kowatch, R. A., M. Fristad, B. Birmaher, K. D. Wagner, et al. "Treatment Guidelines for Children and Adolescents with Bipolar Disorder," *Journal of the American Academy of Child and Adolescent Psychiatry* 3 (2005): 213–235. The Child Psychiatric Workgroup on Bipolar Disorder collaborated with authors.

26. Breggin, Peter R. *Brain Disabling Treatments in Psychiatry* (New York: Springer Publishing, 2008).

27. Sinaikin, P. "How I Learned to Stop Worrying and Love the DSM." *Psychiatric Times* (February, 2004): 103–105.

28. Levine, M. *A Mind at a Time* (New York: Simon and Schuster, 2002).

CHAPTER 4

Epigraph: Mercogliano, Chris. *Teaching the Restless: One School's Remarkable No-Ritalin Approach to Helping Children Learn and Succeed* (Boston: Beacon Press), p. 33.

1. These words, coined by Peter Breggin and introduced in his book *Toxic Psychiatry,* refer to the collaboration between psychiatry and the pharmaceutical empire; this collaboration serves the fiscal interests of both by promoting biochemical treatments for emotional distress.

2. All names are pseudonyms.

3. Zito, Julie Magno, Daniel J. H. Safer, Susan dosReis, James F. Gardner, et al. "Psychotropic Practice Patterns for Youth: A 10-Year Perspective." *Archives of Pediatric and Adolescent Medicine* 157 (January, 2003): 17–25. Accessed March 15, 2009, at http://www.archpediatrics.com.

4. Zito, Julie Magno, Daniel J. Safer, Susan dosReis, James F. Gardner, et al. "Trends in the Prescribing of Psychotropic Medications to Preschoolers." *Journal of the American Medical Association* 283 (2000): 1025–1030.

5. Carey, Benedict and Gardiner Harris. "Psychiatric Group Faces Scrutiny Over Drug Industry Ties." The *New York Times*, July 12, 2008.

6. Whitaker, Robert. "Anatomy of an Epidemic: Psychiatric Drugs and the Astonishing Rise of Mental Illness in America." *Ethical Human Psychology and Psychiatry* 7 (Spring 2005): 23–35.

7. Vedantam, Shankar. "More Children Now Taking Psychiatric Drugs." The *Washington Post,* January 14, 2003. Accessed March 15, 2009, at http://www.stevequayle.com/News.alert/03_Global/030114.more.kids.psych.dru.html.

8. Mental Health E-News, "W. Post: More Kids Receiving Psychiatric Drugs," New York Association of Psychiatric Rehabilitation Services. Accessed March 15, 2009, at http://www.nyaprs.org/Pages/Printable/View_Enews.cfm?EnewsID=2321.

9. Chansky, Tamar. *Freeing Your Child from Obsessive-Compulsive Disorder* (New York: Three Rivers Press, 2000).

10. Natural Solutions Foundation. Accessed March 19, 2009, at http://www.healthfreedomusa.org/?p=558.

11. Texas Office of the Comptroller. Carole Keeton Strayhorn. *Texas Health Care Claims Study—Special Report on Foster Children*. December 14, 2006.

12. Advisory from the Committee on Ways and Means, Subcommittee on Income Security and Family Support. Press release. "Rep. Jim McDermott Introduces The Investment in Kids Act—Calls for Most Comprehensive Reform of Child Welfare in Nearly 30 Years." February 14, 2008.

13. Advisory from the Committee on Ways and Means, Subcommittee on Income Security and Family Support. Press release. "McDermott Announces Hearing on the Utilization of Psychotropic Medication for Children in Foster Care." May 1, 2008.

14. National Alliance for the Mentally Ill. "House Passes Child Medication Safety Act," A report, News of Spring 2003 at NAMI Web site. Accessed March 20, 2009, at http://www.namiscc.org/News/2003/Spring/ChildMedicationSafetyAct.htm.

15. Information accessed from GovTrack.us, Tracking the 110th United States Congress. Accessed January 29, 2008, and March 20, 2009, at http://www.govtrack.us/congress.

16. Preventive Psychiatry E-Newsletter #292, edited by Gary Kohl, M.D. "Psychotropic Drugs Are Toxins Given in Sublethal Doses." March 6, 2007.

17. Moncreiff, Jonanna."Understanding Psychotropic Drug Action: The Contribution of the Brain-Disabling Theory." *Ethical Human Psychology and Psychiatry* 9 (2007): 170–179.

18. Jackson, Grace E. "Chemobrain—A Psychiatric Drug Phenomenon." Paper presented at the International Center for the Study of Psychiatry and Psychology Annual Convention, Arlington, VA, October 13–14, 2007.

19. Diller, Lawrence. *Should I Medicate My Child? Sane Solutions for Troubled Kids With—and Without—Psychiatric Drugs* (New York: Basic Books, 2002), p. 123.

20. Ibid. p. 121.

21. Jackson, Grace E. in *Rethinking Psychiatric Drugs* (Bloomington, IN: Author House, 2005), pp. 12–13.

22. Ibid. pp. 260–263.

23. Snyder, Solomon H. *Drugs and the Brain* (New York: Scientific American Library, 1999).

24. Gross, Mortimer D. "Origin of Stimulant Use for Treatment of Attention Deficit Disorder." *American Journal of Psychiatry* 152 (1995): 298–299.

25. The Carlat Psychiatry Blog. Accessed February 6, 2008, at http://carlatpsychiatry.blogspot.com/search/label/ADHD.

26. Jackson, Grace E. *Rethinking Psychiatric Drugs* (Bloomington, IN: Author House, 2005), pp. 264–265.

27. Diller, Lawrence. *Should I Medicate My Child? Sane Solutions for Troubled Kids With—and Without—Psychiatric Drugs* (New York: Basic Books, 2002), p. 133.

28. Jackson, Grace E. *Rethinking Psychiatric Drugs* (Bloomington, IN: Author House, 2005), p. 289.

29. Stein, David B. *Ritalin Is Not the Answer Action Guide* (San Francisco: Jossey-Bass, 2002), p. 24.

30. Breggin, Peter. "Upcoming Government Conference on ADHD and Psychostimulants Asks the Wrong Questions." Peter Breggin Web site. http://www.breggin/consensuswrong.html.

31. Breggin, Peter. Interview for "Medicating Children," *Frontline*, PBS, April 10, 2001.

32. Accessed May 30, 2008, at http://www.drugs-forum.co.uk/forum/showthread.php?t=2669.

33. Diller, Lawrence. "Bitter Pill." *Psychotherapy Networker,* January/February 2005.

34. Ravenel, DuBose. "A New Paradigm for ADD/ADHD and Behavioral Management Without Medication." *Ethical Human Sciences and Service* 4 (Summer, 2002): 93–106.

35. Jackson, Grace E. *Rethinking Psychiatric Drugs* (Bloomington, IN: Author House, 2005), pp. 274–276.

36. Doheny, Kathleen. "Treating ADHD: Drugs or Therapy Work." *WebMD*, July 20, 2007. Accessed March 20, 2009, at http://www.webmd.com/add-adhd/news/20070720/treating-adhd-drugs-or-therapy-work.

37. DeNoon, Daniel. "ADHD Drug Does Stunt Growth." *WebMD*, July 20, 2007. Accessed March 20, 2009, at http://www.webmd.com/add-adhd/news/20070720/adhd-drug-does-stunt-growth.

38. Glasser, Howard. NHA Advanced training, Tucson, AZ, February 16–20, 2004.

39. Greene, Alan, "Canada Bans Adderall XR . . ." Accessed June 9, 2009, at http://www.webmd.com/add-adhd/canada-bans-adderall-xr.

40. Szabo, Liz. "New Warnings Due for ADHD Drugs." *USA Today*, June 29, 2005.

41. Gardner, Amanda. "FDA Gets Tough on ADHD Drugs." *HealthDay News*, June 29, 2005.

42. *Atlanta Constitution*, July 30, 2005 (author's name not available). This report and the preceding one were e-mailed to our clinic by enews@nyaprs.org on July 1, 2005.

43. Stein, David B. *Stop Medicating, Start Parenting* (Lanham, MD: Taylor Trade Publishing, 2004), p. 41.

44. Diller, Lawrence. *Should I Medicate My Child? Sane Solutions for Troubled Kids With—and Without—Psychiatric Drugs* (New York: Basic Books, 2002), p. 175.

45. Fischer, Vernon W. and Hendrick Barmer. "Cardiomyopathic Findings Associated With Ritalin (Methylphenidate)." *Journal of the American Medical Association* 238 (1977): 1497.

46. Henderson, T. A. and V. W. Fischer. "Effects of Methyphenidate (Ritalin) on Mammalian Myocardial Ultrastructure." *The American Journal of Cardiovascular Pathology* 5 (1994): 68–78.

47. Wang, G. J., N. D. Volkow, J. S. Fowler, R. Ferrieri, et al. "Methylphenidate Decreases Regional Cerebral Blood Flow in Normal Human Subjects." *Life Science* 54 (1994): PL143–PL146.

48. Nasrallah, H. J., J. Joney, S. Olson, M. McCalley-Whitters, et al. "Cortical Atrophy in Young Adults with a History of Hyperactivity in Childhood." *Psychiatry Research* 17 (1986): 241–246.

49. Cole, Krystle A. "The Effects of Long-term Ritalin (Methyphenidate) Use." Accessed March 21, 2009, at www.neurosoup.com/pdf/effects_of_longterm_ritalin_use.pdf.

50. DeNoon, Daniel, "ADHD Drug Does Stunt Growth." *WebMD*, July 20, 2007. Accessed March 20, 2009, at http://www.webmd.com/add-adhd/news/20070720/adhd-drug-does-stunt-growth.

51. International Center for the Study of Psychiatry and Psychology Web site posting at http://www.icspp.org.

52. Stein, David B. *Ritalin Is Not the Answer Action Guide* (San Francisco: Jossey-Bass, 2002), p. 24.

53. DeNoon, Daniel, "ADHD Drug Does Stunt Growth." *WebMD*, July 20, 2007. Accessed March 20, 2009, at http://www.webmd.com/add-adhd/news/20070720/adhd-drug-does-stunt-growth.

54. Karch, Steven B. *Pathology of Drug Abuse* (Boca Raton, FL: Taylor & Francis Group, 2009). This is the newest edition. Information not available for the edition cited by Baughman.

55. Johnson, Linda A. "Study (Survey): ADHD Drugs Send Thousands to ERs." Associated Press, May 24, 2006.

56. Vetter, Victoria L., Josephine Eliz, Christopher Erickson, Stuart Berger, et al. "Cardiovascular Monitoring of Children and Adolescents With Heart Disease Receiving

Stimulant Drugs: A Scientific Statement From the American Heart Association Council on Cardiovascular Disease in the Young Congenital Cardiac Defects Committee and the Council on Cardiovascular Nursing." *Circulation* (2008): 2407–2423. Accessed May 24, 2008, at http://circ.ahajournals.org/cgi/content/full/117/18/2407.

57. Jackson, Grace. *Rethinking Psychiatric Drugs* (Bloomington, IN: Author House, 2005. Jackson cites Kathryn Schultz and David Healy for this information).

58. Ibid. pp. 70–71.

59. Ibid. p. 72. Jackson cites Steven M. Stahl; Kalnya Z. Bezchlibynk-Butler and J. Joel Jeffries; Y. G. Ni and R. Miledi; and J. Garcia-Colunga, et al.

60. Zito, Julie Magno, Daniel J. Safer, Susan dosReis, James F. Gardner, et al. "Rising Prevalence of Antidepressants Among U.S. Youths." *Pediatrics* 109 (2002): 721–727. Accessed June 12, 2006, at http://www.pediatrics.org.

61. Delate, T., A. J. Galenberg, V. A. Simmons, and B. R. Motheral. "Trends in the Use of Antidepressants in a National Sample of Commercially Insured Pediatric Patients." *Psychiatric Services* 55 (2004): 387–391. Accessed March 22, 2009, at http://psychservices.psychiatryonline.org/cgi/content/full/55/4/387.

62. Olfson, Mark, Carlos Blanco, Linxu Liu, Carmen Moreno, and Gonzalo Laje. "National Trends in the Outpatient Treatment of Children and Adolescents with Anti-psychotic Drugs." *Archives of General Psychiatry* 63 (June, 2006): 679–685.

63. Breggin, Peter R. and David Cohen. *Your Drug May Be Your Problem* (New York: Perseus Publishing, 1999), p. 67.

64. Baum Hedlund Web site, "National Class Action Filed Against Drug-Maker for Paxil-Induced Suicides in Youth," at http://www.baumhedlundlaw.com. Accessed March 24, 2006.

65. Breggin, Peter R. "The Proven Dangers of Antidepressants." Report to the FDA, August 23, 2004.

66. Breggin, Peter R. "Suicidality, Violence and Mania Caused by Selective Serotonin Reuptake Inhibitors (SSRIs): A Review and Analysis." *International Journal of Risk & Safety in Medicine* 16 (2003/2004): 31–49.

67. This is taken from Breggin's Report to the FDA, cited above, endnote #65. Other trials are from the citation in endnote #66.

68. Emslie, G. J., A. J. Rush, W. A. Weinberg, R. A. Kowatch, et al. "A Double-Blind, Randomized, Placebo-Controlled Trial of Fluoxetine in Children and Adolescents with Depression." *Archives of General Psychiatry* 54 (1997): 1031–1037.

69. King, R., M. Riddle, P. Chappell, M. Hardin, et al. "Emergence of Self-destructive Phenomena in Children and Adolescents During Fluoxetine Treatment." *Journal of the American Academy of Child and Adolescent Psychiatry* 30 (1991): 179–186.

70. Jackson, Grace E. *Rethinking Psychiatric Drugs* (Bloomington, IN: Author House, 2005), pp. 91–92.

71. Crenson, Matt. "Some Say Ending Antidepressants Daunting." Associated Press Release, August 6, 2006.

72. Laurance, Jeremy. "Antidepressant Drugs Don't Work—Official Study." *The Independent*, Health and Well Being Section, February 26, 2008. Accessed June 9, 2009, at http://www.independent.co.uk/life-style/health-and-families/health-news/anti depressant-drugs-udontu-work-ndash-official-study-787264.html.

73. Jackson, Grace E. *Rethinking Psychiatric Drugs* (Bloomington, IN: Author House, 2005), p. 98.

74. Schwartz, et al. Endnote #16, chapter 2.

75. Leo, Jonathan. "The SSRI Trials in Children: Disturbing Implications for Academic Medicine." *Ethical Human Psychology and Psychiatry* 8 (Spring, 2006): 29–41.

76. Gever, John. "Negative Trial Results Given to FDA May Go Unpublished or Sanitized." *MedPage Today,* November 25, 2008. Accessed June 9, 2009, at http://www.medpagetoday.com/PublicHealthPolicy/ClinicalTrials/11912.

77. Official Wire, "Psychiatrists Advised FDA Fourteen Years Ago Not to Act on Suicide and Homicidal Antidepressant Risks," Web site of Official Wire, http://www.officialwire.com/main.php?action=posted_news&rid=20630. Accessed March 24, 2009.

78. "Antidepressant Drug Induced Suicides: Evidence of 'Iceberg Effect' Revealed," posted by Vera Sharav, June 10, 2004. Accessed June 9, 2009, at http://ahrp.org/infomail/04/06/10.php.

79. Sherman, Carl. "No Credible Evidence for Anti-Suicidal Effect from Psychtropic Drugs." *Clinical Psychiatry News Online* 30 (August, 2002). Accessed June 9, 2009, at http://nourishingdestiny.com/discussions/544.

80. Brody, Michael. "Child Psychiatry, Drugs, and the Corporation." In *No Child Left Different,* ed. Sharna Olfman (Westport, CT: Praeger Publishing, 2006), pp. 91–1050.

81. Emslie, G. J., A. J. Rush, W. A. Weinberg, R.A. Kowatch, et al. "A Double-Blind, Randomized, Placebo-Controlled Trial of Fluoxetine in Children and Adolescents with Depression." *Archives of General Psychiatry* 54 (1997): 1031–1037.

82. Healy, David. *Let Them Eat Prozac.* Cited by Brody, p. 103.

83. Leo, Jonathan. "The SSRI Trials in Children: Disturbing Implications for Academic Medicine." *Ethical Human Psychology and Psychiatry* 8 (Spring, 2006): 29–41.

84. Emslie, G. J., J. Heiligenstein, K. D. Wagner, S. L. Hoog, et al. "Fluoxetine for Acute Treatment of Depression in Children and Adolescents: A Placebo-Controlled, Randomized Clinical Trial." *Journal of American Academy of Child and Adolescent Psychiatry* 41 (2002): 1205–1215.

85. Baum Hedlund Web site, "National Class Action Filed Against Drug-Maker For Paxil-induced Suicides in Youths." Accessed April 27, 2006, at http://www.baumhedlundlaw.com/media/ssri/PaxilSuicideClassAction.htm.

86. Ibid. "Federal Judge Rules Against GSK and Allows Teenage Paxil Suicide Case to Go to Trial," and "Judge Approves $40 Million Settlement in Second Phase of National Pediatric Paxil Class Action—Insurance Companies to Be Reimbursed."

87. Since that time, Risperdal has been approved to treat bipolar in youth aged 10 to 17.

88. Harris, Gardiner. "Use of Antipsychotics in Children Is Criticized." The *New York Times,* November 19, 2008. Accessed November 22, 2008, at http://www.nytimes.com/2008/11/19/health/policy/19fda.html.

89. Olfson, Mark, Carlos Blanco, Linxu Liu, Carmen Moreno, and Gonzalo Laje. "National Trends in the Outpatient Treatment of Children and Adolescents With Anti-psychotic Drugs." *Archives of General Psychiatry* 63 (June, 2006): 679–685.

90. Boyles, Salynn. "More Kids Get Antipsychotic Drugs." *WebMDHealthNews,* May 3, 2006. Accessed June 9, 2009, at http://www.webmd.com/mental-health/news/20060503/more-kids-antipsychotic-drugs.

91. Whitaker, Robert. *Mad in America* (New York: Perseus Publishing, 2002), pp. 203–208.

92. Article distributed via e-mail by Gary Kohl on March 19, 2008. He cites as his source: http://www.mindfreedom.org/kb/psychiatric-drugs/antipsychotics/areford-neuroleptics.

93. Breggin, Peter R., and David Cohen. *Your Drug May Be Your Problem* (New York: Perseus Publishing, 1999), pp. 69–70.

94. Jackson, Grace E. (*Rethinking Psychiatric Drugs.* Bloomington, IN: Author House, 2005), pp. 236–239.

95. Harris, Gardiner, Benedict Carey, and Janet Roberts. "Psychiatrists, Children and Drug Industry's Role." The *New York Times*, May 10, 2007.

96. *Science Daily* Web site, "Antipsychotic Drugs Linked To Insulin Resistance In Children," October 21, 2004. Accessed July 3, 2008, at http://www.sciencedaily.com/releases/2004/10/041021084911.htm.

97. Elias, Marilyn. "New Antipsychotic Drugs Carry Risks for Children." *USA Today,* May 2, 2006.

98. Hansen, Ben. "Michigan Lawsuit Uncovers Psychiatry's Dark Secret: Drug-Induced Movement Disorders in Young Children." *ICSPP Newsletter* (Spring, 2007): 4–5.

99. Boyles, Salynn. "Newer Antipsychotics No Better in Kids." *WebMD Health News*, September 15, 2008. Accessed March 26, 2009, at http://www.rxlist.com/script/main/art.asp?articlekey=92675.

100. Jackson, Grace E. *Rethinking Psychiatric Drugs* (Bloomington, IN: Author House, 2005), pp. 239–240.

101. Drugs.com Web site at http://www.drugs.com/depakote.html. Accessed July 7, 2008.

102. RxList Web site at http://www.rxlist.com/catapres-drug.htm. Accessed March 27, 2009.

103. Angell, Marcia. *The Truth About the Drug Companies* (New York: Random House, 2004), pp. 6–10.

104. Whitaker, Robert. *Mad in America* (New York: Perseus Publishing, 2002), pp. 261–265.

105. Harris, Gardiner. "Psychiatrists Top List in Drug Maker Gifts." The *New York Times*, June 27, 2007.

106. Crosby, Andrew. "Psychiatric Rights on Trial: Faith Myers and Jim Gottstein Win One For Us." *ICSPP Newsletter* 4 (2006): 14–16.

107. Crosby, Andrew. "Jim Gottstein and Friends Meet Eli Lilly: The Legal Battle Over the Zyprexa Documents." *ICSPP Newsletter* 1 (2007): 7–9.

108. Gottstein, Jim. "CriticalThinkRx and PsychRights' Lawsuit Against the State of Alaska's Psychiatric Drugging of Children." Presentation at the annual conference of the International Center for the Study of Psychiatry and Psychology. October 10–12, 2008.

109. Demer, Lisa. "Foster Kids Say Medication Is Overprescribed," *Anchorage Daily News,* November 15, 2008. Accessed June 11, 2009, at http://www.adn.com/life/health/v-printer/story/589914.html.

110. Harris, Gardiner, Benedict Carey, and Janet Roberts. "Psychiatrists, Children and the Drug Industry's Role." The *New York Times*, May 10, 2007.

CHAPTER 5

Epigraph: Pipher, Mary. *In the Shelter of Each Other. Rebuilding Our Families* (New York: Ballantine Books, 1996), pp. 116, 122.

1. Alliance for Human Research Protection (AHRP) Web site. Sharav was interviewed by *New York Times* reporters Marc Santora and Benedict Carey on April 13, 2005 for an article, "Depressed? New York City Screens for People at Risk." The Web site reproduced the article. Accessed February 25, 2009, at http://www.ahrp.org/infomail/05/04/13.php.

2. Web site of TeenScreen. Accessed February 24, 2009, at http://www.teenscreentruth.com/TeenScreens_New_Consent_Procedures.pdf.

3. Web site of TeenScreen. Accessed February 24, 2009, at http://www.teenscreentruth.com/TeenScreens_New_Consent_FactSheet.pdf.

4. If Aliah were truly suicidal, the evaluator was seriously irresponsible to wait six weeks before taking preventive action. Moreover, six weeks after the evaluation Aliah was reportedly functioning normally, throwing considerable doubt on her suicidality.

5. Accessed February 10, 2009, at http://teenscreen-locations.com/noteenscreen.htm.

6. U.S. Department of Health and Human Services. *Report of the Surgeon General's Conference on Children's Mental Health: A National Action Agenda.* Rockville, MD: U.S. Department of Health and Human Services, Department of Education, Department of Justice, 2001, p. 3.

7. U.S. Department of Health and Human Services. "Surgeon General Releases a National Action Agenda on Children's Mental Health." Embargoed for Release by *HHS News*, January 3, 2001, 12:00 A.M., E.D.T. Accessed March 8, 2007, at http://www.hhs.gov/surgeongeneral/news/pressreleases/pressreleasechildren.htm.

8. New Freedom Commission on Mental Health, *Achieving the Promise: Transforming Mental Health Care in America. Final Report.* DHHS Pub. No. SMA-03-3832. Rockville, MD: 2003.

9. Ibid. p. 58.

10. Accessed May 9, 2007 at http://wrightslaw.com/advoc/articles/alessi_problems_blame.html.

11. Lenzer, Jeanne. "Bush Launches Controversial Mental Health Plan," *BMJ,* August 14, 2004. Accessed March 24, 2005, at http://www.bmj.com/cgi/content/full/329/7462/367-a. (Emphasis added.)

12. Fisher, Daniel. "Screening Kids Poses Risk of Harm." *Boston Globe,* October 3, 2007. Letters to Editor. Accessed February 4, 2009, at http://www.boston.com/news/globe/editorial_opinion/letters/articles/2007/10/03/screening_kids_poses_risk_of_harm/.

13. Goldberg, Carey. "Mental Screening for Young to Begin: Mass. Doctors to Offer Questionnaires to Children on Medicaid." *Boston Globe*, December 27, 2007. Accessed March 10, 2008, at http://www.boston.com/news/health/articles/2007/12/27/mental_screening_for_young_to_begin/.

14. Boyles, Salynn. "More Kids Get Antipsychotic Drugs." *WebMDHealth News,* May 3, 2006. Accessed June 11, 2009, at http://www.webmd.com/mental-health/news/20060503/more-kids-antipsychotic-drugs.

15. U.S. Department of Health and Human Services. *Mental Health: A Report of the Surgeon General.* Rockville, MD: U.S. Department of Health and Human Services, Substance Abuse and Mental Health Services Administration, Center for Mental Health

Services, National Institutes of Health, National Institute of Mental Health, 1999. Executive Summary.

16. Ibid.

17. Accessed February 11, 2009, at http://www.accessiblesociety.org/topics/ada/olmsteadoverview.htm.

18. U.S. Department of Health and Human Services. *Report of the Surgeon General's Conference on Children's Mental Health: A National Action Agenda.* Rockville, MD: U.S. Department of Health and Human Services, Department of Education, Department of Justice, 2001, pp. 6–7.

19. Vitiello, Benedetto. "Psychopharmacology for Young Children: Clinical Needs and Research Opportunities." *Pediatrics* 108 (2001): 983–989. Accessed March 12, 2008, at http://pediatrics.aappublications.org/cgi/content/full/108/4/983.

20. Ibid.

21. New Freedom Commission on Mental Health. *Achieving the Promise: Transforming Mental Health Care in America. Final Report.* DHHS Pub. No. SMA-03-3832. Rockville, MD: 2003, p. 57.

22. Ibid. p. 57.

23. Mental Health Commission. "Report of the Subcommittee on Consumer Issues: Shifting to a Recovery-Based Continuum of Community Care." March 5, 2003. Accessed March 31, 2005, at http://www.mentalhealthcommission.gov/subcommittee/Consumer_022803.doc.

24. New Freedom Commission on Mental Health. "The Report of the Subcommittee on Rights and Engagement." March 2003. Accessed March 31, 2005, at http://www.mentalhealthcommission.gov/subcommittee/rights_022803.doc.

25. USMI Roundtable Discussion. Executive Summary, "The Changing Face of Mental Health Services In The Veterans Health Administration." Washington, D.C. October 18, 2004. Accessed February 14, 2009, at http://usminstitute.org/pdf/MHExecSummaryOct04.pdf.

26. Web site of the Mental Illness Research, Education, and Clinical Center (MIRECC), U.S. Department of Veterans Affairs. Accessed June 11, 2009, at http://www.desertpacific.mirecc.va.gov/conferences/rehab-and-recovery/handouts/murphy.pdf.

27. Disabled American Veterans Web site. Accessed February 14, 2009, at http://www.dav.org/voters/documents/statements/Atizado20080401/pdf.

28. Policy Options: Subcommittee on Evidence-Based Practices on Mental Health Policy and Psychotropic Drugs. February 6, 2003. Accessed March 31, 2004, at http://www.mentalhealthcommission.gov/subcommittee/MEDICATIONS_012903.doc.

29. New Freedom Commission on Mental Health. *Achieving the Promise: Transforming Mental Health Care in America. Final Report.* DHHS Pub. No. SMA-03-3832. Rockville, MD: 2003, p. 63.

30. Murray, Melissa. "A Model for Diagnosing Mental Health Problems in the Young." *The Journal of the College of Physicians and Surgeons of Columbia University* 18 (Fall, 1998). Accessed February 17, 2009, at http://cpmcnet.columbia.edu/news/journal/journal-o/archives/jour_v18no3/model.html.

31. Sharav, Vera. "TeenScreen—Under Intense Criticism Nationally." *Arkansas Democrat Gazette.* March 11, 2006. Accessed April 17, 2008, at http://www.ahrp.org/cms/content/view/106/31/.

32. Ibid.

33. This may explain the unethical manner in which Chelsea Rhoades was treated when she was tested at her school, as well as the botched process that led to Aliah Gleason's travesty.

34. NAMI booklet. *Help and Hope—Caring for Your Child's Mental Health,* May 11, 2000. (Emphasis added.)

35. REACH Institute Web site. Accessed February 16, 2009, at http://reachinstitute. net/Jensenbionew.html.

36. NAMI Web site. Accessed February 16, 2009, at http://nami.org/Template. cfm?Section=Press_Release_Archive&template=/contentmanagement/contentdisplay.cfm& contentID=5790&title=NAMI+Joins+In+Announcing+New+Center+For+The+ Advancement+Of+Children+MentalHealth.

37. Pringle, Evelyn. "Meet Laurie Flynn TeenScreen's Top Pusher." *Counterpunch,* June 5, 2005. Accessed February 17, 2009, at http://www.counterpunch.org/ pringle06062005.html.

38. Gaouette, Nicole. "Grassley Probes Financing of Advocacy Group for Mental Health," *Bloomberg.com*, April 6, 2009. Accessed June 16, 2009, at http://www.psychrights. org/Articles/090406BloombergOnGrassleyNAMILtr.htm.

39. TeenScreen Web site. Accessed Feburary 16, 2009, at http://www.TeenScreen.org.

40. Pringle, Evelyn. "TeenScreen—The Law Suits Begin," *Scoop Independent News,* June 13, 2005. Accessed February 17, 2009, at http://scoop.co.nz/stories/ HL0506/S00168.htm.

41. Sharav, Vera. "TeenScreen—Under Intense Criticism Nationally," *Arkansas Democrat Gazette,* March 11, 2006. Accessed April 17, 2008, at http://www.ahrp.org/ cms/content/view/106/31/.

42. *Health Supreme* Web site. Hasslberger, Sepp. "Psychiatric Drugs: TeenScreen Draws Criticism, Legal Challenge," June 17, 2005. Accessed February 17, 2009, at http://www.newmediaexplorer.org/sepp/2005/06/17/psychiatric_drugs_teenscreen_draws_ criticism_legal_challenge.htm.

43. Pringle, Evelyn. "TeenScreen—The Law Suits Begin." *Scoop Independent News*, June 13, 2005. Accessed February 17, 2009, at http://scoop.co.nz/stories/ HL0506/S00168.htm.

44. Ibid.

45. Accessed March 10, 2009 at http://www.teenscreen-locations.com/noteenscreen. htm and http://www.teenscreen-locations.com/photos.htm.

46. Sharav, Vera. "TeenScreen—Under Intense Criticism Nationally." *Arkansas Democrat Gazette*, March 11, 2006. Accessed April 17, 2008 at http://www.ahrp.org/ cms/content/view/106/31/.

47. Tracy, Ann Blake. Response to article by Charly Groenendijk, Bush Administration, Columbia University & TeenScreen program, June 23, 2004. Accessed April 13, 2005, at http://www.antidepressantsfacts.com/Bush-TeenScreen-Program.htm.

48. TeenScreen Web site. Accessed February 16, 2009, at http://www.teenscreen.org.

49. Ibid.

50. Sharav, Vera. "TeenScreen—Under Intense Criticism Nationally." *Arkansas Democrat Gazette,* March 11, 2006. Accessed April 17, 2008 at http://www.ahrp.org/ cms/content/view/106/31/.

51. U.S. Preventive Services Task Force. *Screening for Suicide Risk: Recommendation and Rationale.* May 2004. Agency for Healthcare Research and Quality, Rockville,

MD. Accessed December 11, 2008, at http://www.ahrq.gov/clinic/3rduspstf/suicide/suiciderr.htm.

52. Effrem, Karen R. *The Dangers of Universal Mental Health Screening: A Briefing Book* (Chaska, MN: EdWatch, 2004).

53. Goldberg, Carey. "Mental Screening for Young to Begin." *Boston Globe,* December 27, 2007. Accessed December 31, 2007, at http://www.mindfreedom.org/kb/youth-mental-health/screening-massachusetts.

54. New Freedom Commission on Mental Health. *Achieving the Promise: Transforming Mental Health Care in America. Final Report.* DHHS Pub. No. SMA-03-3832. Rockville, MD: 2003, p. 69.

55. Effrem, Karen R. *The Dangers of Universal Mental Health Screening: A Briefing Book* (Chaska, MN: EdWatch, 2004), p. 34.

56. Wilson N. "Psychiatric Drugs." *KEYE News Investigates,* July 23, 2004; "Drugs and Your Tax Dollars." *KEYE News Investigates,* September 30, 2004. Accessed June 10, 2009, at http://www.keyetv.com/mediacenter/local.aspx.

57. Garza, Stephany. "Allegations Halt Drug Recommendations." The *Daily Texan,* August 25, 2008. Accessed June 10, 2009, at http://familyrights.US/news/archives/2008/aug/allegations_halt_drug_recommendations.html.

58. Lenzer, Jeanne. "Whistleblower Charges Medical Oversight Bureau with Corruption." Accessed July 20, 2009, at http://www.psychrights.org/States/Pennsylvania/BMJonkruszewski.pdf.

59. Lenzer, Jeanne. "Bush Plans to Screen Whole U.S. Population for Mental Illness: Sweeping Initiative Links Diagnoses to Treatment with Specific Drugs." *WorldNetDaily,* June 21, 2004. Accessed March 24, 2005, at http://www.worldnetdaily.com/news/article.asp?ARTICLE_ID=39078.

60. Garza, Stephany. "Allegations Halt Drug Recommendations." The *Daily Texan,* August 25, 2008. Accessed June 10, 2009, at http://familyrights.US/news/archives/2008/aug/allegations_halt_drug_recommendations.html.

61. Effrem, Karen R. *The Dangers of Universal Mental Health Screening: A Briefing Book* (Chaska, MN: EdWatch, 2004), p. 22.

62. APA Web site. *Advocacy News,* July, 2004, Item 11, "Freedom Commission Roadmap Awaited." Accessed June 6, 2009, at http://psychrights.org/Issues/Screening/July2004AdvocacyNews.htm.

63. Effrem, Karen R. *The Dangers of Universal Mental Health Screening: A Briefing Book* (Chaska, MN: Publication of EdWatch, 2004), p. 28.

64. *Project THRIVE* and *About Early Childhood Comprehensive Initiatives.* Accessed February 7, 2009, at http://www.nccp.org/projects/thrive.html and http://www.nccp.org/projects/thrive_abouteccs.html, respectively.

65. Ringwalt, S. *Developmental screening and assessment instruments with an emphasis on social and emotional development for young children ages birth through five,* (Chapel Hill: The University of North Carolina, FPG Child Development Institute, National Early Childhood Technical Assistance Center, 2008). Accessed June 6, 2009, at http://www.nectac.org/~pdfs/pubs/screening.pdf.

66. Chang, Kiki. "The Medicated Child." *Frontline,* PBS, October 8, 2007. Accessed February 3, 2008, at http://www.pbs.org/wgbh/pages/frontline/medicatedchild/interviews/chang.html.

67. Post, R. M. and S. R. B. Weiss. "Kindling and Manic-Depressive Illness." In *The Clinical Relevance of Kindling,* ed. T.G. Bolwig and M.R. Trimble (no more information available).

68. Personal communication with neurologist Fred Baughman, April 4, 2009, confirms no such EEG can diagnose "kindling" in non-epileptic children or adults.

69. Rosemond, John and Bose Ravenel. *The Diseasing of America's Children* (Nashville: Thomas Nelson, 2008), p. 32. (Emphasis added.)

70. *The Bitter Pill* Web site. "Barack Obama vs. John McCain: On Mental Health," September 9, 2008. Accessed February 2, 2009, at http://uniteforlife.wordpress.com/2008/09/09/barack-obama-vs-john-mccain-on-mental-health/.

71. President's New Freedom Commission on Mental Health: *Report to the President*, Figure 4.1. Accessed March 8, 2007, at http://www.mentalhealthcommission.gov/reports/reports.htm.

72. National Physicians Center for Family Resources Web site. Review of infant and toddler home visiting programs with regard to scientific validity and effectiveness by Karen Effrem, M.D. Accessed March 10, 2009, at http://www.physicianscenter.org/v1/positions_home_visitation.php.

73. Effrem, Karen. Response to Hearing on "Perspectives on Early Childhood Home Visitation Programs" and HR 3628, address to Subcommittee on Education Reform of the U.S. House Committee on Education and the Workforce. July 17, 2007.

74. Dalmia, Shikha and Lisa Snell. "Universal Preschool Hasn't Delivered Results." *San Francisco Chronicle,* October 17, 2008. Accessed March 10, 2009, at http://www.sfgate.com/cgi-bin/article.cgi?f=/c/a/2008/10/17/EDQC131SN1.DTL&type=education.

75. Accessed October 15, 2008, at http://www.edwatch.org/updates08/031908-emotionalharmw.pdf.

76. Ibid. Effrem cites Baker, Michael, Jonathan Gruber, and Kevin Milligan. "What Can We Learn from Quebec's Universal Childcare Program?" e-brief of the C.D. Howe Institute, February, 2006.

77. Reedy, Yvonne B. "A Comparison of Long Range Effects of Participation in Project Head Start and Impact of Three Differing Delivery Models" for Pennsylvania State University, 1991.

78. Nicholi, Armand. *The Harvard Guide to Psychiatry,* 3rd edition (Cambridge MA: Belknap/Harvard Press, 1999), p. 623.

CHAPTER 6

Epigraph: Burston, Daniel. "Diagnosis, Drugs, and Bipolar Disorder in Children" In *No Child Left Different,* ed. Sharna Olfman (Westport, CT: Praeger Publishers, 2006), pp. 121–140, p. 136.

1. Effrem, Karen R. *The Dangers of Universal Mental Health Screening*: *A Briefing Book* (Chaska, MN: EdWatch, 2004), p. 7.

2. Eberhart, Dave. "Congress Funds Psychological Tests for Kids." *NewsMax.com,* November 23, 2004. Accessed April 2, 2005, at http://archive.newsmax.com/archives/articles/2004/11/22/215244.shtml.

3. Cuddy, Dennis L. "Mental Health and World Citizenship." *NewsWithViews.com,* August 11, 2004. Accessed May 14, 2008, at http://www.newswithviews.com/Cuddy/dennis14.htm. The following section is taken from this source. Page numbers are not available.

4. Breggin, Peter R. and Ginger Ross Breggin. *The War Against Children of Color* (Monroe, ME: Common Courage Press, 1998. Chapter 5 unless otherwise noted).

5. Sharav, Vera Hassner. "Screening for Mental Illness: The Merger of Eugenics and the Drug Industry." *Ethical Human Psychology and Psychiatry* 7 (Summer, 2005): 111–124. Reproduced with permission of Springer Publishing Company, LLC, New York, NY 10036.

CHAPTER 7

Epigraph: House, Edward Mandell. *Philip Dru: Administrator*. Project Gutenberg e-book #6711, October 2004 (this file was first posted on January 17, 2003).

1. Glasser, Howard and Jennifer Easley. *Transforming the Difficult Child: The Nurtured Heart Approach* (Tucson: Howard Glasser, 1998 (revised in 2002).

2. Grove, Tom, Howard Glasser, and Melissa Lynn Block. *The Inner Wealth Initiative: The Nurtured Heart Approach for Educators* (Tucson: Nurtured Heart Publications, 2007).

3. Stein, David B. *Ritalin Is Not the Answer: A Drug-Free, Practical Program for Children Diagnosed with ADD or ADHD* (San Francisco: Jossey-Bass, 2001).

4. Armstrong, Thomas. *The Myth of the A.D.D. Child* (New York: Putnam Plume, 1995).

5. Oas, Peter T. *Curing ADD/ADHD Children* (Raleigh, NC: Pentland Press, 2001).

6. Rosemond, John. *A Six-Point Plan for Raising Happy, Healthy Children* (Kansas City: Andrews & McMeel, 1989).

7. Bowlby, John. *A Secure Base: Parent-Child Attachment and Healthy Human Development* (New York: Basic Books, 1988).

8. Timimi, Sami. "Developing Nontoxic Approaches to Helping Children Who Could Be Diagnosed with ADHD and Their Families: Reflections of a United Kingdom Clinician." *Ethical Human Psychology and Psychiatry* (Spring, 2004): 41–52.

9. Diller, Lawrence. "The Last Normal Child." In *Childhood in America*, Sharna Olfman, Series Editor (Westport, CT: Praeger, 2006).

10. Diller, Lawrence. *"Should I Medicate My Child? Sane Solutions for Troubled Kids With—& Without—Psychiatric Drugs"* (New York: Basic Books, 2002), p. 220. Diller also devotes an entire chapter to the evaluation process.

11. Ravenel, DuBose. "A Child of Competence and Character: A Parent-Training Curriculum for Modeling and Training a Child for Self-control." Copyright 2006, DuBose Ravenel, M.D., F.A.A.P., F.C.P. For more information, see Web site: www.drbose.com.

12. Baumrind, D. "The Discipline Controversy Revisited." *Family Relations* 45 (1996): 405–414.

13. Baumeister, R. F., J. D. Campbell, U.I. Krueger, and K. D. Vohs. "Does High Self-Esteem Cause Better Performance, Interpersonal Success, Happiness, or Healthier Lifestyles?" *Psychological Science in the Public Interest* 4 (2003): 1–44.

14. Strayhorn, J. M. "Self-Control: Theory and Research." *Journal of the American Academy of Child and Adolescent Psychiatry* 41 (2002): 7–16. And "Self-Control: Toward Systematic Training Programs." *Journal of the American Academy of Child and Adolescent Psychiatry* 41 (2002): 17–27.

15. Christakis, D. A., B. E. Ebel, F. P. Rivara, and F. J. Zimmerman. "Television, Video, and Computer Game Usage in Children Under 11 Years of Age." *Journal of*

Pediatrics 145 (2004). Stevens, L. J. *12 Effective Ways to Help Your ADD/ADHD Child—Drug-Free Alternatives for Attention-Deficit Disorders* (New York: Avery, 2000).

16. Ravenel, S. D. "A New Paradigm for ADD/ADHD and Behavioral Management Without Medication." *Ethical Human Sciences and Services* 4 (2002): 93–106. Revised 2003. A synopsis is posted on Internet at http://www.dbpeds.org/articles/detail.cfm?TextID=256. Marcon, R. A. "Moving Up the Grades: Relationship Between Preschool Model and Later School Success." *Early Childhood Research and Practice* 4 (2002). Posted on Internet at http://ecrp.uiuc.edu/v4n1/marcon.html.

17. Mendelsohn, Roberts. *How to Raise a Healthy Child . . . in Spite of Your Doctor* (New York: Ballantine, 1984), p. 226.

18. Wallis, Claudia. "Hyper Kids? Check Their Diet." *Time,* September 24, 2007.

19. Accessed August 31, 2004, at http://www.homeschoolmath.net/other_topics/add-adhd-diet.php.

20. Ulrich, Laura. "Schools See Exercise As Natural Remedy." *Ithaca Journal,* September 2006.

21. Ibid.

22. Nufer, Kathy Walsh. "Physical Activity and Learning Go Hand in Hand, Expert Says." *Appleton Post-Crescent,* August 16, 2006. Accessed July 26, 2008, at http://actionbasedlearning.com./article10.shtml.

23. *Learning With the Body in Mind* was published in 2000 by The Brain Store, Inc. in San Diego. Eric P. Jensen has written a number of books on strategies to enhance brain development in young children. It is likely all were published by The Brain Store. They can be obtained at www.amazon.com.

24. Curtis, Polly. "Study Shows Exercise Helps Dyslexia, ADD, ADHD." *The Guardian*, May 20, 2004. Accessed July 26, 2008, at http://www.actionbasedlearning.com/article07.shtml.

25. Reynolds, Gretchen. "Lobes of Steel." The *New York Times,* August 19, 2007. Accessed July 26, 2008, at http://www.nytimes.com/2007/08/19/sports/playmagazine/0819play-brain.html?_r=1&oref.

26. Barros, Romina M. "Recess Makes for Better Students." The *Washington Post,* January 26, 2009. Accessed June 13, 2009, at http://yourtotalhealth.ivillage.com/recess~makes-better-students.hrmlp . . . Her study was published in *Pediatrics*, the February 2009 issue.

27. Breggin, Peter R. and Ginger Ross Breggin. *The War Against Children of Color* (Monroe, ME: Common Courage Press, 1998), pp. 171–173.

28. Ibid. p. 173.

29. Barsamian, David. Interview with Adrienne Anderson, *Alternative Radio*, NPR, May 6, 2003.

30. Moberg, David. "Obama's Community Roots." *The Nation*, April 3, 2007. Accessed September 2, 2008, at http://www.thenation.com/doc/20070416/moberg/print.

31. Whitaker, Robert. *Mad in America* (New York: Perseus Publishing, 2002), pp. 226–229.

32. Ibid. pp. 220–226.

33. Ibid. And Mosher, Loren R., Voyce Hendrix, and Deborah C. Fort. *"Soteria: Through Madness to Deliverance"* (USA: Xlibris, 2004).

34. Ibid., (Mosher, Loren R.). Foreword, xiv–xv.

CHAPTER 8

Epigraph: Cited in *The War Against Children of Color* by Peter R. and Ginger Ross Breggin, pp. 190–191. Herbert, W. "Politics of Biology." *U.S. News and World Report*, April 21, 1997, pp. 72–80.

1. Garbarino, James. *Raising Children in a Socially Toxic Environment* (San Francisco: Jossey-Bass Publishers, 1995), pp. 42–43.

2. Bezruchka, Stephen. "Is America Driving You Crazy?" *Alternative Radio*, NPR, October 16, 2006.

3. Stolzer, Jeanne. "ADHD in America: A Bioecological Analysis." *Ethical Human Psychology and Psychiatry* 7 (Spring, 2005): 65–75. Reproduced with the Permission of Springer Publishing Company, LLC, New York, NY 10036.

4. Maslow, A. and I. Szilagy-Kessler. "Security and Breastfeeding." *Journal of Abnormal and Social Psychology* 41 (1946): 83–85,

5. Holloway, A. R. "Early Self Regulation of Infants and Later Behavior in Play Interviews." *American Journal of Orthopsychiatry* 19 (1949): 612–613.

6. Fogal, A. *Infancy: Infant, Family and Society* (Belmont, CA: Wadsworth Publishing, 2001).

7. Baumslag, N. and D. L. Michels. *Milk, Money and Madness: The Culture and Politics of Breast-feeding* (London: Bergin and Garvey, 1995).

8. Pellegrini, A.D. "Elementary School Children's Rough-and-Tumble Play." *Early Childhood Research Quarterly* 4 (1988): 245–260.

9. Baughman, Fred. *The ADHD Fraud: How Psychiatry Makes "Patients" of Normal Children* (Victoria, BC: Trafford Publishing, 2006).

10. Glasser, Howard and Jennifer Easley. *Transforming the Difficult Child: The Nurtured Heart Approach* (Tucson: Howard Glasser, 1999).

11. Bowlby, John. *A Secure Base: Parent-Child Attachment and Healthy Human Development* (New York: Basic Books, 1988).

12. Jensen, Peter S., David Mrazek, Penelope K. Knapp, Laurence Steinberg, et al. "Evolution and Revolution in Child Psychiatry: ADHD as a Disorder of Adaptation." *Journal of the American Academy of Child & Adolescent Psychiatry* 36 (1997): 1672–1679. Accessed June 4, 2009, at http://www.ohsu.edu/psychiatry/pdfs/course%20lectures%20&%20lecture%20materials%20-%20child%20psychiatry%20handout%20b.pdf?fix.

13. Burstyn, Varda and David Fenton. "Toxic World, Troubled Minds." In *No Child Left Different,* ed. Sharna Olfman (Westport, CT: Praeger Publishers, 2006), pp. 49–71.

14. Picard, A. "Flame Retardants Building Up Within Us: Highest Levels Found in Babies as PBDEs Emanate from Carpets, Furniture to Form DustBalls. The *Globe and Mail*, February 15, 2005.

15. Watson, J. "Toxic Chemicals in Our Veins." *Scotsman*, November 24, 2003.

16. Greater Boston Physicians for Social Responsibility. *In Harm's Way: Toxic Threats to Child Development.* Cambridge, MA, 2000. Available at http://www.igc.org/psr.

17. Children's Environmental Health Network. "Why Children Are Not Adults." Washington, DC: CEHN, 1998. http://www.cehn.org. CEHN is a national multidisciplinary organization whose mission is to protect the fetus and the child from environmental health hazards and promote a healthy environment.

18. Hu, H. "Human Health and Heavy Metals Exposure." In *Life Support: The Environment and Human Health,* ed. Michael McCally (Cambridge, MA: MIT Press, 2002), chapter 4.

19. Needleman, H. L. "Childhood Lead Poisoning: The Promise and Abandonment of Primary Prevention." *American Journal of Public Health* 88 (1998): 1871–1877.

20. Organic Consumers Association Web site. "Strong Links Between Lead Poisoning and Violent Behavior." *Rachel's Environment and Health News,* August 5, 2004. http://www.organicconsumers.org/school/lead081004.cfm.

21. Masters, R., M. Coplan, B. Hone, and J. Dykes. "Association of Silicofluoride Treated Water With Elevated Blood Lead." *Neurotoxicology* 21 (2000): 101–110.

22. Anderson, Adrienne. "Planetary Casualties: The Hidden Costs of War." Interviewed by David Barsamian, *Alternative Radio,* NPR, May 6, 2003.

23. Hu, H. "Human Health and Heavy Metals Exposure." In *Life Support: The Environment and Human Health,* ed. Michael McCally (Cambridge, MA: MIT Press, 2002), chapter 4.

24. Trasande, L., et al. "Public Health and Economic Consequences of Methyl Mercury Toxicity to the Developing Brain." *Environmental Health Perspectives* 113 (2005): 590–596.

25. Olmstead, D. "The Age of Autism: Mercury in the Air." *UPI,* May 5, 2005. http://www.upi.com/Science_News/2005/05/05/The-Age-Of-Autism-Mercury-in-the-air/UPI-76151115265900/. The Age of Autism is an ongoing UPI series tracking the roots and rise of autism. The authors also reference Ackerman, T. "Study Links Mercury from Power Plants to Autism." *Houston Chronicle*, March 18, 2005.

26. "Mercury Study Identifies Problem Spots." *Environmental News Network,* Associated Press, March 9, 2005.

27. Needleman, Herbert and Philip Landrigan. *Raising Children Toxic Free: How to Keep Your Child Free from Lead, Asbestos, Pesticides and Other Environmental Hazards* (New York: Perennial Currents, 1995).

28. Rapp, D. *Our Toxic World: A Wake Up Call* (Buffalo, NY: Environmental Medical Research Foundation, 2002).

29. See: Burstyn, V. and G. Sampson. "Technoenvironmental Assaults on Childhood in America." In *Childhood Lost,* ed. Sharna Olfman (Westport, CT: Praeger Publishers, 2005), pp. 155–183.

30. California Safe Schools Web site, "Children's Advocates Celebrate Six Years of Protecting Student Health: Reformed Pesticide Policy Sets National Model." http://calisafe.org.

31. Healy, Jane M. *Endangered Minds* (New York: Simon and Schuster, 1990). My source was the *New Horizons for Learning* Web site. Accessed March 31, 2009, at http://www.newhorizons.org/future/Creating_the_Future/crfut_healy.html.

32. Healy, Jane M. *Failure to Connect: How Computers Affect Our Children's Minds and What We Can Do About It* (New York: Simon and Schuster, 1998.) My source was *Salon,* accessed January 24, 2008, at http://archive.salon.com/21st/books/1998/08/26books.html.

33. Harvey, Matthew. "A Lack of Natural Play in Early Childhood Could Be the Cause of ADHD." *New York Times*, February 1, 2008, Educational Supplement.

34. Olfman, Sharna. "Where Do the Children Play?" In *Childhood Lost,* ed. Sharna Olfman (Westport, CT: Praeger Publishers, 2005), pp. 203–215.

35. Alvarez, L. "Flocking to Finland, Land of Literate Children." *Suutarila Journal, New York Times*, April 9, 2004.

36. Clouder, C. "Early Childhood Education: Lessons from Europe." In *All Work and No Play: How Educational Reforms Are Harming Our Preschoolers*, ed. Sharna Olfman (Westport, CT: Praeger Publishers, 2003), pp. 71–80.

37. House of Commons. *Education Select Committee's Report,* December 2000.

38. Garbarino, James. *Raising Children in a Socially Toxic Environment* (San Francisco: Jossey-Bass, 1995), pp. 12–13.

39. Paley, V. *Wally's Stories: Conversations in the Kindergarten* (Cambridge, MA: Harvard University Press, 1983).

40. Louv, Richard. *Last Child in the Woods: Saving Our Children From Nature-Deficit Disorder* (Chapel Hill, NC: Algonquin Books, 2005).

41. Roszak, Theodore. *The Voice of the Earth: An Exploration of Ecopsychology* (New York: Simon & Schuster, 1992).

42. Ibid. p. 44.

43. Berk, L. *Awakening Children's Minds* (New York: Oxford Press, 2001).

44. Kane, J. and H. Carpenter. "Imagination and the Growth of the Human Mind." In *All Work and No Play: How Educational Reforms Are Harming Our Preschoolers,* ed. Sharna Olfman (Westport, CT: Praeger Publishers, 2003), pp. 125–142.

EPILOGUE

Epigraph: Holy Bible, Authorized King James Version. (Grand Rapids, MI: Zondervan Publishing House, 1986).

1. Goldstein, Jacob. "Grassley Questions Stanford Psychiatrist's Industry Ties," The *Wall Street Journal*, June 25, 2008. Accessed June 15, 2009, at http://blogs.wsj.com/health/2008/grassley-questions-stanford-psychiatrists-industry-ties/.

2. Silverman, Ed. "Grassley Intensifies Probe Into NIH & Stanford," *Pharmalot.com*, August 1, 2008. Accessed June 15, 2009, at http://www.pharmalot.com/2008/08/grassley-intensifies-probe-into-nih-stanford/.

3. Silverman, Ed. "Under Pressure, Stanford Pulls Schatzberg Grant," *Pharmalot.com*, August 1, 2008. Accessed at http://www.pharmalot.com/2008/08/under-pressure-stanford-pulls-schatzberg-grant/.

4. Diller, Lawrence. "Are Our Leading Pediatricians Drug Industry Shills?" *San Francisco Chronicle*, July 13, 2008. Accessed June 14, 2009, at http://www.sfgate.com/cgi-bin/article.cgi?f=/c/a/2008/07/12/IN7G11L6TL.DTL.

5. Harris, Gardiner, Benedict Carey, and Janet Roberts. "Psychiatrists, Children and Drug Industry's Role." The *New York Times*, May 10, 2007.

6. Levitz, Jennifer. "Drug Researcher Agrees to Curb Role." *Wall Street Journal*, December 30, 2008.

7. Harris, Gardiner, Benedict Carey, and Janet Roberts. "Psychiatrists, Children and Drug Industry's Role." The *New York Times*, May 10, 2007.

8. Peale, Cliff. "UC to Keep Closer Eye on Prof's Income." *The Enquirer*, April 21, 2008. Accessed June 14, 2009, at http://tmap.wordpress.com/2008/04/21/UC-to-keep-closer-eye-on-profs-income/.

9. Murphy, Shelley. "Doctor Is Sued in Death of Girl, 4—Her Psychiatrist Treated Her with Powerful Drugs." *Boston Globe*, April 4, 2008. Accessed May 17, 2008, at

http://tmap.wordpress.com/2008/04/04/doctor-is-sued-in-death-of-girl-4-her-psychiatrist-treatedher-with-powerful-drugs/.

10. Garza, Stephany. "Allegations Halt Drug Recommendations." *The Daily Texan*, August 25, 2008. Accessed June 14, 2009, at http://tmap.wordpress.com/2008/08/25/allegations-halt-drug-recommendations/.

11. News Sentinel Staff. "Bristol-Myers Case Lands State $3.5M." *Knoxville News Sentinel*, July 29, 2008. Accessed June 14, 2009, at http://www.knoxnews.com/news/2008/jul/29/bristol-myers-case-lands-state-35m/. Also: "Mass. Gets $9.2M as Drug Maker Settles with States," The *Boston Globe*, (Business in Brief) July 16, 2008. Accessed June 14, 2009, at http://www.boston.com/business/articles/2008/07/16/mass_gets_92m_as_drug_maker_settles_with_states/?page=full Jefferson, Brandie. "Pharmaceutical Company Settles with Rhode Island for $600,000+." *Providence Journal*, August 8, 2008.

12. *Pharmalot* Web site. Silverman, Ed. "NY Senator: Probe Psychiatric Drugs & Medicaid," February 4, 2008. Accessed July 21, 2008, at http://www.pharmalot.com/2008/02/ny-senator-probe-psychiatric-drugs-medicaid/.

13. *Pharmalot* Web site. Silverman, Ed. "Lawmaker Asks NJ AG To Probe Antipsychotics," March 26, 2008. Accessed March 28, 2008, at http://www.pharmalot.com/2008/03/lawmaker-asks-nj-ag-to-probe-antipsychotics/.

14. Russell, John. "Judge: Case Against Lilly May Go To Trial." *Indianapolis Star*, July 3, 2008. Accessed July 8, 2008 at http://www.indystar.com/apps/pbcs.dll/article?AID=20080703/BUSINESS/807030475/1001/NEWS.

15. Eder, Andrew. "Astra CEO in London for Seroquel Trial Disposition." *delawareonline*, July 27, 2009. Accessed June 23, 2008. Available at *delawareonline: The News Journal* Archives http://pqasb.pqarchiver.com/delawareonline/results.html?st=basic&QryTxt=Eder,+Andrew+Astra+CEO+in+London+for+Seroquel+Trial+and+Disposition.

16. Eder, Andrew. "AstraZeneca Defends Drug's Soaring Sales." *delawareonline*, August 3, 2008. Except for my anecdotal comment, this whole section originated with this source. Accessed July 27, 2009. *delawareonline*: The News Journal Archives ID: wil27298005 http://pqasb.pqarchiver.com/delawareonline/results.html?st=basic&QryTxt=Eder,+Andrew+AstraZeneca+Defends+Soaring+Sales.

17. Vedantam, Shankar. "A Silenced Drug Study Creates An Uproar." The *Washington Post,* March 18, 2009. Accessed June 15, 2009, at http://www.laleva.org/eng/2009/03/a_silenced_drug_study_creates_an_uproar.html.

18. United States Senate Special Committee on Aging. Press Release. "Grassley, Kohl Continue Campaign to Disclose Financial Ties Between Doctors and Drug Companies." January 22, 2009. Accessed April 1, 2009, at http://aging.senate.gov/record.cfm?id=307097.

19. Hundley, Kris. "Approval Process Lowers the Number of Kids on Atypical Prescriptions." *St. Petersburg Times*, March 29, 2009. Accessed April 2, 2009, at http://www.tampabay.com/news/health/article987612.ece.

20. Ramshaw, Emily. "Legislation Requires Doctors to Get State Permission Before Prescribing Psychiatric Drugs for Kids on Medicaid." *Dallas Morning News,* April 1, 2009. Accessed April 2, 2009, at http://www.dallasnews.com/sharedcontent/dws/news/dmn/stories/040109dnmetpsychdrugs.3c447d2.html.

21. Sharfstein, Steven S. "Big Pharma and American Psychiatry: The Good, the Bad, and the Ugly." *Psychiatric News*, August 19, 2005. My source is an e-mail distributed by enews@nyaprs.org to my workplace on August 24, 2005. The URL is that of Mental Health e-news, from the New York Association of Psychiatric Rehabilitation Services.

22. American Medical Student Association. Press Release. "Thousands of Medical Students Call on Schools to Eliminate Pharmaceutical Marketing Influence." October 22, 2007. Received via e-mail from Gary Kohls on November 1, 2007.

Recommended Reading

Abramson, John. *Overdosed America: The Broken Promise of American Medicine*. New York: HarperCollins, 2004.

Angell, Marcia. *The Truth About the Drug Companies*. New York: Random House, 2004.

Armstrong, Thomas. *The Myth of the A.D.D. Child*. New York: Putnam Plume, 1995.

Breggin, Peter R. *Medication Madness: The Role of Psychiatric Drugs in Cases of Violence, Suicide, and Crime*. New York: St. Martin's Press, 2008.

Breggin, Peter R. *Brain Disabling Treatments in Psychiatry*. New York: Springer Publishing Co. Inc., 2008.

Breggin, Peter R. & Ginger Ross Breggin. *The War Against Children of Color*. Monroe, ME: Common Courage Press, 1998.

Breggin, Peter R. *The Heart of Being Helpful*. New York: Springer Publishing Co. Inc., 1997.

Breggin, Peter R. *Toxic Psychiatry*. New York: St. Martin's Press, 1991.

Breggin, Peter R. & David Cohen. *Your Drug May Be Your Problem*. New York: Perseus Publishing, 1999.

DeGrandpre, Richard. *Ritalin Nation*. New York: W.W. Norton & Co, 2000.

Diller, Lawrence H. *Should I Medicate My Child?* New York: Basic Books, 2000.

Garbarino, James. *Raising Children in a Socially Toxic Environment*. San Francisco: Jossey-Bass Publishers, 1995.

Glasser, Howard & Jennifer Easley. *Transforming The Difficult Child: The Nurtured Heart Approach*. Tucson: Nurtured Heart Publications, 1999.

Grove, Tom, Howard Glasser, & Melissa Lynn Block. *The Inner Wealth Initiative: The Nurtured Heart Approach for Educators*. Tucson: Nurtured Heart Publications, 2007.

Jackson, Grace E. *Rethinking Psychiatric Drugs*. Bloomington, IN: Author House, 2005.

Kutchins, Herb & Stuart A. Kirk. *Making Us Crazy: The Psychiatric Bible and the Creation of Mental Disorders*. New York: The Free Press, 1997.

Lauv, Richard. *Last Child in the Woods: Saving Our Children from Nature-Deficit Disorder*. Chapel Hill, NC: Algonquin Books, 2005.

Mendelsohn, Robert S. *How to Raise a Healthy Child . . . in Spite of Your Doctor*. New York: Ballantine Books, 1984.

Mercogliano, Chris. *Teaching the Restless: One School's Remarkable No-Ritalin Approach to Helping Children Learn and Succeed*. Boston: Beacon Press, 2003.

Mosher, Loren R. & Voyce Hendrix with Deborah C. Fort (2004). *Soteria: Through Madness to Deliverance*. USA: Xlibris, 2004.

Oas, Peter T. *Curing ADD/ADHD Children*. Raleigh, NC: Pentland Press, Inc., 2001.

Olfman, Sharna (Ed.). *All Work and No Play: How Educational Reforms are Harming Our Preschoolers*. Westport, CT: Praeger Publishers, 2003.

Olfman, Sharna (Ed.). *Childhood Lost*. Westport, CT: Praeger Publishers, 2005.

Olfman, Sharna. (Ed.). *No Child Left Different*. Westport, CT: Praeger Publishers, 2006.

Petersen, Melody. *Our Daily Meds: How the Pharmaceutical Companies Transformed Themselves Into Slick Marketing Machines and Hooked the Nation on Prescription Drugs*. New York: Sarah Crichton Books, 2008.

Rosemond, John. *A Six-Point Plan for Raising Happy, Healthy Children*. Kansas City: Andrews & McMeel, 1989.

Rosemond, John K. & S. DuBose Ravenel. *The Diseasing of America's Children: Exposing the ADHD Fiasco and Empowering Parents to Take Back Control*. Nashville, TN: Thomas Nelson, 2008.

Stein, David B. *Stop Medicating, Start Parenting: Real Solutions for Your "Problem" Teenager*. New York: Taylor Trade Publishing, 2004.

Stein, David B. *Ritalin Is Not the Answer*. San Francisco: Jossey-Bass Publishers, 2001.

Whitaker, Robert. *Mad in America*. New York: Perseus Publishing, 2002.

Index

Abilify, 43, 82, 83, 84

Abramson, John, 5, 62

Achieving the Promise: Transforming Mental Health Care in America, 99, 100, 101, 102, 103, 104, 105, 107, 108, 110, 114, 115

Adderall, 60

Adderall XR (d-amphetamine and amphetamine mixture), 60, 67

The ADHD Fraud: How Psychiatry Makes Patients of Normal Children, 15

Administration for Children and Families, 122

AdmoCare, 112

aerobic exercise, 143, 145

Ages and Stages questionnaires (ASQ), 119, 120

agitation, 67, 74, 81

AHA *see* American Heart Association (AHA)

AHRP *see* Alliance for Human Research Protection (AHRP)

akathisia, 74, 85, 107

Alaska Mental Health Consumer Web, 91

Alaska Youth Initiative, 148

Albee, George, 3

Alessi, Galen, 100

Alfred, Graham, 78

Allen, Paul G., 7

Allen, Scott, 34

Alliance for Human Research Protection (AHRP), 96, 110, 113, 114, 115, 129, 172

All Things Considered, 46

Alternative Radio, 160

Altern Medical Review, 142

Ambien, 81

Ameen, Shahul, 6

Amen, Daniel G., 28

Amen Clinics, 28

American Academy of Child and Adolescent Psychiatry, 47

American Academy of Neurology, 14

American Association of Physicians and Surgeons, 117

American Eugenics Society, 130

American Heart Association (AHA); and cardiovascular warnings, 70–71

American Journal of Psychiatry, 130

American Medical Student Association (AMSA), 182

American Psychiatric Association (APA), 5, 118, 129, 173, 181

American Psychoanalytic Association, 114

American Psychological Association, 16

Americans With Disabilities Act, 104

aminoketone, 73

amphetamines, 59, 60, 62, 63, 69, 72

About the Author

Elizabeth E. Root, MSW, MS Ed, is a Licensed Clinical Social Worker, now retired, whose employment spanned five counties of upstate New York. She worked in the public sector with children and families for 18 years.